D1299416

PMP® Exam Prep

Questions, Answers & Explanations

PMP® Exam Prep

Questions, Answers & Explanations

Christopher Scordo, PMP, ITIL

Professional. Measurable. Realistic.

Copyrighted Material

© Copyright 2011 by SSI Logic. Printed and bound in the United States of America. All rights reserved. No part of this book may be reproduced or transmitted in any form or by any means, electronic or mechanical, or incorporated into any information retrieval system, electronic or mechanical, without the written permission of the copyright owner.
Edition 2011.

Although the author and publisher of this work have made every effort to ensure accuracy and completeness of content entered in this book, we assume no responsibility for errors, inaccuracies, omissions, or inconsistencies included herein. Any similarities of people, places, or organizations are completely unintentional.

Published by SSI Logic
PO Box 39038
Washington, DC 20016

ISBN-10: 0-9825768-0-3
ISBN-13: 978-0-9825768-0-9

All inquiries should be addressed via email to:
support@ssilogic.com

or by mail post to:
SSI Solutions, INC
PO Box 39038
Washington, DC 20016

"PMI", "PMP", "CAPM" and "PMBOK" are trademarks in the United States and other nations, registered to the Project Management Institute, Inc.

Table of Contents

Introduction

Practice Exams and Quizzes

Additional Resources

INTRODUCTION

Welcome

Thank you for selecting SSI Logic's *PMP® Exam Prep – Questions, Answers, and Explanations* for your PMP study needs. The goal of this book is to provide condensed mock exams and practice tests which allow you to become comfortable with the pace, subject matter, and difficulty of the PMP exam.

The content in this book is designed to optimize the time you spend studying in multiple ways.

1. Practice exams in this book are condensed to be completed in one hour; allowing you to balance your time between practice tests and offline study.

2. Passing score requirements in this book are slightly higher than the real exam; allowing you to naturally adjust to a higher test score requirement.

3. Practice exams included in this book cover the entire scope of the PMP exam, while shorter quizzes focus only on specific PMBOK® Knowledge Areas.

The practice exam content in this book is structured into two general types of exam preparation:

- "Lite" Mock Exams, which allow you to test your knowledge across condensed versions of the PMP exam; designed to be completed within one hour.

- Knowledge Area Quizzes, which reflect brief practice tests focused on specific PMBOK® Knowledge Areas; designed to be completed in 15 minutes.

We wish you the best of luck in your pursuit to become a certified PMP.

PMP® Exam Overview

The PMP practice questions in this book reflect the PMP exam version based on the PMBOK® Guide - Fourth Edition.

About the Project Management Professional (PMP) Certification

The PMP certification is managed by the Project Management Institute (PMI®) and reflects the PMI's project management processes as published in the Project Management Body of Knowledge (PMBOK®) Guide. Since 1984, the PMP certification has become one of the most sought after internationally recognized management credentials available. The average salary of a PMP certified manager is 14% higher than individuals without the PMP certification.

The PMP certification is a globally recognized credential, and individuals are encouraged to remain active via PMI's Continuing Certification Requirements (CCRs). Only individuals who maintain active PMP credentials may refer to themselves as Project Management Professionals. Individuals do not need to be a member of PMI to earn a PMP credential.

The minimum requirements in attaining the PMP certification:

- Education: At a minimum, A high school diploma is required
- Project management experience

  - 36 months and 4500 hours of professional experience for individuals with a Bachelor's degree or global equivalent (within the past 8 years)
  - 60 months and 7500 hours of professional experience for individuals without a Bachelor's degree or equivalent (within the past 8 years)
- Project Management Education: 35 contact hours of formal education
- Ethics: Agree to PMI's Code of Ethics and Professional Conduct
- **Pass the PMP Exam**

PMP Exam Details

The PMP exam is designed to objectively assess and measure project management knowledge. Concepts covered in the PMP exam are directly derived from the Project Management Body of Knowledge (PMBOK®) Guide. The PMBOK® Guide is an internationally recognized standard (IEEE Std 1490-2003) which outlines project management fundamentals; and is applicable to a wide range of industries.

The actual exam is offered in both a computer based testing (CBT) environment, as well as through proctored paper-based exams. A summary of the exam structure and passing requirements are as follows:

- There are 200 total multiple choice questions which make up the PMP exam

- 25 randomly placed "pretest questions" are included, and do not count towards the pass/fail determination
- Individuals have 4 hours to complete the exam
- Individuals must score 61% or higher to pass the exam (106 of 175 questions)

The Nine PMBOK® Knowledge Areas

The nine PMBOK® Knowledge Areas covered by the PMP exam are listed below.

- Project Integration Management
- Project Scope Management
- Project Time Management
- Project Cost Management
- Project Quality Management
- Project Human Resource Management
- Project Communications Management
- Project Risk Management
- Project Procurement Management

Additionally, the PMP practice exam content in this book include questions on the overall Project Management Framework and Professional Responsibility; reflecting the real PMP exam.

The nine PMBOK® Knowledge Areas contain a total of 42 processes which are applied to **five basic process groups**.

These five basic process groups, which are common across all projects, are listed below along with the percentage of questions one should expect on the PMP exam:

1. Initiating (11%)
2. Planning (23%)
3. Executing (27%)
4. Controlling and Monitoring (21%)
5. Closing (9%)

The remaining 9% of the exam covers Professional Responsibility.

PRACTICE EXAMS AND QUIZZES

PMP Lite Mock Exam 1
Practice Questions

Test Name: PMP Lite Mock Exam 1
Total Questions: 50
Correct Answers Needed to Pass:
35 (70.00%)
Time Allowed: 60 Minutes

Test Description

This is a cumulative PMP Mock Exam which can be used as a benchmark for your PMP aptitude. This practice test includes questions from all PMBOK knowledge areas, including the five basic project management process groups.

Test Questions

1. You are the project manager of a construction project to build an Industrial Technology Park in a foreign country. You find that you need to transport large machinery and equipment to the construction site and this may potentially cause some disturbance to traffic in the vicinity. You therefore plan to schedule this for a time which is considered off peak-hour traffic. Your liaison in the country informs you that you need to pay a fee to the local administration to do this. How would you handle this?

A. You would pay this only if it was part of the initial project estimate else you would need to check with your customer on whether this fee can be billed to the customer.

B. You would pay the amount in question and adjust the same in another activity during billing since this cannot be justified.

C. Payment of any fee for such a reason would be perceived as a bribe. Hence you would not pay the fee.

D. You would first check with your legal team on whether such a fee is a requirement and complies with the local regulations.

2. If there are 10 people working on a project, how many total communication channels are there?

A. 100 channels

B. 20 channels

C. 45 channels

D. 10 channels

3. A fundamentally functional organization creates a special project team to handle a critical project. This team has many of the characteristics of a project team in a project organization and has a project manager dedicated to the project. Such an organization would be called:

A. A projectized organization

B. A functional organization.

C. A strong matrix organization

D. A composite organization

4. As you are creating the Activity List, which technique is recommended for subdividing the project into smaller components called activities?

A. Decomposition

B. Rolling Wave Planning

C. Define Activities

D. Deconstruction

5. If you would like to base your project cost estimate on historical data and statistical analysis, which cost estimation technique would you use?

A. Parametric Estimating

B. Analogous Estimating

C. Vendor Bid Analysis

D. Bottom-up Estimating

6. The Create WBS process identifies the deliverables at the _____ level in the Work Breakdown Structure (WBS).

A. Lowest

B. Any

C. Tenth

D. Highest

7. What is the primary risk with including reserves or contingency allowances in your cost estimate?

A. Cancelling your project

B. Understating the cost estimate

C. Overstating the cost estimate

D. Tracking the funds

8. Which of the following statements most accurately describes a project scenario?

A. Changes in project scope during the initial phases of the project are very expensive.

B. The influence of the stakeholders is the same all through the project.

C. Staffing peaks up during the execution phase of a project.

D. The next phase of a project should never start until the deliverables for the previous phase have been completely reviewed and approved.

9. Which of the following is not an organizational process asset used in the Develop Human Resource Plan process?

A. Template for organizational charts

B. Template for position descriptions

C. Standardized role descriptions

D. Standardized stakeholder list

10. Which of these is not a typical constraint on the project team's personnel options?

A. Organization structure

B. Collective bargaining agreements

C. Physical location

D. Economic conditions

11. Perform Integrated Change Control includes several configuration management activities. Which of these is not part of Perform Integrated Change Control?

A. Configuration Preparation

B. Configuration Verification

C. Configuration Status Accounting

D. Configuration Identification

12. After brainstorming potential project risks, what is the recommended method for prioritizing these risks and their mitigation plans?

A. RACI chart

B. Control chart

C. Fishbone Diagram

D. Probability and impact matrix

13. If you are influencing factors that create changes to the cost of the project, which process are you using?

     A. Negotiate Costs

     B. Estimate Costs

     C. Control Costs

     D. Determine Budget

14. If you are requesting a vendor quote for a defined scope, what is the recommended contract type?

     A. Fixed price

     B. Commission

     C. Cost reimbursable

     D. Time and materials

15. Within the cost reimbursable contracts, which of these is not a common type of contract?

     A. Cost-Plus-Award-Fee

     B. Cost-Plus-Fixed-Time

     C. Cost-Plus-Fixed-Fee

     D. Cost-Plus-Incentive-Fee

16. In what sequence would the following Project Scope Management processes be used?

     A. Create WBS, Collect Requirements, Define Scope, Verify Scope, and Control Scope

     B. Define Scope, Collect Requirements, Create WBS, Verify Scope, and Control Scope

     C. Collect Requirements, Define Scope, Create WBS, Verify Scope, and Control Scope

     D. Collect Requirements, Define Scope, Verify Scope, Create WBS, and Control Scope

17. The most detailed level of the WBS is called the _____ .

     A. WBS element

     B. Work package

     C. Project scope

     D. Deliverable

18. Risk categories often include technical, external, organizational, and _____ risks.

A. environmental

B. safety

C. consumer

D. project management

19. Which of the following is a tool or technique used in the Monitor and Control Project Work process?

A. Expert judgment

B. Rejected change requests

C. Earned value technique

D. Project management information system

20. Two of the organizational process assets updated as a result of the Close Project or Phase process are:

A. Project management plan, project charter

B. Project charter, project calendar

C. Project management plan, RBS

D. Project management plan, risk register

21. During the Plan Procurements phase, the make-or-____ analysis must be completed. This technique prompts the project team to determine the source of their item.

A. lease

B. buy

C. find

D. ignore

22. Which of these precedence relationships is least commonly used in Precedence Diagramming Method?

A. Start to Start

B. Finish to Finish

C. Finish to Start

D. Start to Finish

23. A RACI chart is an example of a _____.

A. Network

B. Flowchart

C. Responsibility assignment matrix

D. Hierarchical-type organization chart

24. If the project's budget at completion (BAC) is $100,000 and the actual amount spent (AC) is $95,000, what is the cost variance of the project?

A. The cost variance is 195000

B. The cost variance is 5000

C. The cost variance is 0.95

D. The cost variance is 10000

25. As project manager, you are having difficulty understanding which tasks each member of your team is responsible for completing. Additionally, people feel like they are not getting sufficient information about the tasks they are not working on. What tool would help clarify these issues?

A. Network

B. Flowchart

C. Hierarchical-type organization chart

D. RACI chart

26. If you are writing a proposal for additional funding, which communication style should you choose?

A. formal and horizontal

B. formal and vertical

C. informal and vertical

D. informal and horizontal

27. If you want a group of experts to identify project risks, but also want unbiased data, what is an appropriate technique to use?

A. Interviewing

B. Delphi technique

C. Assumption analysis

D. Brainstorming

28. If you are working on a project with constantly changing scope, which contract type would work best when hiring an outside vendor to complete a portion of the work?

A. Cost reimbursable

B. Lump sum

C. Time and material

D. Fixed price

29. Which process of integrative project management documents the actions necessary to define, prepare, integrate, and coordinate all subsidiary plans into a project management plan?

A. Direct and Manage Project Execution

B. Monitor and Control Project Work

C. Develop Project Charter

D. Develop Project Management Plan

30. What is the most effective means of resolving issues and communicating with key stakeholders?

A. Email

B. Face to face meetings

C. Official reports

D. Telephone conversations

31. A project manager scheduled a review at the end of a phase, with the objective of obtaining authorization to close the current one and initiate the next one. Which of the following is an incorrect way of describing this review?

A. Phase gate.

B. Phase point.

C. Kill point.

D. Phase exit.

32. If you are measuring the quality of an item on a pass/fail basis, what is that called?

A. Attribute

B. Tolerances

C. Variable

D. Prevention

33. The Requirements Traceability Matrix helps in tracing all of the following except:

A. Requirements to project objectives

B. Requirements to project scope

C. Requirements to test strategy

D. Requirements to project risk

34. Which of the following should you NOT use as an input into creating the WBS structure?

A. Bill of Material (BOM)

B. Project scope statement

C. Organizational process assets

D. Requirements documentation

35. What are some of the outputs of following the Plan Quality process?

A. Quality Management Plan, Process Improvement Plan, and Cost-Benefit Analysis

B. Quality Management Plan, Design of Experiments, and Benchmarking

C. Quality Management Plan, Quality Checklists, and Quality Metrics

D. Quality Management Plan, Quality Metrics, and Cost of Quality

36. Which term best describes the Identify Risk process?

A. Finite

B. Redundant

C. Iterative

D. Inconsequential

37. During the Plan Risk Management process, assigning _____ will help you and the project team identify all important risks and work more effectively during the identification process.

A. risk factors

B. blame

C. risk mitigation plans

D. risk categories

38. Which of these processes is NOT a project time management process?

A. Create WBS

B. Develop Schedule

C. Define Activities

D. Sequence Activities

39. The technique most commonly used by project management software packages to construct a project schedule network diagram is:

A. Activity-On-Node (AON)

B. Finish-to-Start (FS)

C. Activity-In-Node (AIN)

D. Node-On-Activity (NOA)

40. Which of the following defines the total scope of the project and represents the work specified in the current approved project scope statement?

A. Work Breakdown Structure (WBS)

B. Bill of Material (BOM)

C. Project Charter

D. Requirements Breakdown Structure (RBS)

41. If you are creating a new WBS for your project, what should you consider to save time during the creation process?

A. Delegate the WBS creation since it is not an important process

B. Skip the WBS process

C. Use a previous WBS from a similar project as a template

D. Create a less detailed WBS

42. Which of these precedence relationships is most commonly used in Precedence Diagramming Method?

A. Finish to Start

B. Start to Finish

C. Start to Start

D. Finish to Finish

43. As the project manager of a project in your organization, you find that you have very little authority and mainly are engaged in project co-ordination activities. Your organization can be best described as:

A. Weak Matrix

B. Strong Matrix

C. Projectized

D. Functional

44. A good quality audit should be:

    A. structured and independent

    B. informal and independent

    C. informal and internal

    D. structured and internal

45. What is the traditional way to display a reporting structure among project team members?

    A. Text-oriented role description

    B. Flowchart

    C. Hierarchical-type charts

    D. Matrix based responsibility chart

46. The Project Charter formally authorizes a project. Who authorizes the project charter?

    A. The project manager

    B. A project sponsor or initiator internal to the project organization

    C. The customer

    D. A project sponsor or initiator external to the project organization

47. In an ongoing project, the project sponsor and a manager of the performing organization have conflicts. What would be your comment on this situation?

    A. The project manager needs to step in and handle stakeholder expectations. Stakeholders may have different objectives and interests in a project.

    B. The project manager needs to step in and handle stakeholder expectations. All stakeholders are supposed to have the same objectives and interests in a project.

    C. The project manager will resolve in favor of the project sponsor since he is providing the funds for the project.

    D. The project manager will resolve in favor of the manager of the performing organization since they are executing the project and need to be kept in good books.

48. Project risks should be identified by:

A. Those invited to the risk identification process only

B. The project stakeholders only

C. The project manager only

D. All project personnel

D. You should use Rolling Wave Planning to help you determine which activities are more important and should be done first.

49. A control chart should always contain:

A. Upper and lower warning limits

B. The cumulative average

C. Upper and lower control limits

D. A target value

50. When would Rolling Wave Planning be useful in a project?

A. You should use Rolling Wave Planning to help you achieve the appropriate level of detail in each work package at the right time.

B. You should use Rolling Wave Planning to determine the correct sequencing for long term items.

C. You should use Rolling Wave Planning to help you organize team member's activities within a large project group.

PMP Lite Mock Exam 1
Answer Key and Explanations

1.   D - A fee is not necessarily a bribe. However, when in doubt on any of the information provided by your local contacts, the project manager should check with the legal team. Depending on the nature of the contract (whether T&M, Fixed price, Cost Reimbursable etc), you should keep your customer appropriately informed on the fees and any charges. [Prof. Responsibility]

2.   C - If n is the number of people, then there are n(n-1)/2 communication channels in the project. [PMBOK Page 253] [Project Communications Management]

3.   D - This organization would be called a composite organization. [Project Integration Management]

4.   A - The decomposition technique allows the project manager to create unique, small, and manageable pieces of work from the larger work packages. [PMBOK Page 134] [Project Time Management]

5.   A - Parametric estimating is the process of using historical data to compare against your project to determine a correlation and thereby a cost estimate for your current project. [PMBOK 150] [Project Cost Management]

6.   A - The Create WBS process identifies the deliverables at the lowest level in the WBS, the work package. Project work packages are typically decomposed into smaller components called activities that represent the work necessary to complete the work package. [PMBOK Page 118/133] [Project Time Management]

7.   C - Contingency funds are used to handle cost uncertainty due to unknown purchases that may be needed during a project. These funds are generally used for items that are likely to occur, but not certain to occur. [PMBOK 173] [Project Cost Management]

8.   C - Staffing is typically the highest during the execution phase of the project. The other three responses may not hold true. Projects can move forward into subsequent phases without the deliverables of the prior phase being completely approved - this is known as fast tracking. Changes during the initial phases of the project are the least expensive. The influence of the stakeholders is the highest during the start of the project and reduces as the project moves to completion. [Project Framework]

9.   D - Standardized stakeholder list is not a valid organizational asset used in the Develop Human Resource Plan process. The others are valid assets. Other assets are: Historical information on org structures that have worked in previous projects and organizational processes and policies. [PMBOK Page 219] [Project Human Resource Management]

10.   C - While the physical location of individuals would have been a constraint in the past, with the technological advances, it is simple to work across countries and time zones using virtual teams. [PMBOK 228] [Project Human Resource Management]

11.   A - Configuration Preparation is not a valid response. The configuration management activities included in the Perform Integrated Change Control process are Configuration Identification, Configuration Status Accounting, Configuration Verification and Auditing. [Project Integration Management]

12.   D - A probability and impact matrix will help filter the high risk items and high impact items from the others so that you can focus your attention on these riskier items. [PMBOK Page 291] [Project Risk Management]

13.   C - Control Costs is the process of managing the project's costs and the changes that threaten the bottom line. [PMBOK 179] [Project Cost Management]

14.   A - The fixed price contract works best with a very well defined project scope. [PMBOK Page 322] [Project Procurement Management]

15.   B - If time is included in the equation, then this should be a time and materials contract instead of a cost reimbursable contract. [PMBOK Page 323 / 324] [Project Procurement Management]

16.   C - The five scope management processes are useful to a project manager and should be performed in order to avoid rework and losses. [PMBOK Page 103/104] [Project Scope Management]

17.   B - The work package is the lowest and most detailed level of the WBS and can be scheduled, cost estimated, monitored, and controlled. [PMBOK Page 116] [Project Scope Management]

18.   D - Project management risks can include risks during the estimating or planning process or during the controlling or communication process. [PMBOK Page 280] [Project Risk Management]

19. A - Expert Judgment is a tool or technique used in the Monitor and Control Project Work process. [Project Integration Management]

20. D - Documentation resulting from the project's activities, such as the project management plan and risk registers are updated as a result of the Close Project or Phase process. [Project Integration Management]

21. B - Make-or-buy is a typical decision point for a project manager. [PMBOK Page 321] [Project Procurement Management]

22. D - Start to Finish relationships indicate that the next task is not able to be completed until the one preceding it has started. This is not commonly used. [PMBOK Page 138] [Project Time Management]

23. C - A RACI chart outlines, in matrix form, the project tasks and who is responsible, accountable, consultable, and informable for each task. [PMBOK 221] [Project Human Resource Management]

24. B - The cost variance (CV) equals the BAC - AC. In this case, the CV = $5000. [PMBOK 182] [Project Cost Management]

25. D - A RACI chart outlines, in matrix form, the project tasks and who is responsible, accountable, consultable, and informable for each task. [PMBOK 221] [Project Human Resource Management]

26. B - Since this will be an official project document, it should be formal in nature. Additionally, since you are requesting money from someone higher up in the organization, you are creating a vertical communication. [PMBOK Page 245] [Project Communications Management]

27. B - The Delphi technique involves anonymous questionnaires circulated to a group of experts and provides an unbiased assessment of the risks. [PMBOK Page 286] [Project Risk Management]

28. C - The Time and Material (T&M) contract will allow the contract to change as the project scope changes. [PMBOK Page 324] [Project Procurement Management]

29. D - This statement describes the Develop Project Management Plan process. [Project Integration Management]

30. B - Face to face meetings allow all of the key players to be in a conversation at the same time and are a very effective communication tool.

[Project Communications Management]

31. B - Phase exits, Phase gates and Kill points refer to the same term and refer to a phase end review with the objective of obtaining authorization to close the current phase and begin on the next one. [PMBOK Page 19] [Project Framework]

32. A - An attribute is a quality characteristic measured on a pass/fail basis, while a variable is measured on a continuous scale. [PMBOK 206] [Project Quality Management]

33. D - Requirements Traceability Matrix is an output of the Collect Requirements process. It is used for tracing requirements to project scope, objectives, and test strategy. Tracing requirements to project risk is not a valid use. [Project Scope Management]

34. A - The Bill of Material (BOM) is not used as an input in the Create WBS process. The other three are valid inputs. [PMBOK Page 116] [Project Scope Management]

35. C - The Plan Quality process is an important process with outputs including the Quality Management Plan, Quality Metrics, Quality Checklists, Process Improvement Plan and Project Document Updates.

[PMBOK 200] [Project Quality Management]

36. C - The Identify Risk process is an ongoing, iterative process as risks are often identified throughout the project's life cycle. [PMBOK Page 282] [Project Risk Management]

37. D - Risk categories provide a structure that ensures a comprehensive process of systematically identifying risks and contribute to the effectiveness and quality of the process. [PMBOK Page 280] [Project Risk Management]

38. A - Create WBS is a process in the Project Scope Management area, while the other options are all Project Time Management processes. [PMBOK Page 129] [Project Time Management]

39. A - The method used by most project management software packages to construct a project schedule network diagram is Activity-On-Node (AON). This uses boxes or rectangles, called nodes to represent activities and connects them with arrows showing the logical relationship between them. [Project Time Management]

40. A - The WBS is a hierarchical decomposition of the work to be executed by the project team and defines the total scope of the project.

It represents the work specified in the current approved project scope statement. [Project Scope Management]

41.   C - Creating the WBS is a very important process, but often a previous WBS can be used as a template to save time and the potential rework of forgetting something important. [Project Scope Management]

42.   A - Finish to Start relationships indicate that the next task is not able to start until the one preceding it is completed. [PMBOK Page 138] [Project Time Management]

43.   A - A project manager's role in a weak matrix organization is that of a project co-coordinator or expeditor. In contrast, a project manager has high authority and complete control in a Projectized organization The project manager does not have complete authority over the project and funding in a Balanced matrix organization, but the organization recognizes the need to have a dedicated project manager. [Project Framework]

44.   A - A quality audit should be a structured process performed by an independent entity to provide the best results. [PMBOK 204] [Project Quality Management]

45.   C - A hierarchical-type organization chart can clearly show roles and reporting relationships within a team. [PMBOK 220] [Project Human Resource Management]

46.   D - A project initiator or sponsor external to the project organization, at a level that is appropriate to funding the project, authorizes the project charter. [PMBOK page 74] [Project Integration Management]

47.   A - The project manager needs to recognize that stakeholders could have conflicting interests and objectives. It is the responsibility of the project manager to successfully manage stakeholder expectations. [Project Framework]

48.   D - While it is not feasible to invite everyone to the risk identification meetings, anyone should be encouraged to identify risks as they encounter them. [PMBOK Page 282] [Project Risk Management]

49.   C - Upper and lower control limits allow the control chart to serve its purpose of indicating when a process is in or out of control. [PMBOK 209] [Project Quality Management]

50.   A - Rolling Wave Planning is a technique used to create a more detailed work plan while keeping the right level of detail for each activity - activities happening sooner have more detail than those further in the future. [PMBOK Page 135] [Project Time Management]

Knowledge Area Quiz
Project Integration Management
Practice Questions

Test Name: Knowledge Area Test: Project Integration Management
Total Questions: 10
Correct Answers Needed to Pass: 7 (70.00%)
Time Allowed: 15 Minutes

Test Description

This practice quiz specifically targets your knowledge of the Project Integration Management knowledge area.

Test Questions

1. What is a recommended method for controlling change within a project?

   A. Have only the project manager able to initiate change

   B. Have each change approved or rejected by a board

   C. Allow each project member ultimate control of changes within their realm of the project without a review process

   D. Freeze scope and allow absolutely no changes

2. The project manager of a project calls you in as a consultant to provide inputs on developing the Project Charter. Your contribution to the project could be best termed as:

   A. Professional Consultant

   B. Expert Judgment

   C. Charter Consultant

   D. Expert Consultancy

3. Which process is concerned with providing forecasts to update current cost information?

   A. Monitor and Control Project Work

   B. Project Management Information System

   C. Close Project or Phase

   D. Direct and Manage Project Execution

4. Which of the following would not be considered as an Enterprise

Environmental Factor during the Develop Project Charter process?

A. Scope Statement

B. Organizational infrastructure

C. Governmental standards

D. Marketplace conditions

5. Which of these activities would the Close Project or Phase process be applicable to?

A. Cancelled projects

B. Completed projects

C. Completed phases in a multi-phase project

D. All of the above

6. Which of these tools and techniques are common to all six Project Integration Management processes?

A. Project management Information System

B. Earned value technique

C. Project   management methodology

D. Expert Judgment

7. You are beginning a new project. When should you use the Perform Integrated Change Control process?

A. Throughout the entire project

B. Only when closing out the project

C. Only after the project is completely funded

D. Only after the project scope is clearly defined

8. The project management team has determined that there some changes to the Scope of the project. Who would be responsible for reviewing, evaluating and approving documented changes to the project?

A. Change Control Board (CCB)

B. Change Configuration Board (CCB)

C. Scope Control Board (SCB)

D. Configuration Control Board (CCB)

9. What is the difference between the Monitor and Control Project Work process and the Direct and Manage Project Execution process?

A. The Monitor and Control Project Work process and the Direct and Manage Project Execution process are the same.

B. The Monitor and Control Project Work process monitors the project performance while the Direct and Manage Project Execution process is concerned with performing the activities to accomplish project requirements.

C. The Monitor and Control Project Work process is a sub-process of the Direct and Manage Project Execution process.

D. There is no such thing as the Monitor and Control Project Work process.

10. Which of these Direct and Manage Project Execution items is not an output of the process?

A. Deliverables

B. Work Performance Information

C. Project management plan

D. Change requests

Knowledge Area Quiz
Project Integration Management
Answer Key and Explanations

1. B - It often works best for all project changes to be reviewed by a consistent group of people so that the changes are integrated and the project deliverables can be appropriately updated. [PMBOK Page 94] [Project Integration Management]

2. B - Expert judgment is the judgment provided, based upon the expertise in an application area, knowledge area, discipline, industry etc. This is available from many sources including consultants. [Project Integration Management]

3. A - The Monitor and Control Project Work process is responsible for keeping track of the project's measures, including cost. [PMBOK Page 89] [Project Integration Management]

4. A - The Scope statement is clearly not an enterprise environmental factor whereas the other three choices - Governmental standards, Organizational infrastructure, and Marketplace conditions are enterprise environmental factors. [Project Integration Management]

5. D - The Close Project or Phase process allows the project manager to close or finish a specific portion of the project. [PMBOK Page 99] [Project Integration Management]

6. D - All six processes of Project Integration Management use Expert judgment as a tool and technique. [PMBOK Page 73] [Project Integration Management]

7. A - Changes can occur in the project at any time, therefore the Perform Integrated Change Control process is valuable for managing and tracking those changes. [PMBOK Page 93] [Project Integration Management]

8. A - The Change Control Board is a group of formally constituted stakeholders responsible for reviewing, evaluating, approving, delaying or rejecting changes to the project. [Project Integration Management]

9. B - The Monitor and Control Project Work process monitors the other project processes, including the Direct and Manage Project Execution process, while the Direct and Manage Project Execution process completes the project scope. [PMBOK Page 83, 89] [Project Integration Management]

10. C - The Direct and Manage Project Execution has several outputs, including deliverables, work performance information, change

requests, project management plan updates, and project document updates. The project management plan is an input to the process. [PMBOK Page 84] [Project Integration Management]

PMP Lite Mock Exam 2
Practice Questions

Test Name: PMP Lite Mock Exam 2
Total Questions: 51
Correct Answers Needed to Pass:
36 (70.00%)
Time Allowed: 60 Minutes

Test Description

This is a cumulative PMP Mock Exam which can be used as a benchmark for your PMP aptitude. This practice test includes questions from all PMBOK knowledge areas, including the five basic project management process groups.

Test Questions

1. Which of the following statements is not true about a subproject?

    A. A subproject is a manageable component of a project.

    B. A subproject is the smallest unit of a project and cannot be broken down further.

    C. A subproject may be created from a project depending on human resource skill requirements.

    D. A subproject can be contracted to an external enterprise or another functional unit in the performing organization.

2. If you are developing a Project Management Plan, how should you determine the level of detail to be included in the plan?

    A. Always only provide a summary or high level plan

    B. Include only the details your manager specifically requested

    C. Always provide the maximum level of detail possible

    D. Provide the level of detail based on the project complexity and application area

3. If you want to have multiple vendors bid on your contract, what is the best way to ensure that all vendors have the same information before bidding?

    A. Issue a standard request for bid and do not allow any questions

    B. Hold a bidder's conference

    C. Communicate only through email

    D. Develop a qualified sellers list

4. Randy is managing a project and identifies that there are 8 stakeholders in the project. He is worried that he might end up with an unmanageable number of communication channels. In your view, how many communication channels does Randy have to plan for?

A. 64 channels

B. 56 channels

C. 8 channels

D. 28 channels

5. You have recently been assigned to be the project manager for a project that is already underway (the previous project manager has been moved to a different project). As you begin to learn about the project, you realize that a project charter was never established. What should you do?

A. Complain about the project charter not being completed.

B. Wait and see if a project charter is needed.

C. Establish a project charter at the point when you enter the project.

D. Assume that it is too late and continue without a project charter.

6. You have been asked to establish a project charter for your new project. According to PMBOK, who normally has the responsibility to authorize the charter?

A. Company president or CEO

B. Project initiator or sponsor

C. Key project stakeholders

D. Project manager

7. In general, Perform Qualitative Risk Analysis is:

A. not often completed

B. complete and 100% accurate

C. in-depth and thorough

D. quick and cost-effective

8. As a project manager, you are performing various project performance measurements to assess the magnitude of variation. You then attempt to determine the cause and decide whether corrective action is required. This would be known as:

A. Scope Analysis

B. Variance Analysis

C. Performance Reporting

D. Configuration Management

9. Two efficiency indicators that reflect the cost and schedule performance of a project are:

A. Cost Projection Index (CPI) and Schedule Projection Index (SPI)

B. Cost Performance Index (CPI) and Schedule Performance Index (SPI)

C. Actual Cost (AC) and Planned Value (PV)

D. Cost Pricing Index (CPI) and Schedule Performance Index (SPI)

10. What tool should you use to help identify project risks and their mitigation plans to support the project schedule?

A. Risk Register

B. Critical Path Method

C. Risk and Evaluation Plan

D. Schedule Network Analysis

11. If you want to compress a project schedule, what are two of the recommended alternatives to consider?

A. Fast Tracking and Schedule Network Analysis

B. Crashing and Fast Tracking

C. Resource Leveling and What-If Scenario Analysis

D. Crashing and Schedule Network Analysis

12. A project manager wishes to expand an existing list of sellers. Which of the following techniques should she consider?

A. Networking

B. Outsourcing

C. Expert Judgment

D. Advertising

13. Which of these tools is NOT part of the Seven Basic Tools of Quality?

A. Control Chart

B. Statistical Sampling

C. Flowcharting

D. Scatter Diagram

14. Which quality control technique or tool should be used when trying to determine the cause of a major defect?

    A. Pareto Chart

    B. Control Chart

    C. Histogram

    D. Fishbone diagram

15. Configuration Status Accounting is an activity that is performed as part of which process?

    A. Monitor and Control Project Work

    B. Close Project or Phase

    C. Collect Requirements

    D. Perform Integrated Change Control

16. Why is it important to have a staff release plan for people within the project team?

    A. It helps people manage their time.

    B. The project protects itself from lawsuit.

    C. It is not important.

    D. The project saves money by releasing people from the project at the right time and morale is also improved.

17. Midway through a project, a project manager determined that the project was running way behind schedule. If the project manager needs to now shorten the project schedule, without changing the project scope, which of the following schedule compression techniques could be applied?

    A. Crashing

    B. Reserve Analysis

    C. Forecasting

    D. Last Tracking

18. At the end of a project, what will your schedule variance be equal to?

A. Zero

B. Five

C. One

D. Hundred

19.   Quantitative risk analysis should be performed:

A. only on risks identified by the project manager

B. only in extreme cases

C. only on prioritized risks

D. on all risks

20.   Project risks should include impacts to project:

A. organization and profitability

B. project scope

C. schedule and cost

D. schedule, cost, quality or performance

21.   While analyzing a project, the project manager calculated the ratio of the Earned Value (EV) to the Actual Costs (AC) and obtained a value of 1.2. The project manager decided that this was an unfavorable condition to the project and decided to take corrective action. What is your view?

A. The project manager is correct. The ratio of EV to AC is called Cost Performance Index and a ratio greater than 1 is unfavorable to the project

B. The project manager is not correct. The ratio of EV to AC is called Cost Pricing Index and a ratio greater than 1 is favorable to the project.

C. The project manager is not correct. The ratio of EV to AC is called Cost Performance Index and a ratio greater than 1 is favorable to the project

D. The project manager is correct. The ratio of EV to AC is called Cost Pricing Index and a ratio greater than 1 is unfavorable to the project

22.   Which of these is not an approved Estimate Activity Durations technique?

A. Three Point Estimating

B. Parametric Estimating

C. Analogous Estimating

D. Critical Path Estimation

23. If you are working on a project where there is no definite project detailed scope, but similar projects have been completed in the past, what is the correct Estimate Activity Durations tool to use?

    A. Analogous Estimating

    B. Parametric Estimating

    C. Critical Path Estimation

    D. Three Point Estimating

24. As project manager, you would like to show the relationship between two variables to help your project team understand the quality impacts better. Which tool should be used?

    A. Scatter Diagram

    B. Run Chart

    C. Fishbone Diagram

    D. Pareto Chart

25. Which of these is not one of the tools and techniques recommended in the Control Schedule process?

    A. Performance Measurement

    B. Expert Judgment

    C. Variance Analysis

    D. Schedule compression

26. In a cause and effect diagram, which of these is not a potential cause?

    A. Personnel

    B. Effect

    C. Time

    D. Material

27. Which of the following is inaccurately represented by the term Progressive elaboration?

    A. Changes to project scope

    B. Rolling wave planning

    C. Detailing out the product requirements which were developed during the initiation process.

D. Production of fabrication and construction drawings from the design drawings for a chemical plant.

28. Which document describes the project's deliverables and the work required to create those deliverables?

    A. Project authorization document

    B. Project scope statement

    C. Project scope management plan

    D. Project charter

29. During a presentation to management, you want to display the project schedule with only the key deliverables displayed. What is the correct tool for this purpose?

    A. Project Schedule Network Diagram

    B. Critical Path Schedule

    C. Milestone chart

    D. Bar chart

30. Which of these is an input to the Collect Requirements process?

    A. Requirements management plan

    B. Risk register

    C. Scope statement

    D. Project charter

31. Which of these items are important to address when determining each person's role in the project team?

    A. Role, authority, responsibility, and competency

    B. Role, responsibility, and competency

    C. Role and responsibility

    D. Role, authority, and competency

32. If you want to reduce the number of quality inspections and thus reduce the cost of quality control for your project, which technique should be used?

    A. Run Chart

    B. Defect Repair Review

    C. Statistical Sampling

    D. Pareto Chart

33. When beginning a new outsourcing project, what is the best way to determine which companies you should request a bid from?

    A. Send your proposal to the company you last worked with

    B. Have someone else manage this part of the process

    C. Send your proposal to everyone

    D. Consult the qualified sellers list

34. Which of the following is not a general management technique used to generate different approaches to execute and perform the project work?

    A. Lateral thinking

    B. Six Thinking Hats

    C. Map Out

    D. Brainstorming

35. During lunch with a project manager from another department, you are given to understand that it is sufficient to adhere to the applicable Standards for the project. Regulations are not necessarily applicable to projects since they are guidelines and you as PM have the option to decide whether they are applicable or not. Your understanding is that :

    A. Standards are guidelines established by consensus and approved by a recognized body whereas Regulations are mandatory, government-imposed requirements.

    B. Standards are mandatory requirements created by the project team whereas Regulations are mandatory requirements issued by the Government.

    C. Standards are internally issued guidelines whereas Regulations are government-issued guidelines.

    D. Both are the same. The usage of the term varies depending on the country in which you operate.

36. Where would you find a detailed list and description of specific project assumptions associated with the project?

    A. Project management plan

    B. Project scope statement

    C. Project configuration document

    D. Change management plan

37. The date through which the project has provided actual status and accomplishments is called:

A. Data Date (DD)

B. Due Date (DD)

C. Project Date (PD)

D. Reporting Date (RD)

38. Which of these is NOT a risk diagramming technique?

A. System or process flow charts

B. Cause and effect diagram

C. RACI chart

D. Influence diagrams

39. Which tools and techniques are recommended for developing a project team?

A. Performance assessment, recognition and rewards, and team building

B. Training, team building, and ground rules

C. Team building, creating organizational charts, and assessing individual's performance

D. Setting ground rules and assessing team members based on those rules

40. A hierarchical structure of resources organized by resource type category and resource type used in resource leveling schedules is known as:

A. Team structure

B. Resource Pool

C. Organization breakdown Structure

D. Resource Breakdown Structure

41. A project manager's primary professional responsibility is towards:

A. The performing organization

B. The project sponsor

C. All stakeholders

D. Customers

42. What does a Cost Performance Index (CPI) of more than 1.0 indicate?

A. The project is over budget.

B. The project is right on budget.

C. The project is under budget.

D. The project is ahead of schedule.

43. Which of the following statements is correct?

A. A collection of unrelated programs can constitute a portfolio.

B. The scope of a portfolio is typically smaller than that of a program.

C. A program is a group of unrelated projects.

D. A program need not consist of projects.

44. A project team member finds that the color scheme of the webpage he is designing appears too gaudy and decides to change it to a mellowed down color scheme. The independent testing team flags this as a defect and there is a heated discussion between the team member and the testing team. What is your view?

A. The testing team is incorrect in flagging this as a defect. This is an example of expert judgment, wherein historical expertise is being brought into the project.

B. The testing team is correct. Even though the new color scheme is more pleasing than the old one, the appropriate change management process has not been followed and the work product is not as per design.

C. The testing team is not right in flagging this down. The color scheme is a simple matter and the new colors are definitely more pleasing than the old ones.

D. The testing team is correct in flagging this down. The team member should have sent a note along with the work product indicating that the color scheme change had been made.

45. Which of the following items needs to be kept in mind when relying on risk identification checklists?

A. They are biased.

B. They are not exhaustive.

C. They are often inaccurate.

D. They are easy to prepare.

46. As an external vendor, you are managing a complex software project that has been contracted on Time & Material (T&M). One of your team-members reports a break-through in automating some of the testing activities. This will potentially result in cost savings to the project as well as the project getting completed ahead of schedule by a month. Which of the following actions would you take?

A. This is confidential information within your project team and need not be shared with the customer. The savings will be additional profits on the project.

B. Communicate the current status and inform the customer that you will be incorporating some additional features to use up the savings in cost and time since it has been budgeted for.

C. Communicate the current status to the customer and indicate the potential changes to cost and schedule.

D. Communicate the savings in cost and time to the customer. At the end of the project, notify your billing department that they need

to prepare an invoice for 50% of the cost being saved.

47. What is the advantage of preparing an estimate of costs by an outside professional estimator?

A. To determine if a lump sum contract should be used

B. To determine the project funding limits

C. To hold vendors accountable to a certain price

D. To serve as a comparison point for incoming estimates

48. Which of the following may help in ensuring that certain bidders in the procurement process do not receive preferential treatment?

A. Use of weighted criteria

B. Use of bidder conferences

C. Use of screening techniques

D. Use of expert judgment

49. If you have an unresolved issue while working on a project, what is the best way to communicate that issue?

A. Assume that someone else is already working on it

B. Write an email describing the issue

C. Create an issue log

D. Complain to a fellow colleague

50. Your manager has asked you to include the Human Resource Plan and Schedule Management Plan in your Project Management Plan. Is this the appropriate place for those items?

A. No, these are stand alone documents only.

B. Yes, you should unquestioningly include anything your manager suggests.

C. No, these documents should not be created until later in the project.

D. Yes, include them in the Project Management Plan.

51. On obtaining the project charter, the project manager of a project immediately put together the project team to execute the project. Is this correct?

A. Yes. Acquisition of the project tam is primarily an Initiating Process Group activity.

B. Yes. The project manager needs to get the team together as soon as the project starts.

C. No. It is the responsibility of the Project sponsor to provide the team for execution.

D. No. Acquisition of the project team is primarily an Executing Process Group activity.

PMP Lite Mock Exam 2
Answer Key and Explanations

1. B - A subproject is not necessarily the smallest unit. On very large projects, the subproject can further consist of a series of even smaller projects. [Project Framework]

2. D - The level of detail required in a Project Management Plan would vary by project and would include only the details necessary for the project. [PMBOK Page 78] [Project Integration Management]

3. B - A bidder's conference is a good way to ensure all bidders have the same information at the same time and to ensure fairness and equity within the bidding process. [PMBOK Page 331] [Project Procurement Management]

4. D - The correct response is 28. The formula to identify the number of communication channels is n X (n-1) / 2 where n is the number of stakeholders. Hence in this case, it works out to 8 X (8-1) / 2 = 8 X 7 / 2 = 56 / 2 = 28. [Project Communications Management]

5. C - Even if done late, a project charter can help establish the legitimacy of a project and should be completed as soon as possible.

[PMBOK Page 73] [Project Integration Management]

6. B - The project initiator or sponsor external to the project authorizes the project charter. However, a project manager should be involved in the process as early as possible. [PMBOK Page 73/74] [Project Integration Management]

7. D - Perform Qualitative Risk Analysis is quicker than Perform Quantitative Risk Analysis which is sometimes not required by the project. [PMBOK Page 289 / 295] [Project Risk Management]

8. B - This is known as Variance Analysis. As project manager, you would then attempt to determine the cause of the Variance, relative to the scope baseline and then decide on whether corrective action is required. [Project Scope Management]

9. B - The CPI and SPI are two efficiency indicators in the project to reflect the cost and schedule performance of the project. [Project Cost Management]

10. A - The risk register helps a project manager identify risks and countermeasures that might impact schedule. [PMBOK Page 288] [Project Risk Management]

11. B - Crashing and fast tracking can increase the project's schedule when necessary, but might come at a higher cost and rework potential. [PMBOK 156 / 157] [Project Time Management]

12. D - Advertising is a good avenue to expand existing lists of sellers. Advertisements can be placed in general circulation publications in order to achieve this. [Project Procurement Management]

13. B - The seven basic tools of quality are: cause and effect diagrams, control charts, flowcharting, histograms, pareto charts, run charts, and scatter diagrams. [PMBOK 208] [Project Quality Management]

14. D - A fishbone diagram, also called a cause and effect diagram, helps identify potential causes of an issue or problem. [PMBOK 208] [Project Quality Management]

15. D - Configuration Status Accounting is a key configuration management activity and is done as part of the Perform Integrated Change Control process [PMBOK page 95] [Project Integration Management]

16. D - A staff release plan provides a clean break point for an individual and saves the project money in the process. [PMBOK Page 224] [Project Human Resource Management]

17. A - Crashing is the technique that can be applied to compress the project schedule without changing the project scope. The other technique is Fast tracking. (That is why one of the choices is given as Last Tracking to confuse the candidate) [Project Time Management]

18. A - The schedule variance is the earned value minus the planned value. At the end of the project, all of the planned values should be earned and the difference should be zero. [PMBOK 182] [Project Cost Management]

19. C - Since the quantitative risk analysis is a more in-depth process, it should only be performed on prioritized risks to minimize impact to the overall project schedule. [PMBOK Page 294] [Project Risk Management]

20. D - Schedule, cost, quality and performance are often the key factors that risks can impact for a project. [PMBOK Page 291] [Project Risk Management]

21. C - The project manager is not correct. CPI = Cost Performance Index, and is the ratio of EV to AC. A value greater than 1 is a favorable condition for the project. The project

manager has incorrectly interpreted the situation. [Project Cost Management]

22. D - Analogous, parametric, and three-point estimating techniques are all accepted practices for determining the correct amount of time required for a portion of the project. [PMBOK Page 149 / 150] [Project Time Management]

23. A - Analogous estimation relies on comparing a project to previous such projects that were similar in nature. [PMBOK Page 149] [Project Time Management]

24. A - A scatter diagram plots several occurrences of two variables (one on each axis). A relationship can then often be determine between the two variables based on how closely they fit a geometric model. [PMBOK 212] [Project Quality Management]

25. B - Expert Judgment is not used as a tool and technique in the Control Schedule process since the focus is on current project performance. [PMBOK 162 / 163] [Project Time Management]

26. B - The potential causes of a specific effect fall into these categories: time, machine, method, material, energy, measurement, personnel, and

environment. [PMBOK 209] [Project Quality Management]

27. A - The distinction between Progressive elaboration and Scope Creep needs to be understood since the two terms are different. The changes to scope (especially in an uncontrolled manner) are called scope creep. In contrast, Progressive elaboration involves building on, or elaborating the output of a previous phase. [Project Framework]

28. B - The project scope statement is the correct response. This document describes the project's deliverables in details and the work that is required to create those deliverables. It also forms the baseline for evaluating whether requests for changes are within or outside the project's boundaries. [Project Scope Management]

29. C - A milestone chart displays only the key deliverables and is simple and easy to understand. [PMBOK 157] [Project Time Management]

30. D - The project charter is an input to the Collect Requirements process. The other choices are not valid. Requirement management plan is an output of the Collect Requirements process. [Project Integration Management]

31. A - All four of these are important to consider when considering someone for a position within the project team: role, authority, responsibility, and competency. [PMBOK Page 222] [Project Human Resource Management]

32. C - Statistical sampling will provide sufficient inspection to ensure a high likelihood of a quality product, while saving money for the project. [PMBOK 212 / 198] [Project Quality Management]

33. D - A qualified seller list is a list of sellers that have been pre-screened for their qualifications and past experience, so that procurements are directed only to likely sellers who can work on the project. [PMBOK Page 330] [Project Procurement Management]

34. C - Alternatives Identification concerns itself with identifying techniques to generate different approaches to execute and perform the work of the project. Map-Out is not a valid technique - the other three namely Brainstorming, Lateral thinking and Six Thinking Hats are techniques used to generate ideas for different approaches. [Project Scope Management]

35. A - Standards are seen more as guidelines, developed by a recognized body, established by consensus. In contrast, regulations are government-imposed requirements. Ex: Building codes are an example of regulation [Project Framework]

36. B - The Project scope statement lists and describes the specific project assumptions associated with project scope and the potential impact of those assumptions if they prove to be false. The assumptions listed in the detailed project scope statement are typically more numerous and detailed than the project assumptions listed in the project charter. [Project Scope Management]

37. A - The date through which the project has provided actual status and accomplishments is called as Data Date. It is also known as as-of Date or status Date [PMBOK Page 159] [Project Communications Management]

38. C - Risk diagramming techniques can include: cause and effect diagrams (also known as fishbone diagrams), flowcharts, and influence diagrams. [PMBOK Page 287] [Project Risk Management]

39. B - Building teamwork and friendliness is important to the project's success. Activities such as team building and recognition and rewards can make a project successful

and help it overcome barriers. [PMBOK Page 232 / 233] [Project Human Resource Management]

40. D - The Resource Breakdown Structure is a hierarchical structure of resources by resource category and resource type used in resource leveling schedules and to develop resource-limited schedules. This may also be used to identify and analyze project human resource assignments. [PMBOK page 145] [Project Time Management]

41. C - The project management team's professional responsibilities are not limited to any one of the stakeholders. The other choices are correct but not complete by themselves. [Prof. Responsibility]

42. C - The CPI is calculated as the earned value divided by the actual cost. An index of greater than one indicates that you have spent less than you forecasted to this point. [PMBOK 183] [Project Cost Management]

43. A - A portfolio refers to a collection of projects of programs that are grouped together to facilitate their effective management. The projects or programs need not be directly related or interdependent. [Project Framework]

44. B - The testing team is correct in their findings. Even though the new color scheme might be a better choice than the old one, all changes need to follow the change management process and go through the appropriate change and approval process. [Project Scope Management]

45. B - While the risk identification checklist is a useful tool, it should be used in combination with the other tools, since it is impossible to cover all scenarios on one checklist. [PMBOK Page 287] [Project Risk Management]

46. C - A project manager should always communicate an accurate statement of the project status. There could be subsequent actions to discuss how the savings could be best utilized, whether there can be any cost sharing etc - but they would need to done following the appropriate procedure. [Project Framework]

47. D - An estimate of costs will serve as a benchmark on proposed responses. Any significant differences in cost estimates can be an indication that the procurement statement of work was deficient, ambiguous or the prospective sellers failed to understand the work. [PMBOK Page 332] [Project Procurement Management]

48. B - Bidder conferences allow prospective sellers and buyers to meet prior to submission of a bid. This ensures that all prospective sellers have a clear and common understanding of the procurement. This usually prevents any bidders from receiving preferential treatment. [Project Procurement Management]

49. C - An issue log allows you to communicate, track, and resolve project issues. [PMBOK Page 263] [Project Communications Management]

50. D - These are subsidiary plans and should be included in the Project Management Plan. [PMBOK Page 82] [Project Integration Management]

51. D - No, the project team is not acquired immediately after signing of the project charter. Acquisition of a project team starts with HR planning in the Planning process group, followed by the Acquisition of the team in the Execution phase. The other answers are wrong because the Acquisition of the project team is mentioned in the wrong phase. It is also not the responsibility of the Project Sponsor to provide the team for execution. [Project Human Resource Management]

Knowledge Area Quiz
Project Time Management
Practice Questions

Test Name: Knowledge Area Test: Project Time Management
Total Questions: 10
Correct Answers Needed to Pass: 7 (70.00%)
Time Allowed: 15 Minutes

Test Description

This practice quiz specifically targets your knowledge of the Project Time Management knowledge area.

Test Questions

1. While planning the schedule for your project, you frequently refer to the project calendar. The project calendar is:

    A. A calendar containing the days on which various meetings are scheduled within the project team.

    B. A calendar of working days or shifts that establishes those dates on which schedule activities are worked.

    C. A calendar containing the list of days on which the project team members will be on leave or take an "off".

    D. A calendar that establishes the dates on which project deliverables are sent to the customer.

2. As a project manager, you are in the process of preparing the project schedule for the project. Which of the following accurately depicts the sequence of your activities before you begin preparing the project schedule?

    A. Sequence Activities, Estimate Activity Resources, Estimate Activity Durations

    B. Sequence Activities, Estimate Activity Durations, Estimate Activity Resources

    C. Estimate Activity Durations, Sequence Activities, Estimate Activity Resources

    D. Estimate Activity Resources, Estimate Activity Durations, Sequence Activities

3. After one year of construction, an office building is scheduled to be completed on 30th January. The

landscaping work needs to start 15 days prior to completion of the building. Which of the following relationships most likely represents the relationship of the start of landscaping work to the completion of the office building?

A. Finish-to-start with a 15 day lead

B. Start-to-finish with a 15 day lead

C. Finish-to-start with a 15 day lag

D. Start-to-finish with a 15 day lag

4. You are the project manager of a project. As part of the planning process, you utilize a planning technique to subdivide the project scope and deliverables into smaller, more manageable components. What is this technique called?

A. Unit task analysis

B. Decomposition

C. Task Breakdown Process

D. Arrow Diagramming Method

5. The accuracy of Activity Duration estimates can be improved by considering the amount of risk in the original estimate. The three types of estimates on which three-point estimates are based are:

A. Budgetary, Ballpark, Order of Magnitude.

B. Best case scenario, Expected scenario and current scenario.

C. Most likely, likely, unlikely

D. Most likely, optimistic, pessimistic

6. You have decided to apply Resource Leveling to a project due to a critical required resource being available only at certain times. Which of the following will likely be true?

A. Resource Leveling is usually applied to a schedule model that has already been analyzed by the Critical Path Method

B. Resource Leveling and analysis of the schedule model by the Critical Path Method can be done in parallel.

C. Fast Tracking and not Resource Leveling needs to be applied in this case.

D. Resource Leveling is usually done before a schedule model has been analyzed by the Critical Path Method

7. Bar charts with bars representing activities show activity start dates as well as end dates and activity durations expected. For control and management communication, the broader, more comprehensive summary activity that is used between milestones is referred to as:

    A. Activity bridge

    B. Milestone chart

    C. Hammock activity

    D. Gantt chart

8. A technique that iterates the project schedule many times, to calculate a distribution of possible project completion dates is called:

    A. Monte Carlo Analysis

    B. Monteford analysis

    C. Pareto Cost chart

    D. Deming Analysis

9. The critical path method (CPM) calculates the theoretical early start and finish dates and late start and finish dates. Critical paths have either:

    A. Zero or positive total float

    B. Positive total float

    C. Positive or negative total float

    D. Zero or negative total float

10. You are managing a project that involves work on a film shoot. The editing activity can happen only after the film has been shot. The logical relationship between the editing and shooting of the film can best be described as:

    A. Finish-to-Finish (FF)

    B. Start-to-Start (SS)

    C. Start-to-Finish (SF)

    D. Finish-to-Start (FS)

Knowledge Area Quiz
Project Time Management
Answer Key and Explanations

1. B - A calendar of working days or shifts that establishes those dates on which schedule activities are worked. It also establishes non-working days that determine dates on which schedule activities are idle, such as holidays, week-ends and non-shift hours. [Project Time Management]

2. A - The correct sequence of processes in the Time Management Knowledge Area is: Define Activities, Sequence Activities, Estimate Activity Resources, Estimate Activity Durations, Develop Schedule, Control Schedule [Project Time Management]

3. A - The landscaping work needs to start on completion of the office building, so it is a finish-to-start relationship. Since it needs to start 15 days before completion of the building, it requires a lead of 15 days. Hence the answer is finish-to-start with a 15 day lead. [Project Time Management]

4. B - Decomposition is the correct response. [Project Time Management]

5. D - The accuracy of Activity Duration estimates can be improved by considering the amount of risk in the original estimate. The three types of estimates on which three-point estimates are based are: Most likely, Optimistic, and Pessimistic. An Activity Duration can be created using a value derived from these three estimated durations. [Project Time Management]

6. A - The correct response is that Resource Leveling is usually applied to a schedule model that has already been analyzed by the Critical Path Method [Project Time Management]

7. C - The correct response is Hammock activity. The comprehensive summary activity that is displayed in bar chart reports for control and management communication is called Hammock activity. [Project Time Management]

8. A - Monte Carlo Analysis is a technique that computes, or iterates, the project cost, or the project schedule many times using input values selected at random from probability distributions of possible costs or durations, to calculate a distribution of possible total project costs or completion dates. [Project Time Management]

9. D - The critical path method (CPM) calculates the theoretical early start and finish dates and late start and finish dates. Critical paths have either

zero or negative total float and schedule activities on this path are called critical activities. Adjustments to activity durations, logical relationships, leads and lags may be required to produce network paths with zero or positive floats. [Project Time Management]

10. D - This is a situation where the Editing activity can happen ONLY after the film shooting has been completed. Hence the logical relationship between the two tasks is Finish to Start (FS). [Project Time Management]

PMP Lite Mock Exam 3
Practice Questions

Test Name: PMP Lite Mock Exam 3
Total Questions: 50
Correct Answers Needed to Pass:
35 (70.00%)
Time Allowed: 60 Minutes

Test Description

This is a cumulative PMP Mock Exam which can be used as a benchmark for your PMP aptitude. This practice test includes questions from all PMBOK knowledge areas, including the five basic project management process groups.

Test Questions

1. The project manager of a software development team for a new credit card product is given a deadline of November 15th to release a new product targeted at Christmas sales. This is an example of:

   A. A Critical success factor

   B. A Deadline

   C. Project constraints

   D. Project scheduling

2. What is the difference between a histogram and a pareto chart?

   A. A histogram is a less accurate version of a pareto chart.

   B. A histogram is a type of pareto chart.

   C. A pareto chart is a type of histogram.

   D. A histogram and a pareto chart simply different terms for the same technique.

3. As a project manager, you are responsible for determining and delivering the required levels of both grade and quality. Select which of the following statements you disagree with.

   A. A product can be of a low quality but high grade.

   B. Low quality and Low grade are always a problem.

   C. A product can be of a high quality but low grade.

   D. Low quality is always a problem but low grade need not always be a problem.

4. Which of the following processes produces WBS as an output?

   A. Create WBS

   B. Define Scope

   C. Develop Project Management Plan

   D. Define Activities

5. The system which includes the process for submitting proposed changes, tracking systems for reviewing and approving proposed changes, defining approval levels for authorizing changes and providing a method to validate approved changes is the:

   A. Change Control Board

   B. Approval Plan

   C. Configuration Management System

   D. Work Authorization System

6. Most project management software packages use a method of constructing a project schedule network diagram known as:

   A. Precedence Diagramming Mode

   B. Precedence Diagramming Method

   C. Project Diagramming Method

   D. Critical Diagramming Method

7. When a negative risk occurs in a project, a response to it would be called:

   A. A contingency plan

   B. Failure planning

   C. A workaround

   D. Backup planning

8. Martin is the project manager of a project that is in an early phase. He needs to estimate costs but finds that he has a limited amount of detailed information about the project. Which of the following estimation techniques would be least suited to his requirements?

   A. Top-down Estimating

   B. Bottom-up Estimating

   C. Analogous Estimating

   D. Budgetary Estimating

9. If you had an experience with a particularly good or poor performing vendor, what is the correct way to document this experience for future projects?

   A. Create a seller performance evaluation

   B. Call the vendor and talk to them about the experience

   C. Tell all your friends about it

   D. Vow to only work with that vendor from now on

10. A project to construct 10 buildings in sequence, is estimated to cost $ 500,000 with a project timeline of 6 months. During a review after 3 months, the project manager finds that only 4 buildings are ready. The Actual Cost is $ 200,000. The Schedule Performance Index (SPI) of the project would then be:

   A. 0.8

   B. 1.25

   C. 1

   D. Cannot be determined since the data is insufficient.

11. Which of these is not a tool or technique for the Administer Procurements process?

   A. Contract change control system

   B. Recommended Corrective Action

   C. Claims administration

   D. Performance reporting

12. You are looking at various process improvement models. Which of the following is not a process improvement model?

   A. Malcolm-Baldrige

   B. Organizational Project Management Maturity Model (OPM3)®

   C. Capability Maturity Model Integrated (CMMI®)

   D. TQM

13. Which of these statement correctly links project and product life cycles?

   A. A product life cycle is generally contained within a project life cycle.

B. A project life cycle is generally contained within a product life cycle.

C. A product life cycle is the same as a project life cycle.

D. The last life cycle for a project is generally the product's retirement.

14. Before closing a contract, the project manager should:

A. consult a lawyer

B. verify that all deliverables were acceptable

C. re-read the contract

D. contact everyone on the project team for approval

15. Mark is the manager of a project to install 600 new desktop computers at a budgeted estimate of $ 60,000. He estimates the project duration as 30 days. After 5 days, Mark finds that he had inaccurately estimated his team's capabilities. His team has now completed the installation of 150 desktops. The Actual cost is $ 10,000. What is the Estimate at Completion (EAC)?

A. $45,000

B. $30,000

C. $55,000

D. $40,000

16. A management control point where scope, budget, actual cost and schedule are integrated and compared to earned value for performance measurement is called a:

A. Code of accounts

B. Control packages

C. Control account

D. Account Plan

17. You are defining the schedule activities for your project and identifying deliverables at the lowest level in the Work Breakdown Structure (WBS). You find that there is insufficient definition of the project scope to decompose a branch of the WBS down to the work package level. You now look at using the last component in that branch of the WBS to develop a high-level project schedule for that component. Such a planning component is called:

A. A planning packet

B. Control system

C. A planning package

D. Control element

18. Which of the following best describes the Verify Scope process?

    A. Verifying that the project quality requirements have been met

    B. Controlling changes to the scope of the project

    C. Obtaining stake holders' formal acceptance of the project deliverables

    D. Verifying that all of the project's objectives have been met

19. As a project manager of a project, you are analyzing the costs which have incurred. Which of the following costs cannot be classified under 'Cost of non-conformance'

    A. Quality Assurance Costs

    B. Warranty costs

    C. Costs due to loss of reputation

D. Rework costs

20. Which of these is not a commonly used Perform Quantitative Risk analysis technique?

    A. Control charting

    B. Expected monetary value analysis

    C. Sensitivity analysis

    D. Decision tree analysis

21. A project manager estimates the work to be accomplished in the near term in detail, at a low level of the Work Breakdown structure (WBS), while he estimates work far in the future as WBS components that are at a relatively high level of the WBS. What is this technique called?

    A. Decomposition

    B. Rolling wave planning

    C. High Level Planning

    D. Future planning

22. Negative risks can either be _____, transferred, or mitigated as a countermeasure.

A. extended

B. avoided

C. expected

D. downplayed

23. Pareto's Law states that eighty percent of the _____ are due to twenty percent of the _____. This is also known as the 80/20 rule.

   A. problems/causes

   B. causes/problems

   C. work/effort

   D. effort/work

24. A technical team can begin editing of a large document 15 days after they begin writing it. What kind of a dependency would this be represented as?

   A. Start-to-start with a 15-day lead

   B. Finish-to-finish with a 15-day lead

   C. Start-to-start with a 15-day lag

   D. Finish-to-start with a 15-day lag

25. Three recommended responses to positive risks are:

   A. share, mitigate, avoid

   B. exploit, share, enhance

   C. exploit, share, extend

   D. exploit, enhance, mitigate

26. A project manager is just finishing a project that has not gone well. Apart from cost overruns and schedule overruns, there have been a lot of quality defects and the project required a lot of senior management intervention to finally reach completion. The project manager should now:

   A. Focus on closing the project and moving on to the next one. Lessons learned is not applicable to this project since it has done badly

   B. Focus on presenting the data in positive light while ensuring that the reasons for the delays and problems are appropriately documented.

   C. Mask bad data and only present good data since his performance appraisal will otherwise be impacted.

D. Document lessons learned from the project and update the lessons learned knowledge database.

27. In a matrix organization, where the team members report to both, a functional manager as well as a project manager, generally, whose responsibility is it to manage the dual reporting relationship?

A. Functional manager

B. HR manager

C. Team members

D. Project manager

28. A first-time project manager wants to know during what phases of the project, Perform Integrated Change Control will be performed. What would you respond?

A. Perform Integrated Change Control is performed only in the execution phase.

B. Perform Integrated Change Control is performed during the project closure phase.

C. Perform Integrated Change Control is performed throughout

the project from project inception through project completion.

D. Perform Integrated Change Control is part of the Build phase and is typically found only in IT projects.

29. A Resource Breakdown Structure (RBS) would be used to breakdown the project by type of resources. The RBS is an example of a:

A. Linear chart

B. Matrix chart

C. Cross-reference chart

D. Hierarchical chart

30. You are gathering information to identify the risks in a project. In order to reach a consensus of experts, which technique might you apply?

A. Delta technique

B. None of these.

C. Monte Carlo method

D. Delphi technique

31. While managing a project, you decide to prepare an email to share with some stakeholders which describes the current project status. This is best described as an example of:

   A. Vertical communication

   B. Para lingual communication

   C. Informal communication

   D. Formal communication

32. Analogous Estimating is an estimation technique that use the values of parameters such as scope, cost, budget and duration from a previous similar activity as the basis of activity and is frequently used to estimate when there is a limited amount of information about the project. This is a form of:

   A. Expert Judgment

   B. Function point estimation

   C. Fixed point estimation

   D. Precision Estimation

33. During the execution of your project, you decide that you would like to have charts of your project status - cost and schedule, display certain key project data, and hold your project meetings in a specific conference room. Such a place would be called:

   A. Team project corner

   B. Team meeting room

   C. Team battle room

   D. Team project room

34. The document that formally authorizes a project is the:

   A. Project SOW

   B. Project Plan

   C. Project Charter

   D. Project Scope Statement

35. You are part of the review team of a running project. Among the various documents, which of these define how the project is executed, monitored, controlled and closed?

   A. Project Scope Management Plan

   B. Project Scope Statement

   C. Project Charter

   D. Project Management Plan

36. You are presented with a situation in a project where you need to measure the performance of the project. Which of these techniques would suit your requirement?

   A. Learned Value Technique

   B. Earned Value Technique

   C. Project Status Review

   D. Expert Judgment

37. A manager asks you to evaluate four new projects that he has suggested for next year. You review the projects and notice that one is not really a project, but more an operational task. Which of these is not a project?

   A. Change the product to enable increased consumer usage

   B. Manage a set of people for the next year to deliver the desired productivity results

   C. Respond to a customer request for different product packaging

   D. Resolve a space constraint issue by building a new addition to the plant

38. Which of the following Project Scope Management processes documents a configuration management system?

   A. Control Scope

   B. Define Scope

   C. Verify Scope

   D. Collect Requirements

39. The stakeholders of a project typically have:

   A. Positive objectives

   B. Negative objectives

   C. Conflicting objectives

   D. Similar objectives

40. A project was estimated to cost $ 200,000 with a timeline of 10 months. Due to a shipment delay, the schedule was slightly delayed. This was however made up by receiving the first batch of materials for the project by air. The net result was that there was some additional cost in the project. At the end of the second month, the project manager reviews the project and finds that the project is 20% complete and Actual Costs are

$ 50,000. The Estimate to complete (ETC) for the project would now be:

A. $160,000

B. $210,000

C. $250,000

D. $200,000

41. You have a team of engineers working on your project. Two of the engineers have frequent disagreements. You ask them to resolve their differences through a discussion. However, that does not yield any results. Subsequently, you get involved and based on an analysis of the situation, suggest some changes in the way they work with each other. This still does not yield results and you find that the project schedule is beginning to suffer. What is you next course of action?

A. Take Disciplinary action, if required, since the needs of the project are not being met.

B. Don't do anything. Differences of opinion amongst the team members is a healthy situation

C. Speak to the two team members and ask them to resolve their conflict amicably.

D. Ensure that they work in different shifts so that they don't clash with each other.

42. As a project manager, where would you document the escalation process to resolve issues that cannot be resolved at a lower staff level?

A. Scope management plan

B. Stakeholder management plan

C. Staffing management plan

D. Communications Management Plan

43. While developing the project schedule, you find that the completion of a successor activity depends on the completion of its predecessor activity. What is this dependency called?

A. Start-to-Finish

B. Start-to-Start

C. Finish-to-Start

D. Finish-to-Finish

44. Which of the following is not a tool and technique of the Collect Requirements process?

   A. Group creativity techniques

   B. Interviews

   C. Questionnaires

   D. Traceability matrix

45. You are planning out the communications methods to use as part of stakeholder management. The most effective means for communicating and resolving issues with stakeholders is:

   A. Status reports.

   B. Electronic mail.

   C. Telephone calls.

   D. Face-to-face meetings

46. A project manager wishes to illustrate the connections between the work that needs to be done and the project team members. The resulting document would be called:

   A. Responsibility Assignment Matrix (RAM)

   B. Resource Planning Chart (RPC)

   C. Task Assignment Model (TAM)

   D. Resource Assignment Chart (RAC)

47. Many project managers have seen a graph which shows "Influence of Stakeholders" starting out high and declining as the project progresses. Conversely, it shows the "Cost of Changes" starting out low and increasing as the project progresses. What is the key message a project manager should obtain from this graph?

   A. Stakeholder influence is not important at the end of the project.

   B. Changes should be made as early in the project as possible.

   C. Money should be set aside for expected changes at the end of the project.

   D. The project should be placed on hold until all changes are made.

48. Which of the following documents is likely to have a very extensive approval process?

A. Scope statement

B. Test plan

C. Requirements management plan

D. Procurement contract

49. A project manager found that some of the project work was not done at the right time and was done in an improper sequence. What do you think was the likely issue?

A. This is a project communications breakdown. The project manager needs to re-develop the communication management plan

B. The Project Scope document was not properly updated.

C. The Work Authorization System was not properly established in the project.

D. This is due to poor teamwork.

50. A contract change control system should include:

A. Vendor contact information, tracking systems, and approval levels necessary for authorizing changes

B. Paperwork, tracking systems, dispute resolution procedures, and approval levels necessary for authorizing changes

C. Information database, dispute resolution procedures, and approval levels necessary for authorizing changes

D. Tracking systems, legal ramifications for certain actions, and approval levels necessary for authorizing changes

PMP Lite Mock Exam 3
Answer Key and Explanations

1. C - Project constraints are factors that limit the project team's options. In this case, the deadline of November 15th is a hard deadline since it is tied down to Christmas season shopping. [Project Scope Management]

2. C - A pareto chart is a type of histogram where the causes are ordered by frequency. [PMBOK 210] [Project Quality Management]

3. B - Quality and grade are not the same. Grade is a category assigned to products or services having the same functional use but different technical characteristics. Quality is the degree to which a set of inherent characteristics fulfill requirements. Low quality is always a problem, low grade need not be. [Project Quality Management]

4. A - The Create WBS activity produces the WBS as an output. [Project Scope Management]

5. C - The Configuration Management system includes the process for submitting proposed changes, tracking systems for reviewing and approving proposed changes, defining approval levels for authorizing changes and providing a method to validate approved changes. In most application areas, the Configuration Management System includes the Change control system. [Project Integration Management]

6. B - PDM uses Nodes to represent Activities and connects the activities with Arrow to show dependencies. This is the most commonly used method by most project management software packages. [Project Time Management]

7. C - A workaround is a response to a negative risk that has occurred. It differs from a contingency plan in that a workaround is not planned in advance of the occurrence of the risk event. [Project Risk Management]

8. B - Bottom-up estimating is a technique that can be applied only when there is a large amount of detail available to the project manager. [Project Cost Management]

9. A - A seller performance evaluation is created by the buyer and provides information about the seller's performance. [PMBOK Page 340] [Project Procurement Management]

10. A - SPI = EV / PV
    Earned Value = $(4 / 10) * 500,000 = 200,000$ since 4 buildings are completed out of 10.

Planned Value = (5 / 10) * 500,000 = 250,000 since 5 of 10 buildings were expected to be completed.
Hence SPI = 200,000 / 250,000 = 4 / 5 = 0.8 [Project Cost Management]

11.   B - Recommended corrective action is not a tool or technique in the Administer Procurements process. [PMBOK Page 338 / 339] [Project Procurement Management]

12.   D - TQM is a Quality Improvement Initiative whereas the rest (Malcolm Baldrige, CMMI® and OPM3®)are Process Improvement models. [Project Quality Management]

13.   B - The product life cycle usually consists of sequential, non-overlapping product phases. The project life cycle is generally contained within one or more product life cycles. [PMBOK page 18] [Project Framework]

14.   B - Closing a contact should be done promptly after all contract work and deliverables are achieved. [PMBOK Page 99, 341] [Project Procurement Management]

15.   The Budget at completion (BAC) = $ 60,000 (given). The Actual Cost (AC) = $ 10,000 (given). The Earned value (EV) = (150 / 600) * 60,000 since 150 desktops have been installed. Hence, Earned Value (EV)

= $ 15,000. CPI = Earned Value / Actual cost = 15,000 / 10,000 = 1.5. This is an instance of a typical situation in the project. The project manager has underestimated the team's capabilities in his original estimate. The calculation used for EAC is:
EAC = BAC / CPI = 60,000 / 1.5 = 40,000 [Project Cost Management]

16.   C - This is a Control Account. Control Accounts are placed at selected management points of the Work Breakdown Structure WBS. Each control account may include one or more work packages, but each of the work packages must be associated with only one control account. [PMBOK page 121] [Project Scope Management]

17.   C - The correct response is Planning package. Control Accounts and Planning packages are two planning components used when the there are insufficient details of the project scope. [Project Time Management]

18.   C - Scope Verification involves obtaining the stakeholders' formal acceptance of project deliverables. [Project Scope Management]

19.   A - The Quality Assurance Costs are part of the cost of conformance. The cost of non-conformance includes the

failure costs. [Project Quality Management]

20. A - Control charting is not used in quantitative risk analysis because it is more of an in process measure. [PMBOK Page 298 / 299] [Project Risk Management]

21. B - In Rolling Wave Planning, the work to be accomplished in the near term is estimated in detail at a low level of the Work Breakdown structure (WBS), while the work far in the future is estimated as WBS components that are at a relatively high level of the WBS. The work to be performed within another one or two reporting periods in the near future is planned in detail during the current period. [Project Time Management]

22. B - You can avoid a risk by revising the project plan to eliminate the risk entirely. [PMBOK Page 303] [Project Risk Management]

23. A - Pareto's Law states that 80% of the problems are due to 20% of the causes. You can use a Pareto chart to illustrate this concept. [PMBOK 210 / 211] [Project Quality Management]

24. C - The relationship between the two tasks would be represented as a start-to-start with a lag of 15 days. A lag

directs a delay in the successor activity. [Project Time Management]

25. B - Positive risks can be capitalized on by using one of these three techniques: exploit, share, or enhance. [PMBOK Page 304 / 305] [Project Risk Management]

26. D - A project manager has a professional responsibility to conduct lessons learned sessions for all projects with key internal and external stakeholders, particularly if the project yielded less than desirable results. [Prof. Responsibility]

27. D - In a matrix organization, where the team members are accountable to both, a functional manager as well as a project manager, the management of the project team can tend to be complicated. Generally, it is considered the responsibility of the project manager to manage this dual reporting relationship. [Project Human Resource Management]

28. C - The Perform Integrated Change Control process is performed from project inception through project completion. This process is necessary for controlling factors that create changes, to make sure those changes are beneficial, determining whether a change has occurred, and managing the approved changes, including when they occur. [Project Integration Management]

29.   D - The Resource Breakdown Structure (RBS) is a hierarchical chart. It is used to break down the chart by type of resources. For example, an RBS can depict all of the welders and welding equipment being used in different areas of a ship even though they may be scattered among different branches of the Organizational Breakdown Structure and RBS. [Project Human Resource Management]

30.   D - Delphi technique is the technique used to reach a consensus of experts. [Project Risk Management]

31.   C - The correct response is that an email is an example of an informal communication. Another example is an ad hoc conversation. Reports, briefings are considered as formal communication. [PMBOK Page 245] [Project Communications Management]

32.   A - Analogous estimating is a form of expert judgment. It is most reliable when the previous activities are similar in fact and not just in appearance, and the project team members preparing the estimates have the needed expertise. [Project Time Management]

33.   B - The correct answer is team meeting room. This is one of the strategies of co-location and enhances the ability of the team to perform in a cohesive manner. [Project Human Resource Management]

34.   C - The document that formally authorizes a project is the Project Charter. It provides the project manager with formal authority to apply organizational resources to a project. [Project Integration Management]

35.   D - The project management plan is one of the major documents in the project and describes how a project will be executed, monitored, controlled and closed. [Project Integration Management]

36.   B - The Earned Value Technique measures performance of the project as it moves from initiation to closure. [Project Integration Management]

37.   B - Managing an operating team does not meet the project definition because it is not temporary or unique. [PMBOK Page 5] [Project Framework]

38.   D - Configuration management activities are documented as part of the requirements management plan which is an output of the Collect

Requirements process. [Project Scope Management]

39. C - Stakeholder expectation management is a key responsibility of a project manager as they often have conflicting objectives. [Project Framework]

40. A - The Budget at completion (BAC) = $ 200,000 (given) The Actual Cost (AC) = $ 50,000 (given) The Earned value (EV) = (2 /10) * 200,000 since 20% of the project is complete i.e. 2 months out of 10. Hence, Earned Value (EV) = $ 40,000. This is an instance of an atypical situation in the project. Late arrival of materials does not mean that all subsequent material will arrive late. Hence, the calculation used for ETC is: ETC = BAC - EV = 200,000 - 40,000 = 160,000. [Project Cost Management]

41. A - After the project manager has tried intervening, it is time to go in for more formal conflict resolution mechanisms, such as disciplinary action. [Project Human Resource Management]

42. D - The correct response is the Communications Management plan. This plan provides the stakeholder communication requirements, details of information to be communicated, person responsible for communicating, person or group who will receive the communication, methods of conveying the communication, frequency of communication and also includes the escalation process - identifying timeframes and the management chain to escalate and resolve issues that are unable to be sorted out at the lower staff levels. Among the other responses, the Staffing management plan might appear as a valid choice. However, the Staffing management plan describes when and how human resource requirements will be met and will not address the escalation process. [Project Communications Management]

43. D - In a Finish-to-Finish dependency , the completion of the successor activity depends upon the completion of its predecessor activity. [Project Time Management]

44. D - The requirements traceability matrix is an output of the Collect Requirements process and not one of its tools and techniques. [Project Scope Management]

45. D - Face to face meetings are the most effective means for communicating and resolving issues with stakeholders. [Project Communications Management]

46. A - The correct response is Responsibility Assignment Matrix

(RAM). This illustrates the connections between the work that needs to be done and the various team members. On larger projects, the RAMs can be developed at various levels. [Project Human Resource Management]

47.   B - Changes should be made as early as possible in the process to avoid additional cost and delays. The influence of stakeholders is high at the start of the project and low towards the end. Vice-versa, the cost of making changes in a project is low at the start of a project and high towards the end of the project. [Project Framework]

48.   D - Due to the legal and binding nature of procurement contracts, they are subjected to an extensive approval process. [PMBOK page 315] [Project Procurement Management]

49.   C - The Work Authorization System is a subsystem of the overall project management system. It is a collection of formal documented procedures that defines how work will be authorized to ensure that work is done by the identified organization at the right time and in the right sequence. It includes the steps, documents, tracking systems and defined approval levels to issue work authorizations. The other responses could be contributory factors, but the most likely reason is that the Work authorization procedure was either not properly established, or not properly followed. [Project Integration Management]

50.   B - Having a contract change control system will allow you to establish the procedures and process should you need to modify a contract. [PMBOK Page 338] [Project Procurement Management]

Knowledge Area Quiz
Project Cost Management
Practice Questions

Test Name: Knowledge Area Test: Project Cost Management
Total Questions: 10
Correct Answers Needed to Pass: 7 (70.00%)
Time Allowed: 15 Minutes

Test Description

This practice quiz specifically targets your knowledge of the Project Cost Management knowledge area.

Test Questions

1. The Cost Performance Baseline is a time-phased budget and is used as a basis to measure, monitor, and control overall cost performance of the project. It is usually displayed in the form of:

   A. An S-curve

   B. An inverted S curve.

   C. Pie-chart

   D. A Z curve

2. Contingency Reserves are estimated costs to be used at the discretion of the project manager to deal with:

   A. Inadequacies in the original estimate

   B. Anticipated but not certain events.

   C. Unanticipated events

   D. Anticipated and certain events

3. A project is estimated to cost $ 50,000 with a timeline of 50 days. After 25 days, the project manager finds that 50% of the project is complete and Actual costs are $ 50,000. What is the Cost Performance Index (CPI) ?

   A. The CPI is 1

   B. The CPI is 1.5

   C. The CPI is 2

   D. The CPI is 0.5

4. Your project is mid-way through a delivery schedule. As project manager, you want to understand how much work is left. Which is the most accurate way to determine the

remaining work to be done by the project team?

A. Rolling wave method

B. Earned Value Technique

C. A Manual forecast

D. Future analysis

5. An estimating technique that uses a statistical relationship between historical data and other variables (for example, square footage in construction, lines of code in software development) is known as:

A. Parametric Estimating

B. Analogous Estimating

C. Bottom-up Estimating

D. Historical Analysis

6. Lucy is a project manager involved in the Estimate Costs process in the initiation phase of a project. Given the limited detail available to her, what would you expect the range of her estimate to be and what would you call such an estimate?

A. -25 to +25 %, Rough Order of Magnitude

B. -10 to +10 %, Budgetary

C. -1 to +1 %, Definitive

D. -50 to +50 %, Rough Order of Magnitude

7. Funding requirements for a project are usually in incremental amounts that are not continuous, and these appear as a step function in the graph depicting Cash flow, Cost baseline and Funding. Any gap at the end of the project, between funds allocated and the cost baseline and cash flow amounts represents:

A. The amount of Management Reserve that was not used

B. The amount of Management Reserve that was not allocated

C. The cost overrun

D. Ineffective utilization of funds

8. As a project manager, you periodically do project performance reviews to compare cost performance over time, schedule activities or work packages over-running and under-running budget, milestones due, and milestones met. Which of the following is not a valid technique that

you would use for performance-reporting?

A. Trend Analysis

B. Earned Value Performance

C. Variance Analysis

D. Integration Analysis

9.   A variance threshold for costs or other indicators to indicate the agreed amount of variation allowed is called:

A. Variance limits

B. Control threshold

C. Cost limit

D. Acceptable threshold

10.   Which of these are not inputs to the Determine Budgets process?

A. Cost baseline, Requirements traceability matrix

B. Project schedule, contracts

C. Basis of estimates, Activity cost estimates

D. Project schedule, Resource calendars

Knowledge Area Quiz
Project Cost Management
Answer Key and Explanations

1. A - The correct response is 'S' curve. The Cost Performance Baseline is a time-phased budget and is used as a basis to measure, monitor, and control overall cost performance of the project. It is usually displayed in the form of: an S curve and is developed by summing estimated costs by period. [Project Cost Management]

2. B - Contingency Reserves are estimated costs to be used at the discretion of the project manager to deal with anticipated, but not certain events. These are also called as "Known unknowns" [Project Cost Management]

3. D - The correct answer is 0.5. The Cost performance Index (CPI) is given by the formula CPI = EV/AC where EV is the Earned Value and AC is the Actual Cost. Earned Value = 50% of $ 50,000 = $ 25,000 since 50% of the project is complete. Hence CPI = 25,000 / 50,000 = 0.5. A value less than 1 indicates cost overruns in the projects. This is quite apparent in the current case since the budgeted cost has already been reached ($ 50,000) [Project Cost Management]

4. C - Although the Earned value technique of determining the balance work in the project is quick and automatic, it is not as valuable or accurate as the manual forecasting of the remaining work by the project team. This however is more time-consuming. [PMBOK Page 184] [Project Cost Management]

5. A - This technique is known as Parametric Estimating and can produce higher levels of accuracy depending on the sophistication, as well as the underlying resource quantity and cost data built into the model. [Project Cost Management]

6. D - During the initial stages of the project, the level of information available will be limited. Hence the Rough Order of Magnitude (ROM) estimate is usually prepared and has an accuracy range of -50 to +50 % [Project Cost Management]

7. A - This represents the amount of management reserve that was not used. [Project Cost Management]

8. D - Integration analysis is not a valid choice. The other three choices, namely Variance Analysis, Trend Analysis and Earned Value Performance, are performance reporting techniques. [Project Cost Management]

9.   B - Control thresholds are variance thresholds for costs or other indicators such as person days and indicate the agreed amount of variation allowed. [Project Cost Management]

10.   A - The Cost baseline and Requirements traceability matrix are not inputs to the Determine Budgets process. The others are valid inputs. [Project Cost Management]

PMP Lite Mock Exam 4
Practice Questions

Test Name: PMP Lite Mock Exam 4
Total Questions: 50
Correct Answers Needed to Pass:
35 (70.00%)
Time Allowed: 60 Minutes

Test Description

This is a cumulative PMP Mock Exam which can be used as a benchmark for your PMP aptitude. This practice test includes questions from all PMBOK knowledge areas, including the five basic project management process groups.

Test Questions

1. Contractual agreements with unions or other employee groups can require certain roles or reporting relationships. This is an example of:

    A. A gating mechanism.

    B. Mandated Resource planning

    C. A constraint that limits the HR planning process.

    D. Politics

2. You are involved as project manager in a fairly large-sized project. You are in the process of making a procurement decision and plan to go with a simple purchase order. However, you are doubtful whether this is the correct thing to do and decide to find out more details about the process to be followed. Based on your findings, which of the following would be correct?

    A. A simple purchase order is not appropriate for project. The project manager should always use the Request for Proposal (RFP) route.

    B. Organizational process assets are guidelines available to the project. As project manager you have the final decision making authority and can decide whether to go in for a simple purchase order or not.

    C. The value of the project is immaterial. As project manager, you have the final decision making authority to go in for a simple purchase order as long as you are contracting with an approved vendor

    D. You would need to verify the policy constraints that form part of the Organizational process assets. Many organizations have policies that constrain procurement decisions and require use of a longer form of contract for projects above a certain value.

3. Which of the following is an output of the Define Activity process?

   A. Milestone list

   B. Project schedule activity diagrams

   C. Resource calendar

   D. Activity duration estimates

4. A control chart is used to determine whether or not a process is stable or has predictable performance. When a process is within acceptable limits, the process need not be adjusted. What are the upper and lower control limits usually set as?

   A. + / - 3 sigma (i.e. 99.73 %)

   B. + / - 6 sigma

   C. + / - 3 sigma (i.e.95.46%)

   D. + / - 1 sigma

5. What are the three-point estimates used during the Estimate Activity Duration process?

A. High probability, Low probability, Most likely

B. Best-case, Worst-case, Mean

C. Most likely, Most dangerous, Average

D. Most likely, Optimistic, Pessimistic

6. As part of a new project that you have just started on as project manager, you are putting together your team and find that one of the critical pieces of work requires a specialist from one of the functional departments. However, you are aware that the functional manager may not be very happy giving the resource to your project since your project is not a very high-profile one. Which of the following techniques will you need to apply:

   A. Acquisition

   B. Coercion

   C. Politics

   D. Negotiation

7. Although not a separate process in the Project Cost Management

knowledge area, the cost management plan is created as a part of what?

A. Develop Project Management Plan process

B. Management Contingency Reserve

C. Reserve Analysis

D. Cost Variance

8. The three categories into which contracts can be broadly classified are:

A. Cost-Reimbursable, Time and Material, Cost plus fixed fee

B. Fixed Price, Cost-Reimbursable and Lump Sum

C. Fixed Price, Cost-Reimbursable , Time and material.

D. Fixed Price, Time and Material, Lump Sum

9. The Plan-Do-Check-Act (PDCA) cycle as the basis for Quality Improvement is generally attributed to:

A. Deming

B. Crosby

C. Juran

D. Pareto

10. You are working on a large project that has been divided into the following phases: feasibility, conceptual, design, prototype, and build. You want to use the process groups with these different phases. What is the recommended approach?

A. Assign one process group to each phase.

B. Eliminate your phase structure and rename each phase with one of the process group names.

C. Skip a couple of the process groups since they don't apply to a large project.

D. Repeat all of the five process groups for each phase.

11. A _____ is a collection of projects or programs grouped together for strategic business needs.

A. Portfolio

B. Management System

C. Enterprise

D. Array

12. In a Finish to Start relationship between predecessor and successor activities, a project manager decides to schedule a successor activity 5 days before its predecessor is complete. This is accomplished by providing 5 days of:

A. Lag

B. Load

C. Fast-tracking

D. Lead

13. While managing a project, you decide to contract to an external enterprise. You enter into a contract where you pay the external enterprise a set amount (as defined by the contract), irrespective of the seller's costs. What would best describe this type of contract?

A. Fixed Price (FP)

B. Firm Fixed Price (FFP)

C. Lump-Sum (LS)

D. Fixed-price-Incentive-fee (FPIF)

14. Which of the following inaccurately describes a prototype?

A. A prototype is tangible and allows stakeholders to fine-tune their expectations.

B. Requirements from a prototype are usually insufficient to move to the design phase.

C. Prototypes support the concept of progressive elaboration.

D. A prototype is a working model of the expected product.

15. Rolling wave planning is a form of:

A. Regressive Elaboration

B. Expert Judgment

C. Progressive Elaboration

D. Historical Analysis

16. The Develop Project Management Plan process includes which of the following?

A. How changes will be monitored and controlled

B. The need for communication among the stakeholders

C. The level of implementation of each selected process

D. All of these

17. Which of these is not an example of an Information Gathering technique used in identifying risk?

A. Interviewing

B. Root cause identification

C. Brainstorming

D. Delta technique

18. Which of the following is accurate regarding Project Integration Management?

A. Project deliverables are not part of Integration Management

B. It involves the integration of individual processes and not process groups

C. The need for it becomes evident in situations where individual processes interact

D. It involves disregarding trade-offs and focuses on clearly articulating how accomplish all requirements by the deadline

19. The project charter should be authorized by the _____

A. Operations manager

B. Project team

C. Project manager

D. Project sponsor

20. You are managing a project team that is distributed across global locations. You communicate via email on a daily basis and have a telephonic status call once a week. Which of the following statements is valid?

A. Plan telephonic status calls every day and follow up every email communication with a telephone call to discuss whether the remote team has understood the task allocation.

B. Remote teams are an overhead on the project and should be avoided as far as possible.

C. The communication of status reports and work allocation can never be done effectively via email. Plan for 50% efficiency for the remotely located team.

D. The receivers of communication at the remote location will not be able to pick up nonverbal cues and this results in a certain loss in communication. You need to factor this in your planning.

21. While the five process groups are typically completed in order, they often overlap with each other throughout the project. Which two process groups should never overlap unless a project is canceled?

A. Initiating and Closing

B. Initiating and Executing

C. Initiating and Monitoring and Control

D. Planning and Closing

22. The five process groups should be done in the correct order to achieve maximum results. What is the correct order for the process groups?

A. Planning, Monitoring and Controlling, Initiating, Executing, Closing

B. Planning, Initiating, Executing, Monitoring and Controlling, Closing

C. Initiating, Monitoring and Controlling, Planning, Executing, Closing

D. Initiating, Planning, Executing, Monitoring and Controlling, Closing

23. What are the outputs of the Plan Procurements process?

A. Procurement management plan, Procurement statements of Work, Qualified sellers lists.

B. Procurement management plan, Qualified sellers lists, Selected sellers

C. Procurement management plan, Procurement statements of Work, Make-or-buy decisions

D. Procurement management plan, Qualified sellers lists, Resource calendars

24. You have met with your project sponsor and have been told that the project MUST be completed by the end of the year, no exceptions. This

should be included in the project scope statement as a:

A. Project Constraint

B. Project Boundary

C. Project Acceptance Criteria

D. Project Assumption

25. As a project manager, you are analyzing a process and looking at the causes for variation. Which of the following is not a classification of the causes?

A. Special causes

B. Random causes

C. Common causes

D. Perpetual causes

26. The change requests created as an output of the Monitor and Control Project Work process may be attributed to all of the following except:

A. Preventive Action

B. Defect Repair

C. Proactive Action

D. Corrective Action

27. Lee is the project manager of a project and is planning responses to a set of risks. As a direct response of implementing this risk response, he anticipates certain other risks to arise. These would be termed as:

A. Secondary risks

B. Primary risks

C. Planned risks

D. Related risks

28. You have been identified as the project manager for constructing a large shopping mall in your city. Which of the following are not necessarily stakeholders in your project?

A. Residents of the county.

B. A contractor from a subcontracting agency involved in the project

C. A senior project manager in your organization who just completed a similar project.

D. Local county administration.

29. A tool that is used for charting human resources is a:

A. Resource Histogram

B. Resource Assignment Chart (RAC)

C. Resource Activity Matrix (RAM)

D. Organization Breakdown Structure (OBS)

30. In the past you have had issues with stakeholders who come back to you a year after you thought the project was complete, so this time you are going to have the stakeholders sign an acceptance of deliverables document. This procedure should be included in what project management plan?

A. Change Management

B. Quality Management

C. Scope Management

D. Risk Management

31. Three strategies that typically deal with negative risks or threats are

A. Risk Avoidance, Risk Mitigation and Risk Analysis

B. Risk Transference, Risk Mitigation and Risk Planning

C. Risk Avoidance, Risk Transference and Risk Acceptance.

D. Risk Avoidance, Risk Transference and Risk Mitigation.

32. Which of the following is least likely to be a project?

A. Regular updates of the company website

B. Responding to a contract solicitation

C. Running a campaign for a political office

D. An endeavor that lasts for ten years.

33. Which of the Project Time Management processes involves identifying and documenting dependencies between schedule activities?

A. Sequence Activities

B. Define Activities

C. Develop Schedule

D. Control Schedule

34. What does it mean if the Earned Value is equal to Actual Cost?

    A. Schedule Variance Index is 1

    B. Project is on budget and on schedule

    C. There is no cost variance

    D. There is no schedule variance

35. You are managing a project to lengthen a runway at a major airport. However, after working on the project for six months and holding weekly status meetings, many of your stakeholders are not satisfied with the deliverables, even with a CPI of 1.0 and an SPI of 1.0. Which of the following phases has probably not been done properly?

    A. Control Scope

    B. Define Scope

    C. Identify Risks

    D. Change Management

36. Steve is the project manager of a global project. He finds that of late, there has been a deterioration in the quality of communication between various team members across the globe. What would you term this?

    A. Noise

    B. Encoding

    C. Static

    D. Disturbance

37. You are the project manager managing a project to design a print head for dot matrix printers. In order to determine ideal settings for print quality, the quality manager of the company suggests trying out various scenarios for printing by varying certain parameters on the print head. Identifying such variables which influence the product or process under development is called:

    A. Design of Quality

    B. Design of Experiments

    C. Statistical Experimentation

    D. Factorial analysis

38. You have recently started working at a company as a senior project manager. The company has no employee training programs in place for junior project managers. Some junior project managers have been asking you for assistance in dealing with some work related issues. You feel that they could benefit from some guidance. Which courses of action would NOT fulfill your responsibility?

A. Do nothing; it was not in your job description to mentor other employees.

B. Suggest that you and other senior project managers develop a mentoring program.

C. Develop a training program for junior project managers.

D. Offer to conduct periodic coaching sessions for the employees seeking assistance.

39. Which of the following statements best describes Time & Material (T&M) contracts?

A. T&M contracts are hybrid type of contractual agreements that could contain aspects of both cost-reimbursable and fixed-price type arrangements

B. T&M contracts are the best form of contracts when the scope of work and the number of hours of work for a specific resource category is clearly known.

C. T&M contracts are the same as Fixed Price contracts except that the total value is calculated using Fixed rates and the effort data is available to the purchaser as well as the seller. Once this is agreed upon, it becomes the same as a Fixed Price project.

D. T&M contracts are very risky since the value of the project is not known. It is best to go in for a fixed price (FP) contract.

40. Cause and Effect diagrams are used to illustrate how various factors might be linked to potential problems or effects. They are also called:

A. Taguchi diagrams

B. Pareto diagrams

C. Ishikawa diagrams

D. Process diagrams

41. When does the Close Project or Phase process need to be performed in case of multi-phased projects?

   A. The Close Project or Phase process needs to be done at the end of each phase of the project; however, it is left to the project manager's discretion on whether he/she wants to perform this process in between phases. It necessarily needs to be done at the end of the project.

   B. The Close Project or Phase process is done at the end of the project in case the work is contracted out to external performing organizations.

   C. The Close Project or Phase process needs to performed at the end of the project and involves closing out the entire project scope.

   D. The Close Project or Phase process needs to be performed at the end of each phase of the project and involves closing out the portion of project scope applicable to that phase.

42. A project manager is about to start on a new project. Where would he find details about his authority level in the project?

   A. The Organization HR manual

   B. The Project Charter

   C. The PMBOK

   D. The Scope statement

43. Which of the following is not true about the WBS?

   A. The project team must be involved in developing the WBS

   B. As a rule of thumb, each activity of WBS should take less than 80 hours

   C. WBS should focus on activities rather than deliverables

   D. WBS is usually represented in a hierarchical fashion

44. Which of the following is accurate regarding the Estimate Activity Resources process?

   A. It determines what resources will be used, but not when each resource will be available

   B. It determines dependencies that may require a lead or lag to define the relationship

C. This process is coordinated independent of the Estimate Cost process

D. It involves determining what and how many resources will be used

45. In a project, Activity A has a duration of 4 days and begins on the morning of Monday the 4th. The successor Activity, B, has a Finish-to-Start (FS) relationship with A. The Finish -to-Start relationship has 2 days of lag, and Activity B has a duration of 3 days. If Saturday and Sunday are non working days, which of the following statements is true?

A. Total elapsed days (completing both activities) is 7 days

B. Activity B will be completed by the end of day on Thursday, 14th

C. Activity B will be completed by the end of day on Friday, 15th.

D. Activity B will be completed by the end of day on Tuesday, 12th

46. Analogous Cost Estimating is which of the following?

A. Uses statistical relationship between historical data and other variables

B. Generally less accurate

C. Bottom-up estimating

D. Generally Accurate

47. What is the BEST way to make an accurate forecasting of ETC?

A. EAC - AC

B. BAC – EV

C. Manual Forecasting of cost of remaining work.

D. (BAC – EV)/CPI

48. Which of the following is not a valid instance of Risk Transference?

A. Use of a Cost Reimbursable contract

B. Warranties

C. Fixed Price contracts

D. Performance bonds

49. Under which of the following scenarios would you not use a Decision tree?

A. When some future scenarios are unknown.

B. When you need to look at the implications of not choosing certain alternatives.

C. When the future scenarios are known.

D. When the outcomes of some of the actions are uncertain.

50. You have been assigned as a project manager of a new project to be executed out of New York. However, you determine that the project requires a Global Positioning Systems Expert who is not available within the company in New York. On doing a little checking, you determine that the company has an expert based in London, who is suitable for the project. However, the London based employee is not willing to relocate to New York for the project. In such a case:

A. Write to the manager of the London based employee and inform him that the employee needs to be convinced to relocate

to New York due to project requirements.

B. You would look at the option of moving ahead with the project by using a virtual team.

C. Manage the project without the key resource and flag this as a risk.

D. Co-location of resources is a key factor for the success of projects. As per PMI guidelines, you will not be able to proceed with the project since the resources is not available in New York.

PMP Lite Mock Exam 4
Answer Key and Explanations

1. C - Constraints limit the flexibility in the HR planning process. Examples are: 1) Organizations whose basic structure is a weak matrix means a relatively weaker role for a project manager. 2) Collective bargaining agreements - contractual agreements with unions or other employee groups can require certain roles or reporting relationships. [Project Human Resource Management]

2. D - Organizational process assets provide the existing formal and informal procurement-related policies, procedures, guidelines and management systems that are considered in developing the procurement management plan and selecting the type of contracts to be used. Organizational policies frequently constrain procurement decisions. They may limit use of simple purchase orders and may require all purchases above a particular value to use a longer form of contract. [Project Procurement Management]

3. A - A milestone list is a valid output of the Define Activity process. [Project Time Management]

4. A - The upper / lower control limits are normally set at + / - 3 sigma -

99.73% (standard deviation) [Project Quality Management]

5. D - Most likely, optimistic, and pessimistic are the three-point estimates used during the Estimate Activity Duration process. [Project Time Management]

6. D - The correct response is Negotiation. This is typically done on many projects. The project management team may need to negotiate with functional managers to ensure that the team receives appropriately competent staff in the required timeframe. They may also need to negotiate with other project management teams. [Project Human Resource Management]

7. A - The activities to create the cost management plan are part of the Develop Project Management Plan process. [Project Cost Management]

8. C - Broadly speaking, contracts can be classified as: 1. Fixed price (Firm Fixed Price, Fixed Price Incentive) 2. Cost reimbursable (Cost Plus Fixed Fee, Cost plus Incentive Fee, Cost Plus Award Fee) 3. Time and Material (T&M) [Project Procurement Management]

9. A - The correct response is Deming. [Project Quality Management]

10. D - Process Groups should not be confused with project phases and each phase should contain all of the process groups. [PMBOK Page 41] [Project Framework]

11. A - A portfolio is the collection of projects or programs and helps facilitate efficient management. [PMBOK Page 8] [Project Framework]

12. D - A lead allows an early start of the successor activity. [Project Time Management]

13. B - This is an example of a Firm-Fixed Price project. [Project Procurement Management]

14. B - Prototypes usually go through multiple feedback cycles after which the requirements obtained from the prototype are sufficiently complete to move to a design or build phase. [Project Scope Management]

15. C - Rolling wave is a form of progressive elaboration planning where the near term work is planned in detail and the work for the far future is planned at much higher level. As the project progresses, the subsequent milestones are planned in greater and greater detail. [Project Time Management]

16. D - All of these items are included in the Develop Project Management Plan process. [Project Integration Management]

17. D - Delta technique is not a valid example of an Information Gathering Technique. [Project Risk Management]

18. C - Project Integration Management is needed more where individual processes interact. [Project Integration Management]

19. D - The project charter is authorized by the project sponsor or initiator who is usually external to the project. [Project Integration Management]

20. D - Nonverbal cues form a significant portion of communication. In the absence of this element, as project manager, you need to take special precautions to ensure that the communication is being properly understood by the remote team. If required, you may look at options such as team-building to improve team cohesiveness and video-conferences to help the communication process on a periodic basis. The other options do not present valid options since they quote invalid inferences. [Project Communications Management]

21. A - Throughout the project, the different process groups often are conducted at the same time except for the initial and the closing, which are separated by the other three groups. [PMBOK Page 41] [Project Framework]

22. D - These process groups should be done in the correct order to obtain maximum results: Initial, Planning, Executing, Monitoring and Controlling, and Closing. [PMBOK Page 41] [Project Framework]

23. C - Procurement management plan, Procurement statements of Work, Make-or-buy decisions are the outputs of the Plan Procurements process. [Project Procurement Management]

24. A - A preimposed deadline or milestone is an example of a constraint. PMBOK Pg. 115 [Project Scope Management]

25. D - Perpetual causes is not a valid cause. Special causes are unusual events and common causes or random causes are normal process variation. [Project Quality Management]

26. C - Proactive Action is not a valid reason for change requests. The other three choices Corrective Action, Preventive Action and Defect Repair are valid reasons for change requests in the Monitor and Control Project Work process. [Project Integration Management]

27. A - Secondary risks are those that arise as a direct response of implementing a risk response. [Project Risk Management]

28. C - Project stakeholders are individuals and organizations that are actively involved in the project, or whose interests may be affected as a result of project execution or project completion. A senior project manager who worked on a similar project may not necessarily be a stakeholder. The other three choices are valid since they have an interest in the project. [Project Integration Management]

29. A - The correct response is Resource Histogram. This bar chart illustrates the number of hours that a project, department or entire project team will be needed each week or month over the course of the project. The chart can include a horizontal line that represents the maximum number of hours available for a particular resource. Bars that extend beyond the maximum available hours indicate the need for a resource leveling strategy. [Project Human Resource Management]

30. C - Any process that formalizes the acceptance of the deliverables of a project should be included in the scope management plan. PMBOK Pg. 82 / 104 [Project Scope Management]

31. D - Risk Avoidance, Risk Transference and Risk Mitigation are the three techniques that deal with Negative Risk. [Project Risk Management]

32. A - Regular updates of the company website is an operational activity and is clearly not a project. 'Responding to a contract solicitation' and 'Running a campaign' are clearly projects. The endeavor lasting for ten years cannot be ruled out as a project just because of the duration. Projects can last from a few weeks to many years. [Project Framework]

33. A - Sequence Activities is the process of identifying and documenting dependencies between schedule activities. [Project Time Management]

34. C - There is no cost variance when Earned Value is equal to Actual Cost. [Project Cost Management]

35. B - With an CPI of 1.0 and an SPI of 1.0, the schedule is on time and on budget, however the stakeholders don't like deliverables. The indicates that the Define Scope phase was not properly done. PMBOK Pg. 183 / 115 [Project Scope Management]

36. A - Anything that interferes with the transmission and understanding of a message is termed noise. Distance would be such an example, as in the case of global teams. [Project Communications Management]

37. B - The correct response is Design of Experiments. [Project Quality Management]

38. A - PMI expects Project Management Professionals to share their knowledge with other professionals. Doing nothing to assist the employees because it does not strictly fall within your job description would not fulfill your responsibility to transfer knowledge to others. Even if the project managers job description does not include helping to transfer knowledge to others it is your responsibility as a project manager to do so. [Prof. Responsibility]

39. A - T&M contracts are hybrid type of contractual agreements that contain aspects of both cost-reimbursable and fixed-price type arrangements. They resemble cost-reimbursable contracts in that they are open ended, but resemble fixed price type contracts where the unit rates can be preset and agreed upon between buyer and seller for a specific resource category. [Project Procurement Management]

40. C - Cause and Effect diagrams are also called Ishikawa diagrams [Project Quality Management]

41. D - In multi-phase projects, the Close Project or Phase process is done at the end of each phase and closes out the portion of project scope and associated activities for a particular phase. [Project Integration Management]

42. B - The project charter contains details of the assigned project manager and authority level. It provides the project manager the authority to apply organizational resources to project activities. [Project Integration Management]

43. C - The WBS puts a greater focus on the deliverables than on actual activities. [Project Scope Management]

44. D - The Estimate Activity Resources process determines what and how many resources will be used. [Project Time Management]

45. B - Activity A has a duration of 4 days and completes by end of the day on Thursday, 7th. There is a 2 day lag and since Saturday and Sunday are non-working, Activity B can begin only on Tuesday, 12th. Activity B has a duration of 3 days and completes by end of the day on Thursday, 14th. [Project Time Management]

46. B - Analogous cost estimating is generally deemed less accurate than other methods of estimation. [Project Cost Management]

47. C - Manual forecasting of costs for remaining work is generally the best means of generating an accurate forecast. [Project Cost Management]

48. A - A Cost reimbursable contract does not transfer risk to the seller, rather, the risk is with the buyer. Risk Transference involves shifting the negative impact of a risk, along with the ownership of the response, to a third party. Risk transference nearly always involves payment of a premium to the party taking on the risk. Examples are use of performance bonds, Warranties, Fixed price contracts. [Project Risk Management]

49. C - You would use a Decision Tree when uncertainty and unknowns exist regarding future scenarios and their outcomes. [Project Risk Management]

50. B - The use of Virtual teams has created possibilities of having teams located in different global locations working towards a common goal. The availability of email, video conferencing has made such teams possible. Virtual teams do present additional challenges, but these can be managed in most cases. The other choices are not valid. [Project Human Resource Management]

Knowledge Area Quiz
Project Quality Management
Practice Questions

Test Name: Knowledge Area Test: Project Quality Management
Total Questions: 10
Correct Answers Needed to Pass: 7 (70.00%)
Time Allowed: 15 Minutes

Test Description

This practice quiz specifically targets your knowledge of the Project Quality Management knowledge area.

Test Questions

1. A project manager is analyzing and evaluating non-conformities. He is planning to use the 80/20 principle. What does this represent?

   A. 80 percent of the problems are caused by 20 percent of the causes

   B. 80 percent of the problems can be resolved while the remaining 20 have no solution.

   C. 20 percent of the problems can be resolved while the remaining 80 have no solution.

   D. 20 percent of the problems are caused by 80 percent of the causes

2. What is a run chart?

   A. A run chart is the same as a Pareto chart and shows the aggregation of defects

   B. A run chart is a pie chart that shows the distribution of various defects during the execution phase.

   C. A run chart is a bar graph that shows the occurrence of defects during the execution phase.

   D. A run chart is a line graph that shows trends in process over time, variation over time or declines/improvements in a process over time.

3. A project manager is unsure of the difference between precision and accuracy and asks for your help in understanding the difference between the two terms. Which of these responses would be the best response to such a question?

A. Precision is consistency that the value of a repeated set of measurements are clustered and have little scatter whereas accuracy is correctness that the measured value is very close to the true value.

B. Accuracy is consistency that the value of a repeated set of measurements are clustered and have little scatter whereas precision is correctness that the measured value is very close to the true value.

C. Accuracy and Precision are equivalent and normally specified in the SOW by the customer who issues the SOW.

D. Accuracy is more important than precision. The project management team must decide the level of accuracy required.

4. The technique of comparing actual or planned project practices to those of other projects to generate ideas for improvement and to provide a basis by which to measure performance is known as:

A. Workbench

B. Benchmarking

C. Quality control

D. Best practices

5. There is a serious defect in the finished product of a project that was completed a few months back and this results in a recall campaign to recall the defective products. What would be the best classification for these types of costs?

A. Cost of Defects

B. Replacement Costs

C. Recall Costs

D. Cost of Quality

6. You are the project manager of a project and have come up with a bar graph of problems and their frequencies. This kind of a chart is called a:

A. Deming chart

B. Pareto chart

C. Ishikawa diagram

D. Control chart

7. What is the process of random selection and inspection of a work product?

    A. Control Charting

    B. Flow Charting

    C. Statistical Sampling

    D. Inspection

8. Which of the following relates to Root Cause Analysis?

    A. Process Analysis

    B. Performance Measurements

    C. Quality Audits

    D. Quality Control Measurements

9. Which of the following tools is used during Trend Analysis?

    A. Control Charts

    B. Scatter Diagram

    C. Run Chart

    D. Cause and Effect Diagram

10. An automotive designer uses a certain technique to determine which combination of suspension and tires will produce the most desirable ride characteristics at a reasonable cost. In order to do this, she works with a statistical framework and systematically changes all of the important parameters instead of changing the factors one at a time. This is known as:

    A. Design of Experiments

    B. Suspension-Tire analysis

    C. Design of Quality

    D. Design of Automobiles

Knowledge Area Quiz
Project Quality Management
Answer Key and Explanations

1. A - The correct response is that 80% of the problems are due to 20% of the causes. This is also known as the Pareto technique and is conceptually related to Pareto's law which holds that a relatively small number of causes will typically produce a large majority of the problems or defects. [Project Quality Management]

2. D - A run chart is a line graph that shows data points plotted in the order in which they occur. It shows trends in process over time, variation over time or declines/improvements in a process over time. It is very useful to perform Trend Analysis. [Project Quality Management]

3. A - Precision is consistency that the value of a repeated set of measurements are clustered, and have little scatter, whereas accuracy is correctness that the measured value is very close to the true value. Precise measurements are not necessarily accurate. A very accurate measurement is not necessarily precise. The project management team must determine how much accuracy or precision or both are required. [Project Quality Management]

4. B - Benchmarking is the technique of comparing actual or planned project practices to those of other projects to generate ideas for improvement and to provide a basis by which to measure performance. [Project Quality Management]

5. D - The correct response is Cost of Quality. This refers to the total cost of all efforts related to Quality and includes operational costs of quality as a result of product recalls, warranty claims and recall campaigns. [Project Quality Management]

6. B - This is an example of a Pareto chart or Pareto diagram. [Project Quality Management]

7. C - Statistical sampling is the process of random selecting and inspection of a work product. [Project Quality Management]

8. A - A Root Cause Analysis is a type of Process Analysis. [Project Quality Management]

9. C - A Run Chart is typically used during trend analysis. [Project Quality Management]

10. A - The correct response is Design of Experiments and this plays a key role in optimization of products or processes. [Project Quality Management]

PMP Lite Mock Exam 5
Practice Questions

Test Name: PMP Lite Mock Exam 5
Total Questions: 50
Correct Answers Needed to Pass:
35 (70.00%)
Time Allowed: 60 Minutes

Test Description

This is a cumulative PMP Mock Exam which can be used as a benchmark for your PMP aptitude. This practice test includes questions from all PMBOK knowledge areas, including the five basic project management process groups.

Test Questions

1. Pierre is a project manager who has just finished a project. This project yielded less than desirable results. Which of the following is an important activity that Pierre must conduct with key internal and external stakeholders?

   A. Lessons learned session

   B. Project party

   C. Fault-finding session

   D. 360 degree session

2. When writing the roles and responsibilities for team members you should include the following in your write up:

   A. Role, Authority, Responsibility, Competency

   B. Role, Action Items, Supervisor, Competency

   C. Training Plan, Project Org Charts, Role , Authority

   D. Action Items, Org Charts, Responsibility, Authority

3. Management Contingency Reserve is identified in which process:

   A. Estimate Costs

   B. Determine Budget

   C. Estimate Activity Durations

   D. Estimate Activity Resources

4. Which of these is not a component of the scope baseline that is contained in the project management plan?

   A. Work Breakdown Structure (WBS)

B. Stakeholder register

C. WBS Dictionary

D. Project Scope Statement

5. You have been asked to provide a somewhat accurate estimate, but not to spend much money generating the estimate, for a project to create material safety data sheets (MSDS) for a chemical company. This is project is similar to one that your company closed last year, so you have decided to gather the project team members from the previous project to discuss and come up with an estimate for your management team. This is an example of what type of estimating?

A. Expert

B. Analogous Estimating

C. Bottom Up

D. Parametric Estimating

6. Project stakeholders are individuals and organizations that are actively involved in the project or have an interest in it. Which of these is a likely stakeholder?

A. Budget Director

B. Public Relations Manager

C. Project Sponsor

D. Fund Manager

7. You have landed your dream job, as project manager working in an exotic sports car factory. Your project involves coming up with a smoother ride for the car. You have tasked the engineers to determine which type of suspension and what type of tires will provide the best ride and the most reasonable cost. This is an example of?

A. Cost Benefit Analysis

B. Monte Carlo Analysis

C. Benchmarking

D. Design of Experiments

8. Report Performance includes information on how resources are being used to achieve project objectives. It should also generally include information on:

A. Cost and Schedule

B. Scope, Schedule, Cost and Quality

C. Scope and Schedule

D. Cost, Schedule and Quality

9. You are about to contract out a project to a service provider. However at the time of awarding the contract, you are not sure of the total effort involved. Which of the following would best suit your purpose?

A. Cost-Plus-Fixed-Fee (CPFF)

B. Time & Material (T&M)

C. Fixed Price (FP)

D. Cost-Plus-Incentive-Fee (CPIF)

10. You are working in the US, but have outsourced programming to India and structural engineering to people in Australia. The project doesn't have the budget to bring all the team together, so you will be relying on e-mail, fax, video conference and chat to work together. This is an example of?

A. Global Team

B. Virtual Team

C. Cross Functional Global Team

D. Diverse Team

11. As an experienced PMP, you have found that running a WBS meeting is tricky because you need to find a balance between decomposition and excessive decomposition. When items are excessively decomposed it leads all of the following, EXCEPT:

A. Too detailed project plan

B. Inefficient use of resources

C. Non productive management effort

D. Decreased efficiency when performing work

12. You are a sponsor of a project that is designed to record phone calls for quality control purposes. You are in the process of writing the charter, what is NOT an input into this document?

A. Organizational standard processes

B. Marketplace conditions

C. Government or industry standards

D. Project Scope Statement

13. John, a project manager, for Code Crashers Inc. has been assigned a project where he must lead a group of inexperienced programmers in developing a software package that creates Material Safety Data Sheets (MSDS) for a chemical company. This is very similar to a project that his colleague, Peter, worked on in 2006, with some junior programmers. If John needs to come up with a rough order of magnitude estimate, what tool or technique should he use?

A. Parametric Estimating

B. Bottom Up Estimating

C. Three-point estimate

D. Analogous Estimating

14. You are an expatriate working in a foreign country and have been asked to offer a cash payment gift to the procurement manager at a company you are bidding on work for. How BEST should you interpret this request?

A. Agree to provide the cash payment because the procurement manager controls whether your bid is accepted.

B. Inform the procurement manager that offering such a payment would violate your professional standards.

C. Base your interpretation of the request on an understanding of the norms of the country you are in.

D. Express your anger at the request and inform the procurement manager that this would never happen in your home country.

15. Lisa is the project manager of a large project. Early on she identifies a number of risks in the project and wants to adequately prepare for them. Which of the following can be used to transfer project risk?

A. Financial contracts

B. Insurance contracts

C. Prototype development

D. Change the project management plan to eliminate risk

16. The project managers have maximum authority in which type of organization?

A. Weak Matrix

B. Strong Matrix

C. Functional

D. Balanced Matrix

17. As the project manager on the construction of a new hotel you have developed a project management plan that you believe is realistic and will be formally approved. The organizational assets that influenced the development of the plan may include all of the following except:

    A. Project management plan templates

    B. Risk register from a past project

    C. Change control procedures

    D. Business case for the project

18. As part of your staffing management plan, you have developed a chart indicating the # of hours (X axis) a senior programmer will be working over the months (Y axis) of the project. This is an example of what?

    A. Pareto Chart

    B. Graph

C. Resource Histogram

D. Staff Acquisition Chart

19. Which of the following is a control tool that helps the project management team quantify and categorize defects according to sources?

    A. Scatter chart

    B. Pareto diagram

    C. Histogram

    D. Cause and effect diagram

20. You have just returned from the weekly change control board meeting where you presented the requested changes to the employee move project. You had five changes approved, however one was denied. You now are updating the project management plan to incorporate the changes. In what project management process would this be done?

    A. Direct and Manage Project Execution

    B. Planning

C. Monitor and Control Project Work

D. Initiation

21. You have successfully passed your PMP and are leading a project to replace the storage devices in a data center. In the following week you and your team of experts will be meeting with a storage device vendor to discuss the status of their deliverables that are due at week's end. What management process do these activities reflect?

A. Inspections and Audits

B. Administer Procurements

C. Procurement Performance Review

D. Report Performance

22. Alan is the project manager of a project with 6 stakeholders. If the number of stakeholders goes up to 8, how many additional channels does he have to manage?

A. 2

B. 14

C. 13

D. 28

23. The project management plan can best be described as:

A. A list of tasks, activities, durations and resources in a software program (e.g., Microsoft Project)

B. Coordinating changes across the entire project

C. Integrating and coordinating all project plans to create a consistent, coherent document

D. Integrating and coordinating all project documents and stakeholder expectations

24. Which of the following is not an example of a procurement document?

A. Tender Notice

B. Letter of Intent

C. Request for Proposal (RFP)

D. Invitation for Negotiation

25. You have been contracted to build a manufacturing plant in Kuala Lumpur, however you are not familiar with the building codes in the city of Kuala Lumpur or in the country of Malaysia, so you are reviewing all of their building codes prior to "putting a shovel in the ground". This is an example of?

A. Mandated quality assurance

B. Quality planning

C. Quality assurance

D. Quality control

26. An organization wishes to ensure that the opportunity arising from a risk with positive impact is realized. This organization should:

A. Exploit the impact.

B. Mitigate the risk

C. Share the risk

D. Avoid the risk

27. Your Vice President has asked you what the Estimate at Completion is going to be for an extremely small project you are working on. You were given a budget of $30, and to date you have spent $20 but only completed $10 worth of work.

A. 60

B. Not enough information to estimate.

C. 30

D. 15

28. You have just sat through an exhausting change control meeting discussing a change in scope to the project you have been working on for the last 7 months. After lengthy discussion the change in scope was approved. As the project manager you should now update all of the following documentation, EXCEPT:

A. Scope Baseline

B. Requirements documentation

C. WBS Dictionary

D. Project charter

29. You work at a software company that authors Material Safety Data Sheets (MSDS) for chemical companies. Prior to releasing the MSDS to the company you have created a list of items to be reviewed to see that they appear on the document such as: chemical name, CAS#, protection required, what to do an emergency,

etc. This is an example of what type of tool?

A. Checklist

B. Process Improvement Plan

C. Quality Management Plan

D. Quality Metrics

30. You are 8 months into a project and you have been given a new resource due to an employee resigning. After a couple weeks on the job, the new resource indicates it isn't clear to him what exactly he should be accomplishing. While this is disturbing to you as the PM, you decide to give him a document that contains detailed descriptions of work packages. What document did you give him?

A. Project Scope Management Plan

B. Activity List

C. WBS Dictionary

D. Project Charter

31. You are the project manager for a large petroleum company and are in the process of writing the project

charter for your sponsor. You have used the following as inputs except:

A. Business case for the project

B. Project statement of work

C. Work breakdown structure (WBS)

D. Project contract

32. Which of these statements is accurate regarding quality management?

A. Modern quality management complements project management

B. Overworking the team to meet requirements is not likely to increase attrition and rework

C. Quality and grade are essentially the same

D. Project requirements are turned into customer needs, wants, and expectations

33. You are a project manager arranging for some interviewing techniques to be applied. This would not apply to which of the following Project Risk Management processes?

A. Perform Qualitative Risk Analysis

B. Perform Quantitative Risk Analysis.

C. Identify Risks

D. Plan Risk Responses

34. The Risk Register is a component of the project management plan. It contains details of all identified risks and current status. It is a document containing the results of:

A. Plan Risk Responses

B. Perform Quantitative Risk Analysis

C. Perform Qualitative Risk Analysis

D. Perform Qualitative Risk Analysis, Perform Quantitative Risk Analysis and Plan Risk Responses

35. The correct sequence of processes in the Risk management area is:

A. Plan Risk Responses, Perform Qualitative Risk Analysis and Perform Quantitative Risk Analysis

B. Perform Quantitative Risk Analysis, Perform Qualitative

Risk Analysis and Plan Risk Responses

C. Plan Risk Responses, Perform Quantitative Risk Analysis and Perform Qualitative Risk Analysis

D. Perform Qualitative Risk Analysis, Perform Quantitative Risk Analysis and Plan Risk Responses

36. You the project manager responsible for building a 100,000 sq ft. data center. One of the schedule activities in your plan is to install the Computer Room Air Conditioning (CRAC) units, however in order to start the installation of the units the raised floor in the data center must be completely installed first, so the units have something to be bolted on to. This is an example of what type of dependency?

A. External

B. Required

C. Discretionary

D. Mandatory

37. Stakeholders have vested interest in the outcome of the project. Which of the following is a role of a stakeholder?

A. Project variable

B. Risk owner

C. Resource contributor

D. Cost reporting

38. You are analyzing the risk in a project and decide to do Sensitivity analysis to determine which risks have the most potential impact on the project. You look at a tool to help compare the relative importance of variables that have a high degree of uncertainty to those that are more stable. One such tool is:

A. S-tree analysis

B. Lightning Curve

C. Risk Curve

D. Tornado Diagram

39. Which of these is accurate regarding the Develop Schedule process?

A. Schedule flexibility is measured by the positive and negative difference between early and late dates

B. The critical path method is a schedule network analysis

technique that is performed using the schedule model

C. Schedule compression shortens the project schedule while changing the project scope

D. Schedule network analysis is a technique that is derived from the project schedule

40. A new CEO has come into your company and promptly shut down your project because it no longer met the business needs of the company. While not pleased with the decision, you document the level and completeness of the project to date. What activity or process is this part of?

A. Close Project or Phase

B. Close Procurements

C. Control Scope

D. Lessons learned

41. When a project is performed under contract, the contractual provisions will generally be considered as _____ for the project.

A. Constraints

B. Exclusions

C. Deliverables

D. Provisions

42. You are the project manager responsible for building a 100,000 sq ft. data center. One of the schedule activities in your plan is to install the Computer Room Air Conditioning (CRAC) units, however in order to start the installation of the units the raised floor in the data center must be completely installed first. This is an example of what type of precedence relationship?

A. Finish to Finish

B. Start to Finish

C. Start to Start

D. Finish to Start

43. The Manage Project Team process is part of what process group?

A. Planning

B. Executing

C. Monitoring and Controlling

D. Closing

44. You have been assigned a project where you are responsible for building a condo complex in a resort town. The project is expected to take 2 years to complete. During your work breakdown structure meeting you have decomposed many deliverables into work packages and schedule activities, however there are some work packages that will be occurring a year from now, so you have elected not to decompose those deliverables and work packages at this time. This is an example of what tool and/or technique?

A. Project Scope Evolution

B. Delayed Planning

C. Rolling Wave Planning

D. Time Delayed Decomposition

45. A Probability and Impact Matrix contains risks prioritized according to their potential implications for meeting the project's objectives. The typical approach is:

A. To use a look-up table or Probability and Impact Matrix with specific combinations of Probability and impact that lead to a risk being rated as "high", "moderate" or "low" importance.

The importance for planning responses to the risk are usually set by the organization.

B. To create a Risk Breakdown Structure with the probabilities and Impacts listed on the individual boxes. The higher the risk, the closer it is towards the Start Node.

C. To use a look-up table or Probability and Impact Matrix with specific combinations of Probability and impact that lead to a risk being rated as "high", "moderate" or "low" importance. The importance for planning responses to the risk are usually set by the project manager.

D. To create a matrix with the Cost, Time, Scope and Quality on one axis and probability of occurrence on the other.

46. You are attempting to estimate the resources required to put the server racks together in the new data center you are building. It has occurred to you that you may be able to compress the schedule if you look at using power tools vs. hand tools to build the racks and use individuals who have worked on this brand of rack in the past. This is an example of what type of resource estimating tool?

A. Top Down Estimating

B. Bottom Up Estimating

C. Alternative Analysis

D. Published Estimating Data

47. A project is contracted as a Time & Material (T&M) type of contract. The service provider initially estimates that the total effort involved would be about 1000 hours of effort. The project is contracted at a rate of US$ 75 per hour of effort. If the project ended up with 1200 hours of effort, what would the contract payout be.

A. US$ 75,000

B. US$ 90,000

C. US$ 82,500

D. US$ 120,000

48. A project is contracted as a Cost-Plus-Incentive-Fee (CPIF) type of contract. The project is negotiated such that if the final costs are less than expected costs, the sharing formula for cost savings is 75:25. The targeted cost is US$ 100,000 with an 8% incentive fee. If the project comes in at US$ 80,000, what would be the cost of the total contract?

A. US$ 108,000

B. US$ 93,000

C. US$ 112,000

D. US$ 91,400

B. Activities

C. Milestones

D. Tasks

49. Organizations strongly influence the project framework. Which of the following are recognized types of organizations?

A. Projectized, Functional

B. Strong Matrix, Organic

C. Weak Matrix, Pre-existing

D. Functional, Transactional

50. During a work breakdown structure meeting you have decomposed the deliverables into work packages and created your WBS dictionary. However, you now want to decompose the work packages to assist you in estimating, executing and control the project. These decomposed work packages are called?

A. Work Packages can't be decomposed into smaller units

PMP Lite Mock Exam 5
Answer Key and Explanations

1. A - The correct response is Lessons Learned Sessions. Lessons learned provide future project teams with the information that can increase effectiveness and efficiency of project management. [Project Communications Management]

2. A - A good role and responsibility document includes: Role, Responsibility, Authority, Competency. PMBOK Pg. 222 / 223 [Project Human Resource Management]

3. B - The Management Contingency Reserve is identified in the Determine Budget Phase. [Project Cost Management]

4. B - The Stakeholder register is not a component of the scope baseline. It contains all details about identified stakeholders. [Project Scope Management]

5. B - The estimate used expert judgment (past team members), costs from an old project and didn't spend a much money getting the estimate is an example of analogous estimating. PMBOK Pg. 171 / 172 [Project Cost Management]

6. C - The Project Sponsor is the most obvious stakeholder. [Project Framework]

7. D - Design of Experiments is a statistical method that helps identify which factors may influence specific variables of a product or process under development or in production. It is a tool in the quality planning process. PMBOK Pg. 197 / 198 [Project Quality Management]

8. B - The Report Performance process involves collection of all baseline data and distribution of performance information to all stakeholders. Generally, the performance reporting should provide information on scope, schedule, cost and quality. [Project Communications Management]

9. B - This type of a project situation calls for a Time & Material type of contract. The contract will be open ended since the effort is not completely known. However, the unit rates will be negotiated and agreed upon for a particular resource category. [Project Procurement Management]

10. B - Any team that doesn't meet face to face, but relies on electronic communications, is an example of a virtual team. PMBOK Pg. 228 [Project Human Resource Management]

11. A - Excessive decomposition can lead to: inefficient use of resources, decreased efficiency and non productive management efforts. PMBOK Pg. 120 [Project Scope Management]

12. D - The project charter is an input to the project scope statement. All the other choices are inputs into the project charter. All the other choices are enterprise environmental factors or organizational process assets. PMBOK Pg. 76 [Project Integration Management]

13. D - Analogous estimating is the correct choice. This technique relies on parameters from a similar previous project and is a gross value estimating approach. It is also generally less accurate. PMBOK Pg. 171, 172 [Project Cost Management]

14. C - It is important to understand the local customs and standards in the area where your project is taking place. This knowledge will ensure your decisions are considered ethical. Project managers have a responsibility to not accept or offer inappropriate payments. In some cultures it would be considered inappropriate to offer a cash payment to a company accepting bids, however, in the scenario presented it may be a lawful and accepted practice of the foreign country you are working in. In such a scenario, offering cash payment would not be an inappropriate payment. [Prof. Responsibility]

15. B - Transferring project risk (to a third party) can be done through tools such as insurance contracts, performance bonds, and warranties. Changing the project management plan is a form of risk avoidance; while developing a prototype would imply risk mitigation. [Project Risk Management]

16. B - A Strong Matrix organization provides project managers with the most authority. [Project Framework]

17. D - The business case for the project is used to develop the project charter and may not play a role in the development of the project management plan. [Project Integration Management]

18. C - A chart representing hours and the time the position, department, company will be working on the project is an example of a resource histogram PMBOK Pg. 224 [Project Human Resource Management]

19. B - A Pareto Diagram helps the management team quantify and categorize defects. [Project Quality Management]

20. A - Adapting changes to the project management plan are part of the Direct and Manage Project Execution. PMBOK Pg. 83 / 85 [Project Integration Management]

21. B - The question is asking for the project management process. The only project management process in the answers is Administer Procurements, a process of the Project Procurement Management knowledge area. The other choices are tools and techniques of Administer Procurements process. PMBOK. 338 & 339 [Project Procurement Management]

22. C - The formula to calculate the number of channels is n*(n-1)/2 where n is the number of stakeholders. In the original situation, with 6 stakeholders, the no. of channels is 6 * (6 - 1) / 2 = 30 / 2 = 15 In the new situation, with 8 stakeholders, the no. of channels is 8 * (8 - 1) / 2 = 56 / 2 = 28. Hence the additional number channels to manage is = 28-15 = 13 [Project Communications Management]

23. C - The Project Management Plan is the combination of all the other management plans such as: scope management plan, risk management plan, cost management plan, etc. PMBOK Pg. 78 [Project Integration Management]

24. B - Letter of Intent (LOI) is not a procurement document. Procurement documents are used to seek proposals from prospective sellers. Examples are: Invitation for bid, Request for proposal, Request for Quotation, tender notice, Invitation for Negotiation and contractor initial response. [Project Procurement Management]

25. B - Any type of quality plans, such as building codes, OSHA guidelines, ISO9000 or company quality plans are examples of Organizational Process Assets which are inputs in the Plan Quality process. PMBOK Pg. 192 / 194 [Project Quality Management]

26. A - Three strategies to deal with risks with potentially positive impacts on project objectives are to exploit, share or enhance the opportunity. [Project Risk Management]

27. A - Estimate at Completion (EAC)=BAC/CPI Budget at Completion (BAC) is $30 in this example Cost Performance Indicator (CPI)= Earned Value (EV) ($10)/Actual Cost ($20), which is .5 EAC=30/.5 EAC=$60 [Project Cost Management]

28. D - It is the project scope statement and not the project charter that should be updated. The project charter only contains the high-level requirements and high-level project description. All of the other documents listed in the question should also be updated. PMBOK Pg. 128 [Project Scope Management]

29. A - The scenario describes a checklist that someone would use to review the document prior to it being released. Creating checklists is a tool in the Plan Quality process. [Project Quality Management]

30. C - The WBS dictionary can include contract information, quality requirements and technical references. All the other documents would help the individual, but not give him an exact idea of what he needs to accomplish. PMBOK Pg. 121 / 122 [Project Scope Management]

31. C - The WBS is not an input to the creation of the project charter. [Project Integration Management]

32. A - As the correct item states, modern quality management complements project management. [Project Quality Management]

33. D - Of the Project Risk Management processes listed as response options, interviewing is a tool or technique which applies to all of them except

for Plan Risk Responses. [Project Risk Management]

34. D - The Risk Register contains the results of the Perform Qualitative Risk Analysis, Perform Quantitative Risk Analysis, and Plan Risk Responses. It details all identified risks, including description, category, cause, probability of occurring, impact(s) on objectives, proposed responses, owners, and current status. [Project Risk Management]

35. D - The correct sequence is: Perform Qualitative Risk Analysis, Perform Quantitative Risk Analysis and Plan Risk Responses. Perform Qualitative Risk Analysis includes methods for identifying risks for further action such as Perform Quantitative Risk Analysis and Plan Risk Responses. [Project Risk Management]

36. D - This is an example of a mandatory dependency, since the units will be bolted to the raised floor. A required dependency is not PMBOK term. PMBOK Pg 139 [Project Time Management]

37. B - Project stakeholders are also risk owners for a given project. [Project Framework]

38. D - A tornado diagram is useful for comparing the relative importance of variables that have a high degree of

uncertainty to those that are more stable. [Project Risk Management]

39. B - The accurate statement regarding the Develop Schedule process is that the critical path method is a schedule network analysis technique that is performed using the schedule model [Project Time Management]

40. A - Documenting the completeness of the project to date in case of premature termination of a project is an activity under the Close Project or Phase process. PMBOK Pg. 99 / 100 [Project Scope Management]

41. A - When a project is performed under contract, the contractual provisions are generally considered as constraints for the project. [Project Integration Management]

42. D - The successor activity, in this case the installation of the CRAC units, can't be started until the raised floor in the data center is finished (i.e., the units need to sit on the floor), therefore this is an example of a finish to start relationship. PMBOK Pg. 138 [Project Time Management]

43. B - The Manage Project Team process is part of the Executing process group. [Project Human Resource Management]

44. C - The correct answer is rolling wave planning. Rolling wave planning is a form of progressive elaboration and is used when the project management team does not have enough information for a phase or deliverable that will occur quite a long way into the future. PMBOK Pg. 120 [Project Time Management]

45. A - A look-up table or Probability and Impact Matrix with specific combinations of Probability and impact that lead to a risk being rated as "high", "moderate" or "low" importance is used. The importance for planning responses to the risk are usually set by the organization. The project manager can tailor this to the specific project during the Plan Risk Management process. [Project Risk Management]

46. C - In this scenario you are looking for alternative ways to compress the schedule by using experienced resources and power tools instead of hand tools. This is an example of alternative analysis. PMBOK Pg. 144 [Project Time Management]

47. B - The correct answer is US$ 90,000. Since this is a T&M contract, the contract is open-ended in value. Hence the contract value is the actual effort multiplied by the agreed rate = US$ 75 X 1200 = US$ 90,000 [Project Procurement Management]

48. B - The correct answer is US$ 93,000. The calculation is as follows: Incentive fee based on budgeted costs = 8% of 100,000 = 8,000 Actual costs = 80,000 Share of cost savings = 25% of 20,000 = 5,000 (since the cost savings is 100,000 - 80,000) Hence the payout = 80,000 + 8,000 + 5,000 = US$ 93,000. [Project Procurement Management]

49. A - Both projectized and functional are formally recognized terms for organizations. [Project Framework]

50. B - Activities represent the effort needed to complete a work package and are an output of the Define Activities process. PMBOK Pgs. 133, 134 & 418 (Definitions) [Project Time Management]

PMP Lite Mock Exam 6
Practice Questions

Test Name: PMP Lite Mock Exam 6
Total Questions: 51
Correct Answers Needed to Pass:
36 (70.00%)
Time Allowed: 60 Minutes

Test Description

This is a cumulative PMP Mock Exam which can be used as a benchmark for your PMP aptitude. This practice test includes questions from all PMBOK knowledge areas, including the five basic project management process groups.

Test Questions

1. You are responsible for measuring the errors in the paint process for the exotic cars that are manufactured at the plant where you work. Your control limits were set previous to your measurement and you found that 95.46% of the paint samples were in the acceptable range, this is an example of?

    A. 1 Sigma

    B. 3 Sigma

    C. 2 Sigma

    D. 6 Sigma

2. Accepted deliverables are an input to the Close Project or Phase process. These deliverables would have been accepted through which of the following processes?

    A. Verify Scope

    B. Perform Quality Control

    C. Accept Scope

    D. Perform Quality Assurance

3. Which of the following is not accurate about the initial phase of a project?

    A. The highest uncertainty is at this stage of the project

    B. The cost associated at the beginning of the project is highest

    C. Stake holders have maximum influence during this phase

    D. None of these statements are accurate

4. As part of the Define Scope process, a project manager documented the

specific project assumptions associated with the project scope in the project scope statement. While reviewing this document, an experienced project manager pointed out that the project manager should also document:

A. The date on which the assumption becomes invalid.

B. The assigned responsibility for each of the assumptions.

C. The potential impact of the assumptions if they proved to be false.

D. An Assumption Management Plan.

5. Your company has been chosen to develop a new line of business for a large insurance company. This is a large and important project for the company and you have told senior management that you will be creating a team meeting room for this project. This is one of the strategies for:

A. Collocation

B. Centralized Team

C. Project Control

D. Develop Project Team

6. Which process group corresponds to the "do" part of the plan-do-check-act cycle?

A. Closing

B. Monitoring and Controlling

C. Planning

D. Executing

7. The Administer Procurements process ensures that the seller's performance meets contractual requirements and that the buyer performs according to the terms of the contract. This process is part of which process group?

A. Executing

B. Closure

C. Planning

D. Monitoring & Controlling

8. Project Cost Management is primarily concerned with the cost of resources need to complete schedule activities. From a broader point of view, it is also concerned with the effect of project decisions on using,

maintaining and supporting the product, service or result of the project. This is referred to as:

A. Life cycle costing

B. Post-project costing

C. Comprehensive project costing

D. Project cycle costing

9.   One of the configuration management activities in the project involved capturing, storing and accessing configuration information needed to manage products and product information. This is known as:

A. Configuration status accounting

B. Configuration auditing

C. Configuration verification

D. Configuration reporting

10.   You and your team have diligently been working on a project over the past 2 years and yesterday you met with the Operations area to turn over the production system to the Operations team. You came back from the meeting with signed formal documentation indicating the project

was completed to specifications and the deliverables have been officially turned over to production for ongoing maintenance. This is an example of what?

A. Contract Closure

B. A new project for Operations

C. Sign-off documentation

D. Project or phase closure documentation

11.   The paint on the exotic cars that are manufactured in your plant is bubbling after about a year of application. What would be the BEST tool for your team to use to find potential causes of the peeling paint?

A. Defect Repair Review

B. Ishikawa Diagram

C. Control Chart

D. Inspection

12.   You are meeting with your team, early in the project, and would like to address all the strengths, weakness, opportunities and threats the project is facing. What tool should be used?

A. SWOT Analysis

B. Interviewing

C. Delphi Technique

D. Brainstorming

13. You are assigned to prepare the Procurement Management Plan for a project that involves setting up an org-wide Supply chain management system. You are looking for a guideline on what type of contracts you can use and what type of contract forms are to be used for this project. Which source will help you obtain this?

   A. Each project is unique so you will need to prepare the necessary documentation for this.

   B. Department process repository

   C. Organizational Process Assets

   D. Integrated project Plan

14. You have run away and joined the carnival as a project manager and are in charge of constructing the Ferris wheel in each town the carnival visits. However, this is something you have never done before and you are getting different opinions from others on how long it takes. Joe, is new and has given you what you believe to be an optimistic estimate of 3 hours, Bill says it will take 10 hours, which seems too long to you and quite pessimistic. Lastly, Margie, who is the most experienced at this task is telling you it will take 8 hours. You are not sure who to believe, so you decide to do a PERT estimation, based on this you have determined it will take how many hours to assemble the Ferris wheel.

   A. 7.5 hours

   B. 8 hours

   C. 21 hours

   D. 7 hours

15. Which technique among the following will help to improve decision making and is often used to reduce cost and execution time and to improve the quality and performance of the project deliverable?

   A. Project Engineering (PE)

   B. Cost Engineering (CE)

   C. Efficiency Engineering (EE)

   D. Value Engineering (VE)

16. A project manager colleague of yours is currently working under contract on a short term project. He has expressed some concerns about finding work after the project ends. The project he is working on is currently ahead of schedule and he expects they will finish a month sooner than initially expected. What advice would be appropriate to provide him?

A. Slow down work on the project to have it finish on schedule.

B. Continue the work within the project's scope and possibly finish ahead of schedule.

C. Exaggerate his experience to the sponsor to try to get a project manager position for him on other upcoming projects.

D. Inform the client the project is behind schedule and it will have to be extended.

17. You have just returned from the weekly change control board meeting where you presented the requested changes to the employee move project. You had five change requests approved, however one rejected request. These are outputs of what process?

A. Expert Judgment

B. Change Control Board

C. Project Management Methodology

D. Perform Integrated Change Control

18. There are two activities on your schedule, which are: 1) Install server in lab 2) Move server into the data center. However, the second task can't start until the server has run in the lab for 5 days without failure. This is an example of what?

A. Fast Track

B. Lead

C. Crashing

D. Lag

19. You just found out that a major subcontractor for your project consistently provides deliverables late. The subcontractor approaches you and asks you to continue accepting late deliverables in exchange for a

decrease in project costs. This offer is an example of:

A. Forcing

B. Smoothing

C. Confronting

D. Compromise

20. At which stage, in a typical project, do stake holders have maximum influence?

A. Middle stage

B. Influence is similar at all stages

C. Final stage

D. Initial stage

21. During your weekly status reports you are reporting the earned value for the project this information is important to you and the stakeholders to gauge the progress of the project. What process is the cost and schedule control part of?

A. Project Closure

B. Perform Integrated Change Control

C. Direct and Manage Project Execution

D. Monitor and Control Project Work

22. You have your project team members record the time they spend on different activities during the day such as: programming, electrical, HVAC, etc. This is an example of a tool and technique in what process?

A. Distribute Information

B. Plan Communications

C. Report Performance

D. Manage Project Team

23. You are working with your team and are looking at the cost risks in the project. For risks with no cost risk they have assigned a value of .05, for risks that will impact cost less than a 10% increase they have assigned a value of .1. For an increase to cost greater than 10% they have assigned a value of .2. With these values the team can build what qualitative risk analysis tool output?

A. Decision Tree Analysis

B. Expected Monetary Analysis

C. Probability and Impact Matrix

D. Modeling and Simulation

24. When solving complex problems with the team, what type of communication should be used extensively?

A. Written

B. Non-verbal

C. Verbal

D. Formal

25. You will be reporting to management, for the week of 07/15, that your project has an EV of $7700 and a PV of $9600. What is the status of your project?

A. Ahead of Schedule

B. On schedule

C. Not enough information provided

D. Behind Schedule

26. You are in the execution stage of your project and you have been informed that "corporate" will be sending in a

team of consultants to review whether your project activities comply with company and PMI policies, standards and procedures. This is an example of?

A. Quality Audit

B. Organizational Process Assets

C. Process Analysis

D. Recommended   Corrective Actions

27. You are in the initiation phase of your project and believe the project can be completed for $100,000. However, you are an experienced project manager and know that many things can happen between the initiation phase and the closure of the project. You have provided an estimate in the project charter of $50,000 - $150,000. This is an example of?

A. Completion Estimate

B. Original Estimate

C. Rough   Order   of   Magnitude Estimate

D. Approximate Estimate

28. PMBOK recognizes five process groups typical of almost all projects. Which of the following is not one of them?

    A. Executing

    B. Monitoring and Controlling

    C. Planning

    D. Time Management

29. A technique that uses a project model to translate the uncertainties specified at a detailed level into their potential impact on objectives that are expressed at the level of the total project is called:

    A. Probabilistic analysis

    B. Theoretical Analysis

    C. Simulation

    D. Effect Analysis

30. Which of the following is not one of the Knowledge Area processes?

    A. Procurement management

    B. Integrations management

    C. Communications management

    D. Execution management

31. A process that states how formal verification and acceptance of the completed project deliverables will be obtained is documented in the:

    A. Scope Management plan

    B. Procurement Management plan

    C. Project Body of Knowledge

    D. Communications Management Plan

32. The WBS is a deliverable-oriented hierarchical decomposition of the work to be executed by the project team, to accomplish the project objectives. This is created as part of:

    A. Project Integration Management

    B. Project Scope Management

    C. Project Procurement Management

    D. Project Time Management

33. In order to better manage your project, you would like the see if you have a concentration of sources of

risks, in any areas of the project. The team could go about this activity using all of the following, EXCEPT

A. RBS

B. Project Phases

C. WBS

D. Process Analysis

34. The process of auditing the quality requirements and the results from quality control measurements to ensure appropriate quality standards and operational definitions are used is the definition of:

A. Quality assurance

B. Quality planning

C. Quality control

D. Quality application

35. Which of the following correctly depicts the most common order in which the project management processes are executed?

A. Perform Quality Assurance is done after Verify Scope

B. Verify Scope is done before Perform Quality Control

C. Perform Quality Control is done before Verify Scope

D. Perform Quality Control is done before Perform Quality Assurance

36. A buyer has just received a final set of deliverables from the seller and finds that they do not conform to the specifications that were originally planned for. Ideally, where would the buyer expect to find documentation on how to handle non-conforming deliverables?

A. Communication Plan

B. The contract

C. Quality Plan

D. Scope Statement

37. A change request that is issued to bring future performance of the project in line with the project management plan would be called:

A. Corrective action

B. Defect Repair

C. Recuperative action

D. Preventive action

38. Two of your team members played the Mega Millions lottery and won! As much as they like working on your team, they have decided to retire. What plan should be updated?

A. Retirement Plan

B. Resource Availability Document

C. Communications Plan

D. Staffing Management Plan

39. You are running one week behind on a project due to a vendor delivering cables late, so you are forced to compress your schedule due to a government mandated end date that constrains your project. After meeting with your team, the decision is to work several tasks in parallel that were scheduled to run consecutively. This is an example of what?

A. Risk Acceptance

B. Crashing

C. Resource Leveling

D. Fast Tracking

40. When developing your project schedule, you have asked everyone to provide a list of planned vacations over the next 3 months and you have applied this into the task that each person is responsible for. This is an example of what tool?

A. Applying Calendars

B. Adjusting Leads

C. Schedule Variances

D. Adjusting Lags

41. A project has gone out of control and the project manager is trying to bring it back under control. There have been a number of changes to the project scope and some of the changes resulted in further changes such that the project cost spiraled and the project went out of schedule. This is known as:

A. Scope creep

B. Scope jump

C. Project creep

D. Scope control

42. You are working on a data center migration project and will be moving a mainframe system to another data center, however you can't have any downtime when performing the move. There are a number of theories that subject matter experts have on how this daunting task can be done, but the group is not coming to consensus. You have decided that you will send out a questionnaire to the subject matter experts to get their views and risks on the project. You will then summarize the risks and approaches and recirculate to the subject matter experts. You are hoping to reach consensus after several rounds of this? What type of tool is being used?

A. Interviewing

B. Brainstorming

C. SWOT Analysis

D. Delphi Technique

43. A software development project that you are managing as project manager will involve working with a remote team. One of the requirements is to set up a secure communication link. The lead-time to setup the link is 45 days. Since the initial phase of the project involves requirements gathering, you feel that the link is required only after 3 months and are

planning accordingly. You would typically do this planning activity in:

A. The Conduct Procurements process

B. The Define Activities phase

C. The Plan Procurements process

D. The Administer Procurements phase

44. You have been pulled into your boss' office and told your "team member of the month" is a bad idea because it is a zero sum reward system. What does this mean?

A. It rewards poor behavior

B. Only a limited number of people can be rewarded

C. Too many team members will win the award

D. No team member is good enough to win the award

45. You are an experienced project manager who managed projects that migrate entire data centers from one facility to another. You have been hired to perform the function again and have pulled together a team and are conducting training on the databases, spreadsheets and management plans you will be using during the lifecycle of the project. This training is a tool and technique in what process?

A. Manage Project Team

B. Acquire Project Team

C. Develop Project Team

D. Train Team

46. You have taken a position as a project manager for an oil drilling company, with oil at $143 per barrel this could be a very lucrative project. However, there is a risk that the price of oil will drop below $105 per barrel, thus eliminating the profit in the project. This is an example of what type of risk?

A. Unforeseeable

B. Technical

C. External

D. Internal

47. During the weekly change control board meeting you invited the facilities manager to speak about the

change request to increase the BTU's to the air conditioning system in the new data center. This is an example of what type of tool and technique in the Perform Integrated Change Control process?

A. Variance Analysis

B. Expert Judgment

C. Project Management Methodology

D. Project Management Information System

48. You are managing a project that has a task to translate several pages of a document into Spanish. This is very similar to a project done last year where a document was translated into German. You are not sure how long it will take to translate into Spanish so you look at the project plan from the German translation and use the activity duration for your project. What type of estimating is this an example of?

A. Hypothesis

B. Parametric Estimating

C. Analogous Estimating

D. What if Scenario Analysis

49. To control the schedule, a project manager is re-analyzing the project to predict project duration. This is done by analyzing the sequence of activities with the least amount of flexibility. What technique is being used?

A. Precedence Diagramming

B. Work Breakdown Structure

C. Flowchart

D. Critical Path Method

50. A project manager creates a component-specific tool to verify that a set of required steps have been performed. This tool is called a :

A. Guide

B. Work list

C. Checklist

D. A plan-list

51. A change request has just been formally documented and approved by the Change Control Board. The project manager now needs to communicate this to a project team member. Which of the following activities must the project manager necessarily do?

A. Telephone the team member and inform him/her about the changes.

B. Plan for a meeting over lunch and detail the changes.

C. Issue a formal communication document informing the team member about the changes.

D. Write an informal memo communicating the changes

PMP Lite Mock Exam 6
Answer Key and Explanations

1. C - 1 Sigma = 68.26% 2 Sigma = 95.46% 3 Sigma = 99.73% 6 Sigma = 99.99985% [Project Quality Management]

2. A - Accepted Deliverables are those that have been accepted through the Verify Scope process.[PMBOK page 101] [Project Integration Management]

3. B - The reason why this response is NOT accurate is because: at the initial stage of a project, the cost is typically not at its highest. [Project Framework]

4. C - It is important to list out the potential impact of assumptions if they prove to be false. The assumptions listed out in project scope are typically more numerous and detailed than the assumptions listed in the project charter. [Project Scope Management]

5. A - Collocation is when all the team members are brought together, such as in a team meeting room. Collocation is highly recommended as a good project management practice. PMBOK Pg. 234 [Project Human Resource Management]

6. D - The "Executing" process group corresponds with the "do" portion of the PDCA cycle. [Project Framework]

7. D - Administer Procurements is part of the Monitoring and Controlling Process Group and is necessary for managing the contract and relationship between the buyer and seller. [Project Procurement Management]

8. A - This is referred to as Life Cycle costing. It refers to the broader view of project cost management and considers the effect of project decisions on the cost of using, maintaining, and supporting the product, service or result. It goes beyond just the costing of the project. [Project Cost Management]

9. A - The correct response is configuration status accounting [Project Integration Management]

10. D - Project closure documents consist of formal documentation and the official turnover to Operations. PMBOK Pg. 102 [Project Integration Management]

11. B - All the choices are tools/techniques in quality control, however the BEST choice would be the Ishikawa or Cause and Effect diagram. PMBOK Pg. 208 / 209 [Project Quality Management]

12. A - A SWOT Analysis chart would be the best choice. SWOT is an

acronym for strengths, weakness, opportunities and threats. PMBOK Pg. 288 [Project Risk Management]

13. C - Organizational process assets provide existing formal and informal procurement-related policies, procedures, guidelines, and management systems that are considered in developing the procurement management plan and selecting the contract type to be used. [Project Procurement Management]

14. A - The PERT formula is Estimate= (Optimistic + (Most Likely *4) + Pessimistic)/6 [Project Time Management]

15. D - This is referred to as Value Engineering. It is a creative approach used to optimize project life-cycle costs, save time, increase profits, improve quality, expand market share, solve problems and/or use resources more effectively. [Project Cost Management]

16. B - It would be appropriate to advise him to continue the work within the project's scope as scheduled. Project managers have a responsibility to act in a truthful and complete manner. Continuing the scheduled work with no hidden slow downs fulfills the responsibility of the project manager to the profession and their client. It is unfortunate that this action will result

in your colleague being without a job a month earlier than anticipated but their reputation and the reputation of other project management professionals will be upheld. [Prof. Responsibility]

17. D - Approved and rejected change requests are outputs of the Perform Integrated Change Control process. [Project Integration Management]

18. D - A Lag is a modification of a logical relationship that directs a delay in a successor activity. In this case, there is a 5 day delay before the server can be moved into the data center. PMBOK Pg. 429 [Project Time Management]

19. D - In this scenario both parties are giving up something, this is an example of compromise. [Project Human Resource Management]

20. D - Stakeholders typically have the most influence during the initial stages of a project. [Project Framework]

21. D - The earned value technique is a tool and technique for managing and controlling the project. PMBOK Pg. 425 [Project Integration Management]

22. C - Time reports and the amount of time expended on a project are part of Performance Reporting. PMBOK

Pg. 270 [Project Communications Management]

23. C - The probability and impact matrix chart is a tool used in the Perform Qualitative Risk Analysis. PMBOK Pg. 291 / 292 [Project Risk Management]

24. A - Any time there are complex issues that need to be solved you should use written communication to ensure that all parties are receiving the same message and are on the "same page". [Project Communications Management]

25. D - Your project is behind schedule. You had expected to have $9600 worth of work completed, that is your planned value (PV). However, you completed $7700 (EV) worth of work. Your schedule variance is -$1900, SV=EV-PV. [Project Time Management]

26. A - Any activity that is a structured and independent review to examine the project is an example of a Quality Audit. A quality audit is a quality assurance tool. PMBOK Pg. 204 [Project Quality Management]

27. C - A ROM estimate is given in the beginning of a project and is defined as +/- 50% of the estimated cost. [Project Cost Management]

28. D - Time Management is not a process group. It is one of the knowledge areas. [Project Framework]

29. C - This is known as simulation. Project simulations use computer models and estimates of risk, usually expressed as a probability distribution of possible costs or durations at a detailed work level, and are typically performed using Monte Carlo Analysis. [Project Cost Management]

30. D - Execution management is not a knowledge area. Note that execution is a process group. [Project Framework]

31. A - The correct response is the Scope Management Plan. This plan provides guidance on how project scope will be defined, documented, verified, managed and controlled by the project management team. [Project Scope Management]

32. B - Creating the WBS is an important activity in the project and it is done as part of Project Scope management under the Define Scope Process. [Project Scope Management]

33. D - The Risk Breakdown Structure would categorize risks by source, the WBS would categorize the work by area affected, project phases would let you know if you have a problem during the lifecycle. The correct answer is, process analysis which is a quality assurance tool [Project Risk Management]

34. A - This is the definition of quality assurance. PMBOK Pg. 189 [Project Quality Management]

35. C - Verify Scope is primarily concerned with the acceptance of all the deliverables whereas Perform Quality Control is primarily concerned with meeting the quality requirements specified for the deliverables. Perform Quality Control is performed before Verify Scope. The other responses are incorrect. Perform Quality Assurance is done before Perform Quality Control. [Project Scope Management]

36. B - The requirements for formal deliverable acceptance and how to address non-conforming deliverables are usually defined in the contract. [Project Procurement Management]

37. A - Change requests that are issued to bring expected future performance of the project in line with the project management plan is called corrective action. [Project Integration Management]

38. D - Any time a team member joins or leaves the team, for any reason the Staffing Management Plan should be updated. PMBOK Pg. 223 [Project Human Resource Management]

39. D - The example provided is the definition of fast tracking. Crashing the schedule would be if you decide to double the amount of resources so the task(s) could be done in half the amount of time. PMBOK Pg. 157 [Project Time Management]

40. A - Project calendars and resource calendars indicate when resource can work or work can be performed, it is called applying calendars. PMBOK Pg. 143 [Project Time Management]

41. A - Scope creep is the term used to refer to uncontrolled changes in scope and can be a project manager's nightmare if not properly managed. [Project Scope Management]

42. D - The exercise described is the Delphi Technique. It is a series of questions that are circulated to experts to reach consensus. PMBOK Pg. 286 [Project Risk Management]

43. C - Determining what to purchase or acquire and when and how it will be purchased or acquired, is done in the Plan Procurements phase. [Project Procurement Management]

44. B - A Zero Sum reward system is a win-lose recognition program. In this case, with an employee of the month program their will only be one or two team members who will win the award each month. Reward programs should be more win-win. PMBOK Pg. 234 [Project Human Resource Management]

45. C - Any type of training that is conducted, whether it be formal, on the job, computer based, etc. is a tool and technique in Develop Project Team. PMBOK Pg. 232 [Project Human Resource Management]

46. C - Market conditions are an example of an external risk. PMBOK Pg. 280 [Project Risk Management]

47. B - The facilities manager would be considered an expert in the A/C system, thus this is an example of Expert Judgment. PMBOK Pg. 98 [Project Integration Management]

48. C - This is an example of analogous estimating because you went back to an old project plan of a similar project to get the estimate. Parametric estimating would be correct if you used the number of words translated (e.g. 1000 words takes 1hr.). PMBOK Pg. 149 [Project Time Management]

49. D - The critical path of a project is the series of activities that have the least amount of float (flexibility). The other logical choice is precedence diagramming, however that shows activity relationships and not schedule flexibility. [Project Time Management]

50. C - Checklists are structured tools used to verify that a set of required steps has been performed. They can be either simple or complex. Many organizations have standardized checklists to ensure consistency in frequently performed tasks. [Project Quality Management]

51. C - The correct response is to issue a formal communication document. Telephoning the team member or planning for an informal lunch meeting may be additional options in the communication process, but a formal document has to be issued indicating the changes. [Project Communications Management]

Knowledge Area Quiz
Project Procurement Management
Practice Questions

Test Name: Knowledge Area Test: Project Procurement Management
Total Questions: 10
Correct Answers Needed to Pass: 7 (70.00%)
Time Allowed: 15 Minutes

Test Description

This practice quiz specifically targets your knowledge of the Project Procurement Management knowledge area.

Test Questions

1. Which of these is an input to the Administer Procurements process?

   A. Qualified seller list

   B. Statement of Work

   C. Source selection criteria

   D. Make or Buy decisions

2. Which of the outputs of the Administer Procurements phase involves written documentation (correspondence) and payments schedules?

   A. Contract Documentation

   B. Organizational Process Assets (Updates)

   C. Recommended Corrective Actions

   D. Requested Changes

3. You have received a proposal from a RFP that was sent to vendors. The vendor has indicated they can do the project for $12,500. There cost for the project is $10,000 and their profit will be $2500. This is an example of what type of contract?

   A. Cost Plus Incentive Fee

   B. Cost Plus Fee

   C. Cost Plus Fixed Fee

   D. Cost Plus Percentage of Cost

4. Your company requires that before you purchase any routers or switches for the data center you are building, you need to solicit quotes from three separate suppliers before submitting the purchase request to the finance

department. What type of input is this in to the procurement process?

A. Organizational Process Assets

B. Enterprise Environmental Factors

C. Procurement Management Process

D. Make or Buy Decision

5. Since it involves verification of all work and deliverables, what process does the Close Procurements process support?

A. Perform Integrated Change Control

B. Close Project or Phase

C. Estimate Activity Durations

D. Control Costs

6. Which of the following is accurate regarding contracts in the Project Procurement Management process?

A. Any stakeholder in the process chain may enter into a contract situation without the consent of the other stakeholders

B. Terms and conditions may are finite and may not include the seller's proposal

C. Contracts are not mutually binding agreements

D. It involves contracts that are legal documents between a buyer and a seller

7. What is the purpose of a bidder conference?

A. Select a vendor

B. Get qualified leads

C. Provide vendors with a clear understanding of the procurement (technical and contract requirements).

D. Develop a seller list

8. Establishing the direction to be provided to sellers on developing and maintaining a work breakdown structure (WBS) is generally included in the:

A. Request for Proposal (RFP)

B. Procurement management plan

C. Procurement statement of work

D. Procurement guide

9.   Different types of contracts are
     appropriate for different types of
     purchases. Which of these is not one
     of the three broad categories of
     contracts?

     A. Cost-reimbursable

     B. Time and Material

     C. Fixed-price or lump-sum

     D. Fixed-assessment

10. You are building a mansion that will
     have copper roofs. The duration of
     the project will be approximately
     three years, so you have built into the
     contract that as the price of copper
     increases the contract allows for price
     increases as a percentage of the cost
     copper. However, all other costs are
     fixed. This is an example of what
     type of contract?

     A. Fixed Price with Economic Price
          Adjustment

     B. Fixed Price Incentive Fee

     C. Unit Price

     D. Time and Materials

Knowledge Area Quiz
Project Procurement Management
Answer Key and Explanations

1. B - The Statement of Work is part of the procurement documents that are an input to the Administer Procurements process. [Project Procurement Management]

2. B - Organizational Process Asset updates are an output of the Administer Procurements phase and include written documentation and payments schedules. [Project Procurement Management]

3. C - The type of contract described in the question is the most common type of cost reimbursable contact. The buyer pays all costs, but the fee (profit) for the vendor is set at a fixed price. [Project Procurement Management]

4. A - Any type of corporate policy or formal procurement procedure is an organizational process asset. PMBOK Pg. 321 [Project Procurement Management]

5. B - Close Procurements supports the Close Project or Phase process. [Project Procurement Management]

6. D - Contracts are indeed legal documents between buyers and sellers. [Project Procurement Management]

7. C - Bidder conferences are also called contractor conferences or vendor conferences. Their purpose is provide all vendors with an understanding of the project requirements and give all vendors equal time to get questions answered. PMBOK Pg. 331 [Project Procurement Management]

8. B - The procurement management plan will generally include guidance for establishing the direction to be provided to sellers on developing and maintaining a work breakdown structure (WBS) [PMBOK page 325] [Project Procurement Management]

9. D - Fixed-assessment is not a category of contracts. [Project Procurement Management]

10. A - Since the price increases are tied only to the rising costs of the copper, this is a Fixed Price with Economic Price Adjustment (FP-EPA) contract. This is common with multiple year contracts. [Project Procurement Management]

PMP Lite Mock Exam 7
Practice Questions

Test Name: PMP Lite Mock Exam 7
Total Questions: 51
Correct Answers Needed to Pass:
36 (70.00%)
Time Allowed: 60 Minutes

Test Description

This is a cumulative PMP Mock Exam which can be used as a benchmark for your PMP aptitude. This practice test includes questions from all PMBOK knowledge areas, including the five basic project management process groups.

Test Questions

1. Lynn is the project manager of a project. She creates a structure similar to the Work Breakdown Structure (WBS). However, instead of being arranged according to the project deliverables, it is arranged according to the team's existing departments and units. The project activities / work packages are listed against each existing department. This would be called:

    A. An Organizational Breakdown Structure (OBS)

    B. A Department Breakdown Structure (DBS)

    C. A Resource Breakdown Structure (RBS)

    D. A Hierarchical Breakdown Structure (HBS)

2. You are negotiating a contract with a seller. You want to go in for a Fixed price type of contract. The seller uses a different terminology for the fixed price type of contract. He is most probably referring to it as a:

    A. Cost-Plus-Fixed-Fee contract

    B. A Time and material contract

    C. Lump sum contract

    D. Cost-Plus-Fee contract

3. A construction project requires that governmental environmental hearings be held prior to site preparation. What kind of a dependency is this?

    A. Mandatory dependency

    B. Discretionary dependency

    C. Soft logic

    D. External dependency

4. A manager asked to see a list of milestones in the project. This would be available as an output from the:

   A. Sequence Activities phase

   B. Define Scope phase

   C. Estimate Activity Durations

   D. Define Activities phase

5. One of the project team members had a teleconference with a customer representative who was reviewing some of the deliverables and discussed some changes in the product requirements. Your project team member discusses the changes with you and feels that these are necessary for the project. You agree with the team member's view. As a project manager, you should ensure that:

   A. Ask the project team member to go ahead with the changes.

   B. The changes are documented and they follow the change management process to become an Approved Change request.

   C. Summarize the changes and archive your discussion with the team member as a future record.

   D. Ask the team member to ignore the changes.

6. A project manager of a project that was contracted on a Time and Material basis finds that some of the tasks have been taking lesser time than planned. On average each team member has required only 30 hours to accomplish work which was planned for 40 hours during the week. The project manager should:

   A. Report the accurate status to your manager and send a separate report stating that each team member was busy for 40 hours

   B. Report this accurately on the status report and ensure that activities are re-planned as necessary, to keep the team completely occupied.

   C. Report on the status report that each team member was busy for 40 hours, and use the time saved for other activities not related to the project.

   D. Avoid mentioning these kinds of savings on status reports.

7.   There are a number of risks that have been identified in your project, however the team has elected not to change the project plan to deal with the risk, but they have established a contingency reserve of money in the event some of these risks are triggered. This is an example of what type of risk mitigation technique?

A.   Contingent Response Strategy

B.   Active acceptance

C.   Passive acceptance

D.   Avoidance

8.   Large variations in the periodic expenditure of funds are undesirable for organizational operations. Therefore the expenditure of funds is frequently reconciled with the disbursement of funds for the project. This is known as:

A.   Disbursement reconciliation

B.   Expenditure Reconciliation

C.   Budget Reconciliation

D.   Funding Limit Reconciliation

9.   The Earned Value Management methodology can be used as a means to:

A.   Forecast future performance based on past performance

B.   Calculate the number of days left in the project

C.   Calculate the value provided to the customer

D.   Calculate the profitability of the project

10. The customer requests a change to the project that would increase the project risk. Which of the following should you do before all others?

A.   Talk to the customer about the impact of the change

B.   Change the risk management plan

C.   Include the expected monetary value of the risk in the new cost estimate

D.   Analyze the impacts of the change with the team

11. A Work Breakdown Structure (WBS) dictionary supports the WBS and is a companion document to the WBS.

Which of the following is not included in the WBS dictionary?

A. List of schedule milestones

B. Resource assigned

C. Contract Information

D. Code of Account Identifier

12. The State of New York has contracted your company to provide a claims payment system for Medicaid benefits. In the contract there is a clause that indicates that the State of New York can review your work processes and deliverables. This is an example of?

A. Performance Report

B. Record Management System

C. Deliverables Checklist

D. Inspections and Audits

13. Control Schedule is part of which Project Management process group?

A. Monitoring and controlling

B. Planning

C. Executing

D. Initiating

14. Mandatory dependencies are those that are inherent in the nature of the work being done. They often involve physical limitations, such as on a construction project where it is impossible to erect the superstructure until the foundation has been built. This type of dependency is also called:

A. Soft logic

B. Unilateral dependency

C. Fixed logic

D. Hard logic

15. You are a project manager for your company. Part of the project requires producing 10,000 widgets, which your company will outsource. The company has agreed to pay all related costs and 5% of the estimated project costs. What type of contract has been negotiated?

A. Time and Material contract

B. Cost-Plus-Fixed-Fee contract

C. Cost-Plus-Incentive-Fee contract

D. Fixed-price contract

16. A special cause may also be referred to as:

    A. Foreign cause

    B. Assignable cause

    C. Atypical cause

    D. Normal cause

17. Jack is the project manager of a project and is looking at the schedule of work. He adjusts a few of the schedule milestones and imposes date constraints for some of the work packages. The most likely reason that may need him to do this is:

    A. Many of the work packages have been completed and he wants to change the dates on subsequent ones.

    B. His manager has requested him to change the milestone dates.

    C. To allow time for a project status presentation.

    D. To regulate expenditure of funds so that they can be reconciled against the disbursement of funds for the project.

18. As a project manager, you are concerned with both Prevention and Inspection of errors in a work product. The difference between Prevention and Inspection is:

    A. Inspection is work done by the Quality Control (QC) team whereas Prevention is work done by the Quality Assurance (QA) team

    B. Inspection refers to keeping errors out of the process whereas prevention refers to keeping errors out of the hands of the customer.

    C. Prevention refers to keeping errors out of the process whereas inspection refers to keeping errors out of the hands of the customer.

    D. Inspection and Prevention refer to the same activity depending on what stage of the project the activity is done.

19. Which of these statements is true?

    A. The cost of correcting mistakes through an inspection is much lesser than the cost of preventing them.

B. The cost of preventing mistakes is generally much lesser than the cost of correcting them as revealed by inspection.

C. It does not matter where a defect is captured as long as the finished work product does not have a defect.

D. The cost of correcting mistakes through an inspection is more or less that same as the cost of preventing them since the same effort goes into both activities.

20. The project manager of a long term project to develop a new medical device waits to include the details of later phase deliverables on the WBS until such time as those deliverables are more clearly defined. This is an example of:

A. Iterative planning

B. Balanced planning

C. Deferred planning

D. Rolling wave planning

21. You have a schedule activity that can be delayed without delaying the early start date of any subsequent activities. This is an example of?

A. Free Float

B. Lead Float

C. Total Float

D. Lag Float

22. As the project manager of a project, you have needed to estimate certain activity durations before all project team members were acquired. On acquisition of the project team, you find that the actual competency levels of the acquired team members are much lower than what you had anticipated. In such a case, you will:

A. Make no changes to the schedule.

B. Ask the project team members to meet the original schedule by putting in overtime if required.

C. Make changes to activity duration and schedule incorporating the changed competency levels.

D. Inform the customer that the project is behind schedule.

23. The Executive VP of Finance has informed you that you will be the project manager for an energy audit the company is performing in order to save expenses. He has tasked you with identifying stakeholders and to start documenting the assumptions and constraints. Your project is in what process group?

A. Initiating

B. Planning

C. Monitoring & Controlling

D. Executing

24. On a control chart, a source of variation that is not inherent in the system, is not predictable and is intermittent is called a:

A. Normal Cause

B. Specific Cause

C. Common Cause

D. Special Cause

25. You are just starting on a project as project manager. The project sponsor indicates to you that she would like to have a monthly Project Status meeting to review the progress of the project. She would also like to receive weekly status updates by email. These requirements are documented in the:

A. Scope statement

B. Communications management plan

C. Project charter

D. Organizational plan

26. As part of the Plan Quality process, you create a document which describes the purpose, start and end of processes, their inputs, outputs, data required and the owner and stakeholders of processes. This is called a:

A. Process metric

B. Process configuration

C. Process chart

D. Process boundary

27. A project manager is managing a project where there are teams located in remote locations in order to obtain cost savings. This is in line with organizational guidelines which require that at least 25% of work should be done from a remote location. This is an example of:

A. A constraint

B. A necessity

C. A choice

D. An assumption

28. The project manager controls the interfacing and overlapping areas of the organization's procurement processes, and the project schedule with processes from this area:

A. Project Human Resource Management

B. Project Scope Management

C. Project Risk Management

D. Project Integration Management

29. Throughout various project meetings you have documented differences in opinion, situations to be investigated and emerging or unanticipated responsibilities. These are all inputs to what document?

A. RACI Chart

B. Issue Log

C. Risk Register

D. Project Performance Appraisals

30. Administrative closure involves all the activities in a step-by-step manner to satisfy various completion and exit criteria for the project. This is part of which Project Management Knowledge Area?

A. Project Communication management

B. Project Scope Management

C. Project Integration Management

D. Project Procurement Management

31. You are working on an upgrade to a call distribution system for a call center, however you are finding it extremely difficult to get the proper resources assigned and tasks completed because the Call Center Manager is in control of the budget. You have just realized that you work in what type of an organization?

A. Balanced Matrix

B. Functional

C. Strong Matrix

D. Projectized

32. You have completed a milestone in your software development project and you are now verifying that the product meets the specifications outlined in the project management plan. What process group is this process in?

  A. Quality Control

  B. Closing

  C. Executing

  D. Monitor and Controlling

33. Project performance appraisals are different from team performance assessment in that project performance appraisals focus on?

  A. Reducing staff turnover

  B. A Team building effort

  C. How an individual team member is performing on the project

  D. An evaluation of the project team's effectiveness

34. You are working on a project where a negative risk has occurred. However, you have no contingency plan for this risk. You call a meeting and a solution is devised to change the workflow until a permanent solution can be implemented. This is an example of?

  A. Work Item

  B. Workaround

  C. Work Package

  D. Reserve plan

35. The Stakeholder Committee has been given a report that shows zero schedule variance. However, the first milestone in the project was missed, and will cause a delay in the project. What type of item was not reported correctly?

  A. Resource management plan

  B. Risk analysis

  C. Critical path status

  D. Communications plan variance

36. Your manager has provided you with a draft project charter and immediately asks you to provide an analysis of the risks on the project. Which of the following would BEST help this effort?

A. A conversation with a team member from a similar project that failed in the past

B. Project Scope statement from the project planning process

C. An article from PM Network Magazine

D. Resource plan from the project planning process

37. Megamart is estimating the cost of a new ERP system using the costs of an earlier ERP system project as the basis for the cost. This is what type of estimating?

A. Analogous

B. Resource-based

C. Judgment-based

D. SWAG

38. Costs incurred in one area of a project can offset costs in another area of the same project. However, it is not the best practice to consider only the costs of project execution when making project decisions. What must also be considered?

A. Return on Investment

B. Total Cost of Ownership

C. Project Lifecycle Costs

D. Environmental Impact

39. Your company is way behind schedule in the deployment of a government mandated change to a health care processing system that must be in production by the end of the year. You and your team have met and decided to hire an additional 50 programmers to work with the existing staff on the activities in order to meet the due date. This is an example of what?

A. Resource Leveling

B. Fast Tracking

C. Crashing

D. Risk Transference

40. The key difference between Verify Scope and Perform Quality Control is:

A. Verify Scope is concerned with meeting the quality standards specified.

B. Verify Scope is concerned with the acceptance of deliverables.

C. Verify Scope does not apply in projects that have been cancelled.

D. Verify Scope can never be performed in parallel with quality control.

41. You are managing a fund raising golf tournament that has a hole-in-one contest. However, your company can't afford to pay the $1,000,000 if someone does get a hole in one, so they have elected to take out an insurance policy in the event that someone does get lucky. This is an example of?

A. Sharing

B. Mitigation

C. Transference

D. Avoidance

42. The Make-or-Buy analysis is a technique that is used as part of the Plan Procurements process. It is used to determine whether a particular product or service can be produced by the project team or should be purchased. The analysis to arrive at a decision should include:

A. Indirect costs only

B. Direct as well as Indirect costs

C. Direct costs only

D. Staffing costs only

43. Fill in the blank: _____ includes the processes required to ensure that the project includes all the work required, and only the work required, to complete the project successfully.

A. Statement of Work

B. Project Time Management

C. Project Scope Management

D. Work breakdown structure

44. Breaking down project deliverables into smaller components is called:

A. Work breakdown structure

B. Deconstruction

C. Tasking

D. Decomposition

45. All of the following are characteristics of a project, EXCEPT:

A. Has a definite beginning and end

B. Temporary

C. Progressively elaborated

D. Ongoing Effort

46. Projects are often started as a result of an external factor such as market demand for a new product, a new legislative or regulatory mandate, or a change in technology. This results in the creation of _____ by an entity or organization external to the project organization.

A. the project charter

B. the project scope

C. the project budget.

D. the project kickoff

47. Bottom-up Cost estimating is typically motivated by the size and complexity of:

A. The project management software

B. The statistical relationship between historical data and other variables

C. The project budget.

D. The individual schedule activity or work package

48. The Quality Policy is the intended direction of a performing organization with regard to quality. As a project manager in a performing organization, you find that the organization lacks a formal quality policy. What should be done in such a case?

A. The project management team need not develop a quality policy since the performing organization does not have one.

B. The project management team needs to obtain the quality policy from the customer.

C. A quality policy is a 'nice-to-have' and is not required for every project.

D. The project management team will need to develop a quality policy for the project.

49. During your weekly project status meetings your set some time aside on the agenda to review the risk register by looking at all the risks, if the response plans are still appropriate

and adding or deleting risks. This is an example of?

A. Performance Measurement

B. Trend Analysis

C. Risk Reassessment

D. Risk Audit

50. The cost estimates for a project are in the range of +/- 5 %. What phase is the project likely to be in?

A. Closing phase

B. Preliminary phase

C. Initial phase

D. Intermediate phase

51. You are setting up your team for the project you are currently working on and you are looking at a chart that shows the programming will be performed by Systems Development, the infrastructure will be implemented by Infrastructure Systems, the customer communication will be handled by the call center. This is an example of what type of chart?

A. RACI

B. Organizational Breakdown Structure (OBS)

C. Work Breakdown Structure

D. Resource Breakdown Structure (RBS)

PMP Lite Mock Exam 7
Answer Key and Explanations

1. A - Organizational Breakdown Structure (OBS) is the correct answer. This is a useful way of listing project activities. An operational department such as Information Technology or purchasing can see all of its project responsibilities by looking at its portion of the OBS. [Project Human Resource Management]

2. C - A fixed price contract is synonymous with a lump sum contract. This type of contract involves a fixed total price or a lump sum for a well-defined product. [Project Procurement Management]

3. D - This is called an external dependency. It involves a relationship between project and non-project activities (for example: governmental environmental hearings). [Project Time Management]

4. D - The list of milestones is available as an output from the Define Activities phase. [Project Time Management]

5. B - All changes should be formally documented in writing. Any verbally discussed but undocumented changes should not be processed or implemented [Project Quality Management]

6. B - You would need to report the status accurately to the customer even if it means losing some revenue. [Prof. Responsibility]

7. B - Recognizing the risk and not changing the plan, but making some contingencies in the event the risk is triggered is an example of active acceptance. Passive acceptance would be if no contingencies were put in place and avoidance would be correct if the project plan were modified. PMBOK Pg. 304 [Project Risk Management]

8. D - This is known as Funding Limit reconciliation. This will necessitate the scheduling of work to be adjusted to smooth or regulate those expenditures. [Project Cost Management]

9. A - The Earned Value Management methodology can be used as a means to forecast future performance based on past performance. [Project Integration Management]

10. D - The first thing you should always do is assess the impact of the change with the team, then determine options and then go to management. [Project Risk Management]

11. B - Resource assignments are not part of the WBS dictionary. [Project Scope Management]

12. D - When a buyer puts in a contract that they can review work and deliverables it is an example of an inspection and audit. PMBOK Pg. 339 [Project Procurement Management]

13. A - Control Schedule is part of the monitoring and controlling process group. [Project Framework]

14. D - Mandatory dependencies are also referred to as hard logic. [Project Time Management]

15. B - This is an example of a Cost-Plus-Fixed-Fee contract. This type of contract determines the profit element as a fixed percentage of the estimated project cost. [Project Procurement Management]

16. B - A special cause is also referred to as an assignable cause. [Project Integration Management]

17. D - Reconciliation of the funding limits is a key reason why scheduling of work may need to be adjusted to smooth or regulate expenditures in relation to the disbursement of funds for the project. [Project Cost Management]

18. C - Prevention refers to keeping errors out of the process whereas inspection refers to keeping errors out of the hands of the customer. [Project Quality Management]

19. B - This is one of the basic tenets of project and quality management. The cost of preventing mistakes is generally much lesser than the cost of correcting them as revealed by inspection. [Project Quality Management]

20. D - Decomposition may not be possible for a deliverable or subproject that will be accomplished far into the future. The project management team usually waits until the deliverable or subproject is clarified so the details of the WBS can be developed. This technique is sometimes referred to as rolling wave planning. [PMBOK Page 134] [Project Scope Management]

21. A - The question given is the definition of free float. PMBOK Pg. 427 [Project Time Management]

22. C - The appropriate action is to make changes to the project schedule and activity durations depending on the actual competency of the team. Asking the project team members to put in overtime or informing the customer that the project is late are too drastic in nature given the stage of the project. [Project Human Resource Management]

23. A - Identifying stakeholders, assumptions and constraints are all part of developing the project charter, which is an output of the Initiating Process Group. PMBOK Pg. 44 [Project Framework]

24. D - These types of causes are called Special causes. [Project Integration Management]

25. B - As part of communication planning, stakeholder communication requirements are gathered and documented in the communications management plan. This forms a subsidiary of the project management plan. [Project Communications Management]

26. D - This is called a Process boundary and increases value to the customer by facilitating the identification of waste and non-value added activity. [Project Quality Management]

27. A - This is an example of a constraint. Constraints are factors that can limit the project management team's options. An organizational mandate requiring that a certain part of the team operate from a different location to obtain cost savings is a constraint that the project management team needs to

incorporate into their planning. [Project Communications Management]

28. D - Project Integration Management includes the processes and activities needed to identify, define, combine, unify, and coordinate the various processes and project management activities within the project management process groups. [PMBOK Page 72] [Project Integration Management]

29. B - These are all inputs to an issue log. The issue log is a written document and helps address obstacles that can prevent the team from achieving its goals. PMBOK Pg. 240 [Project Human Resource Management]

30. C - The Administrative Closure activities are part of the Close Project or Phase process under the Project Integration Management knowledge Area. [Project Integration Management]

31. B - The functional manager, in this case, the Call Center Manager, controls the budget in Functional and Weak Matrix organizations. PMBOK Pg. 28 [Project Framework]

32. B - Verifying a product meets specifications, is part of the closing process group. Verify Scope would be part the monitoring and controlling group. PMBOK Pg. 99 & 102 [Project Framework]

33. C - Project performance appraisals deal with how each team member is performing work, rather than how well the team is working together. [Project Human Resource Management]

34. B - Any time there is no contingency plan in place, but the risk must be addressed it is a workaround. PMBOK Pg. 445 [Project Risk Management]

35. C - The critical path is the sequence of schedule activities that determines the duration of the project. [PMBOK Page 423] [Project Time Management]

36. A - Since you were handed a draft project charter the project is still in the initiation phase. Therefore, the only correct answer is talk to a team member from a similar project that failed. [Project Risk Management]

37. A - Analogous cost estimating means using the actual cost of previous, similar projects as the basis for estimating the cost of the current project. Analogous cost estimating is frequently used to estimate costs when there is a limited amount of detailed information about the project (e.g., in the early phases). [PMBOK Page 171] [Project Cost Management]

38. C - Project Cost Management is primarily concerned with the cost of the resources needed to complete schedule activities. However, Project Cost Management should also consider the effect of project decisions on the cost of using, maintaining, and supporting the product, service or result of the project. [PMBOK Page 167] [Project Cost Management]

39. C - Crashing is a specific type of project schedule compression technique performed by taking action to decrease the total project schedule duration. Typical approaches for crashing a schedule include reducing activity durations and increasing the assignment of resources. PMBOK Pg. 423 [Project Time Management]

40. B - Verify Scope differs from Perform Quality Control in that Verify Scope is primarily concerned with the acceptance of the deliverables, while Perform Quality Control is primarily concerned with meeting the quality requirements specified for the deliverables. [PMBOK Page 123] [Project Scope Management]

41. C - The use of insurance to shift the negative impact of a risk, in this case the payment of $1,000,000 is an example of transference. PMBOK Pg. 303 [Project Risk Management]

42. B - The analysis should include both indirect as well as direct costs. [Project Procurement Management]

43. C - Project scope management is primarily concerned with defining and controlling what is and is not included in the project. [PMBOK Page 103] [Project Scope Management]

44. D - Decomposition is the subdivision of project deliverables into smaller more manageable components, until the work and deliverables are defined to the work package level. [PMBOK Page 118] [Project Scope Management]

45. D - Projects are not repeated on an ongoing basis (e.g. quarterly) these are classified as Operations. PMBOK Pg. 5 [Project Framework]

46. A - A project initiator or sponsor external to the project organization, at a level that is appropriate to funding the project, issues the project charter in response to some sort of stimulus. [PMBOK Page 74} [Project Integration Management]

47. D - Bottom-up estimating involves estimating the cost of individual work packages or individual schedule activities with the lowest level of detail. Generally activities with smaller associated effort increase the accuracy of the schedule activity cost estimates. [PMBOK Page 172] [Project Cost Management]

48. D - The project management team will need to develop a quality policy for the project if the performing organization does not have a formal policy. It is also the responsibility of the project management team to ensure that the project stakeholders are fully aware of the policy. [Project Quality Management]

49. C - All of the answers listed are tools/techniques of Monitor and Control Risks. The regular review of your risk register for appropriateness (e.g., responses, identified risks, etc.) is an example of risk reassessment. PMBOK Pg. 310 [Project Risk Management]

50. A - The project is likely to be in a closing phase since the range of estimates is quite narrow. Early on in the project, there is less cost information available and the range of estimates is much higher. As the project progresses, the degree of accuracy improves. [Project Cost Management]

51. B - A hierarchically organized depiction of the project organization arranged so as to relate the work

packages to performing organizational units is an example of Organizational Breakdown Structure (OBS) PMBOK Pg. 431 [Project Time Management]

.

Knowledge Area Quiz
Project Management Framework
Practice Questions

Test Name: Knowledge Area Test: Project Management Framework
Total Questions: 10
Correct Answers Needed to Pass: 7 (70.00%)
Time Allowed: 15 Minutes

Test Description

This practice quiz specifically targets your knowledge of the Project Management Framework knowledge area.

Test Questions

1. Fill in the blank: A _____ is a document established by consensus and approved by a recognized body that provides, for common and repeated use, rules, guidelines or characteristics for activities or their results, aimed at the achievement of the optimum degree of order in a given context.

   A. Advisory

   B. Standard

   C. Regulation

   D. Policy

2. A company that designs and manufactures a series of new bicycles each year may manage the effort more efficiently how?

   A. As a program

   B. As separate design and engineering projects.

   C. As separate UPC codes

   D. As independent product lines

3. The transition from one phase to another within a project's life cycle (e.g. design to manufacturing) is typically marked by:

   A. Technical transfer or handoff

   B. Deliverables

   C. Milestones

   D. Reviews

4. Ongoing operations and a project both have Initiating Processes, but only a project has _____.

   A. Planning Processes

B. Closing Processes.

C. Control processing

D. Executing Processes

5. Which of the following are enterprise environmental factors influencing a project's success?

A. Stakeholder risk tolerances

B. Political climate

C. Marketplace conditions

D. All of the above

6. Estimating the type and quantities of material, people, equipment or supplies required to perform each activity is:

A. Estimate Activity Workload

B. Estimate Activity Input

C. Activity Resource Requirements

D. Estimate Activity Resources

7. Organizations can be categorized according to their operations style. Which two types of organizational

systems are recognized by the PMBOK?

A. Project -based and Non-project based

B. Management driven or revenue driven

C. Mature or immature

D. Project management or program management

8. Fill in the blank: _____ means developing in steps and continuing by increments.

A. Progressive management

B. Iterative elaboration

C. Waterfall development

D. Progressive elaboration

9. Defining the requirements for a new product is what type of activity?

A. Initiating process group

B. Planning process

C. Scope management process

D. Control process

Knowledge Area Quiz Project Management Framework - Practice Question

10.   Project scope, time, and cost are often referred to as the:

A. Three-legged stool

B. Triple constraint

C. Project drivers

D. Standard constraints

Knowledge Area Quiz
Project Management Framework
Answer Key and Explanations

1. B - Standards ensure reproducible results or products, within a specific set of parameters. Examples of standards are USB 2.0 and the octane rating of gasoline. [PMBOK Page 442] [Project Framework]

2. A - A program is a group of related projects managed in a coordinated way to obtain benefits and control not available from managing them individually. [PMBOK Page 9] [Project Framework]

3. A - The transition from one phase to another within a project's lifecycle generally involves, and is usually defined by, some form of technical transfer or handoff. [PMBOK Page 19] [Project Framework]

4. B - A project is a finite effort; the Initiating Process Group starts the cycle, and the closing Process Group ends the cycle. [PMBOK Page 39] [Project Framework]

5. D - All the three listed factors are enterprise environmental factors that influence a project's success. Enterprise environmental factors may enhance or constrain project management options. [Project Framework]

6. D - Estimate Activity Resources is the process of estimating the type and quantities of material, people, equipment or supplies required to perform each activity. [PMBOK Page 141] [Project Framework]

7. A - Project-based organizations are those whose operations consist primarily of projects. Non-project based organizations often may lack management systems designed to support project needs efficiently and effectively. [Project Framework]

8. D - Progressive elaboration is a characteristic of projects that allows a project management team to manage it to a greater level as the project evolves. [PMBOK Page 7] [Project Framework]

9. A - The Initiating process group consists of the processes performed to define a new project or a new phase of an existing project by obtaining authorization to start the project of phase. [PMBOK Page 44] [Project Framework]

10. B - Project quality is affected by balancing project scope, time, and cost. High quality projects deliver the required product, service, or result within scope, on time, and within budget. [Project Framework]

PMP Lite Mock Exam 8
Practice Questions

Test Name: PMP Lite Mock Exam 8
Total Questions: 51
Correct Answers Needed to Pass:
36 (70.00%)
Time Allowed: 60 Minutes

Test Description

This is a cumulative PMP Mock Exam which can be used as a benchmark for your PMP aptitude. This practice test includes questions from all PMBOK knowledge areas, including the five basic project management process groups.

Test Questions

1. For many procurement items, the procuring organization can either prepare its own independent estimates or have an estimate of costs prepared by an outside professional estimator. This estimate serves as a:

    A. Potential-cost estimate

    B. Expected-cost estimate

    C. Benchmark estimate

    D. Must-cost estimate

2. A large construction project for a logistics company will require the expenditure of a large amount of capital. The finance group works with the project manager to project set limits when expenses will be incurred in a given project, and determine if there are ways to smooth out or levelize the spending to avoid a single large expenditure one quarter and none the next. This is an example of:

    A. Levelized Billing

    B. Funding Limit Reconciliation

    C. A financial review

    D. Rescheduling

3. Calculation of late finish dates and late start dates for the uncompleted portion of the project is called_____.

    A. A schedule network analysis

    B. An arrow diagram

    C. A backward pass

    D. A forward pass

4. The following text is an example of _____. "WBS Element 2.3.1.8. - System Deployment Testing Planning - This element includes the effort to identify requirements for and methodology of testing systems to be deployed."

   A. a resource breakdown structure

   B. a scope baseline

   C. a bill of materials

   D. a WBS dictionary entry

5. Which of the following is not a Project Time Management process?

   A. Source Activities

   B. Estimate Activity Resources

   C. Define Activities

   D. Sequence Activities

6. While rating a proposal, one of the requirements was "The proposed project manager needs to be a certified Project Management Professional, PMP® " This is an example of:

   A. Constraints

   B. Evaluation Criteria

   C. Assumptions

   D. Requirements

7. Which of the following is Deming's formula for continuous improvement?

   A. Plan-Act-Check-Do

   B. Plan-Do-Check-Act

   C. Check-Plan-Do-Act

   D. Plan-Check-Do-Act

8. A decision tree is a Perform Quantitative Risk Analysis technique that is structured around using a Decision Tree Diagram. It describes a situation under consideration and the implications of each of the available choices and the possible scenarios. A Decision Tree Diagram shows how to make a decision between alternative capital strategies known as:

   A. Alternative nodes

   B. Questionpoints

   C. Decision nodes

   D. Checkpoints

9. As part of the Close Procurements process, the project manager prepared a complete set of indexed contract documentation, including the closed contract, to include with the final project files. This is called a:

    A. Procurement file

    B. Documentation file

    C. Closure report

    D. Closure file

10. Clear criteria for rewards and a planned system for their use promotes and reinforces desired behaviors in the project. Creating a plan with established times for rewards ensures that recognition takes place and is not forgotten. This is usually part of the:

    A. Project Dashboard

    B. Company HR plan

    C. Communications Management Plan

    D. Staffing Management Plan

11. A project manager determines that there are 15 communication channels in the project. The number of stakeholders in the project must then be:

    A. 15 stakeholders

    B. 6 stakeholders

    C. 8 stakeholders

    D. 105 stakeholders

12. A summary milestone schedule would normally be part of which document?

    A. Project sign-off document

    B. Project charter

    C. Project requirements document

    D. Project scope statement

13. Which of the following processes deals with maintaining the integrity of baselines by releasing only approved changes for incorporation into the project management plan?

    A. Perform Integrated Change Control

    B. Direct and Manage Project Execution

C. Develop Project Management Plan

D. Monitor and Control Project Work

14. Defense Dynamics has been awarded a fixed price project to design and build a military cargo jet. The design team is looking at ways to increase the cargo capacity of the plane while keeping manufacturing costs and the fuel efficiency of the final product within specific limits. The engineers on this team have identified factors that affect capacity, costs, and fuel efficiency and have created a statistical model of how these factors impact each other. The outcome of this model is a design with the highest cargo capacity and fuel efficiency at the lowest cost possible. What type of mathematical model is this called?

A. Outcome-based Hypothesis

B. Basis Benchmarking

C. Cost of Quality

D. Design of Experiments

15. Anne is the project manager of a project. She has evaluated certain responses from prospective sellers and wants to select a contract model which will transfer risk to the seller. Which of the following should she select in order to achieve this?

A. Time and Material contract

B. Cost-Plus-Fixed-Fee contract

C. Cost-Plus-Incentive-Fee contract

D. Fixed price contract

16. Indicating the need for catering services to be provided to consultants during the entire first month of a special event can be noted on the schedule with a _____

A. Critical resources

B. Hammock Activity

C. Direct activity

D. Resource Identifier

17. The formula for Cost Variance is:

A. CV=EV-AC

B. CV=AC-EV

C. CV=BAC-(AC-EV)

D. CV=SV-BC

18. Select the best answer: Continuous process improvement reduces _____ and _____, which allows processes to operate at increased levels of efficiency and effectiveness.

   A. Process and policy overhead.

   B. Departmental and organization processes

   C. Cost and scope

   D. Waste and non-value added activities.

19. A detailed milestone list is created as an output of what process?

   A. Sequence Activities

   B. Define Activities

   C. Develop Project Charter

   D. Develop Schedule

20. Analysis of project spending against project budget and calculating the percentage complete of tasks currently underway are examples of:

   A. Delivery management

   B. Earned value

   C. Work performance information

   D. Baseline variance

21. You are managing the communication requirements for your project. You find that certain general management skills come into play as part of managing stakeholder requirements and that there are different dimensions to communication that you have to plan for as the sender of information. Which of the following is not a dimension of communicating?

   A. Vertical / Horizontal communication

   B. Forward / backward communication

   C. Formal / Informal communication

   D. Internal / external communication

22. Accounting for the limited resources in the project schedule is called:

   A. Forward pass

   B. Critical chain method

C. Backward Pass

D. Critical Path Method

23. You find out that a project team member has been stealing some material from the work place. You accidentally discover this and he says that he is very sorry about it, and will not repeat it again. You will:

A. Get a statement in writing from the project team member saying that he will not repeat such an activity.

B. Document the matter for your archives.

C. Inform your HR department about the matter

D. Keep quiet until it repeats for a second time

24. As part of the Develop Team process, the project manager of a project has planned for some Team Development activities. Team Development Activities should take place throughout the project life cycle, but have greater benefit when conducted:

A. On a need-basis.

B. At the end of the project life cycle

C. Early in the project life cycle

D. In the middle of the project life cycle.

25. _____ is the authorized budget for the work scheduled to be completed on an activity or WBS up to a given time. The projected cost of all painting from a January 3rd start to a February 15th milestone is an example of this.

A. Planned Value

B. Earned Value

C. Midpoint cost

D. Interim cost

26. Collect Requirements, Develop Schedule and Perform Qualitative Risk Analysis are all part of what process group?

A. Planning

B. Scope Planning

C. Monitor and Controlling

D. Executing

27. You have assembled a group of subject matter experts (SME's) to perform an exercise where they are going to complete a probability and impact matrix chart. You and your team are still in what process group?

A. Risk

B. Monitor and Controlling

C. Quantitative Analysis

D. Planning

28. Stakeholders can be identified in which management process group(s)?

A. Planning

B. Planning and Monitoring & Controlling

C. Initiating and planning

D. All

29. A project is being done for an external customer. Which of the following is an input to the Develop Project Charter process?

A. Contract

B. Business Case

C. Project Statement of Work

D. All of the above

30. Which document defines how the project is to be executed, monitored, controlled, and closed?

A. Project scope

B. Project charter

C. Project management information system

D. Project management plan

31. You have the project management responsibility of a virtual team comprising team members from the same company who live in widespread geographic areas, employees who work from home-offices and employees with mobility handicaps. Which of the following is a key planning activity that you need to undertake?

A. Plan Communications

B. Plan Quality

C. Develop Human Resource Plan

D. Distribute Information

32. The term _____ indicates the degree to which a particular product or service meets requirements, while _____ indicates a category or rank used to distinguish that item from other similar items.

    A. Quality, grade

    B. Grade, standard

    C. Grade, quality

    D. Quality, standard

33. Visiting a construction site to ensure the work being done is the same work called out in the requirements is called:

    A. Site auditing

    B. Scope verification

    C. Quality control

    D. Requirements traceability

34. A Responsibility Assignment Matrix illustrates the connections between the work that needs to be done and the project team members. A RACI chart is a type of Responsibility

Assignment matrix where the names of the roles being documented are:

    A. Responsible, Administration, Check and Inform

    B. Reportable, Actionable, Check and Inform

    C. Responsible, Accountable, Consult and Inform

    D. Reportable, Actionable, Consult and Implement

35. It has come to your attention that you can't accurately estimate the resources needed for the schedule activity "Build Racks for Data Center", so in order to get an accurate number or skill of resources required to present to your Human Resource department later in the week, you have decided to decompose the schedule activity of "Build Racks for Data Center" into smaller components such as: take equipment out of box, review equipment for completeness, build frame and install rails and estimate the number of resources for each smaller component and then roll it up into an aggregate. This is an example of?

    A. Aggregate Estimating

    B. Alternative Analysis

C. Bottom Up Estimating

D. Rolling Wave Estimating

36. Due to the unexpected release of a similar product from a competitor, the Widgets International executive team has stepped up the pressure on the product team to release the Widget product 3 months earlier. The project manager uses what technique to shorten the schedule but maintain the project scope?

A. Schedule compression

B. Rolling wave planning

C. Schedule network analysis

D. Schedule management planning

37. _____ is widely used to forecast project costs at completion.

A. Cumulative CPI

B. Earned Value

C. Schedule Performance Index

D. Total CPI

38. A project to design and build a new aircraft is cancelled after the project has been underway for some time. What process is invoked to document what work was done, and to what extent it was completed?

A. Manage Scope

B. Close Scope

C. Perform Quality Control

D. Close Project or Phase

39. The project manager of a large construction project is responsible for ensuring that all changes to the building plans are approved and tracked before they are implemented. These activities form part of which process?

A. Manage Scope

B. Perform Configuration Management

C. Perform Integrated change control

D. Perform Quality Control

40. Vendor selection and management and documentation of lessons learned are tasks that fall under this process area:

A. Procurement management

B. Deliverable management

C. Direct and manage project execution

D. Scope management

41. The Conduct Procurements process receives bids or proposals and applies criteria to select one or more sellers who are both qualified and acceptable as a seller. Which of the following techniques is not a valid technique for this process?

A. Make-or-buy analysis

B. Proposal Evaluation

C. Advertising

D. Bidder Conferences

42. You are managing a project which requires an environmental permit to do work. The approval is in the final stages of being granted when a confidential, reliable report is brought to your notice which indicates that there is a high risk of an environmental hazard due to the

project. Your manager tells you that it is better to keep quiet at this stage since the loss due to non-starting/execution of the project is very high. You will:

A. Send an email to your manager documenting the matter and disowning ownership of the project.

B. Inform the necessary authorities of the hazard, even if it means that the project will be cancelled.

C. Wait for the project to start and see if the information in the report was true.

D. Keep quiet about the matter since you will follow your manager's instructions.

43. A Work Breakdown Structure is a hierarchical illustration of all the work to be done in a project. A WBS component can represent:

A. products

B. results

C. services

D. All of the above

44. A project manager assigned values of 0.2, 0.4, 0.6 and 0.8 to the impacts of certain threats to the projects. What kind of numeric scale does this represent?

   A. Logarithmic scale

   B. Linear scale

   C. Sine value scale

   D. Non-linear scale

45. The business case to justify a project typically contains:

   A. The business need and the market demand

   B. The business need and the cost-benefit analysis.

   C. The cost-benefit analysis and the market demand

   D. The cost-benefit analysis and the strategic plan

46. Which of the following is not a Risk-Diagramming Technique?

   A. Influence diagrams

   B. Control diagrams

   C. Cause-and-Effect diagrams

   D. System flowcharts

47. The Cost of Quality principle includes:

   A. The costs of ensuring conformance to requirements.

   B. The costs involved when changes are made to the requirements.

   C. The cost of deploying a project Configuration Management System

   D. The costs associated with eliminating requirements.

48. The most recent analysis of Microcorp's new fabrication facility renovation shows a CPI value of less than 1.0 What does this indicate?

   A. The cost has overrun estimates.

   B. The cost has underrun estimates.

   C. The project is running ahead of schedule.

   D. The schedule has slipped.

49. As a project manager it is important to determine risk tolerances to help:

A. The team rank project risks

B. the team schedule the project

C. the project manager estimate the cost of the project

D. management know how other managers will act on the project

B. Upgrade the configuration management database with new controls.

C. Replanning

D. Root cause analysis of the cause of the variance relative to the scope baseline.

50. Probability distributions are frequently used in Perform Quantitative Risk Analysis. Which of these is not a valid example of such a distribution?

A. Theta distribution

B. Logarithmic distribution

C. Triangular distribution

D. Beta distribution

51. Project performance measurements are used to assess the magnitude of variation from the original scope baseline. Once the degree of scope variation is known, what step is performed next?

A. Audit the project team

PMP Lite Mock Exam 8
Answer Key and Explanations

1. C - This serves as a benchmark estimate. Significant differences in estimates can be an indication that the procurement statement of work was deficient or the prospective sellers either misunderstood or failed to respond fully to the procurement statement of work.[PMBOK page 332] [Project Procurement Management]

2. B - Large variations in the periodic expenditure of funds are usually undesirable for organizational operations. Therefore, the expenditure of funds is reconciled with the funding limits set by the customer or performing organization on the disbursement of funds for the project. [PMBOK Page 178] [Project Cost Management]

3. C - Calculation of late finish dates and late start dates for the uncompleted portion of the project is called a backward pass. [PMBOK Page 419] [Project Time Management]

4. D - The WBS dictionary is a companion document to the WBS. The detailed content of the components contained in the WBS, including work packages and control accounts, can be described in the WBS dictionary. [PMBOK Page 121] [Project Scope Management]

5. A - The Project Time Management processes include Define Activities, Sequence Activities, Estimate Activity resources, Estimate Activity durations, Develop Schedule, and Control Schedule. [PMBOK Page 131] [Project Time Management]

6. B - This is an example of an evaluation criterion used to rate or score proposals. [Project Procurement Management]

7. B - Deming's model is Plan-Do-Check-Act [PMBOK Page 191] [Project Quality Management]

8. C - The decision points are known as Decision nodes. The decision tree incorporates the cost of each available choice, the possibilities of each of the available choices and possible scenarios. It shows how to make a decision between alternative capital strategies (decision node) when the environment is not known with certainty. [Project Risk Management]

9. A - This detailed set of documentation is called a Procurement file [Project Procurement Management]

10. D - The plan for rewards and recognition is part of the Staffing Management plan. The recognition and rewards are developed as part of

the Develop Human Resources Plan process. [Project Human Resource Management]

11. B - The correct answer is 6. The number of channels = n(n-1)/2 where n is the number of stakeholders. The answer cannot be 105 since the number of stakeholders will be less than the communication channels. The option 15 is eliminated since it is the same as the number of stake holders. Options remaining are 6 and 8. Calculating with 6 gives 6 X 5 / 2 = 15 and with 8 gives 8 X 7 /2 = 28. So the answer is 6. [Project Communications Management]

12. B - The summary milestone schedule is normally included as part of the project charter which documents the business need, understanding of customer's needs and other high-level items. [Project Integration Management]

13. A - Maintaining the integrity of baselines is done in the Perform Integrated Change Control process. This process is conducted from project inception through project completion. [Project Integration Management]

14. D - Design of Experiments is a statistical method that helps identify which factors may influence specific variables of a product or process

under development or in production [PMBOK Page 197 / 198] [Project Quality Management]

15. D - A Fixed price contract allows the buyer to transfer risk to the seller. [Project Risk Management]

16. B - A broader more comprehensive summary activity is sometimes referred to as a hammock activity, and extends over an entire segment of a project. [PMBOK Page 157] [Project Time Management]

17. A - CV equals earned value (EV) minus actual cost (AC) [PMBOK Page 182] [Project Cost Management]

18. D - Continuous process improvement reduces waste and non-value-added activities, which allows processes to operate at increased levels of efficiency and effectiveness. [PMBOK Page 202] [Project Quality Management]

19. B - A detailed milestone list is created as an output of the Define Activities process and includes information on whether the milestone is mandatory or optional. Note that the project charter also contains milestone information, but at a high level. [Project Time Management]

20. C - Information on the status of the project activities being performed to accomplish the project work is routinely collected as part of the project management plan execution. [PMBOK Page 87] [Project Integration Management]

21.   B - General management skills include the art of managing stakeholder requirements. The sender is responsible for making the information clear and complete so that the receiver can receive it in its entirety and correctly. There are different dimensions to communicating, but the response "Forward/Backward communication" is an invalid response. [Project Communications Management]

22.   B - The Critical Chain Method is a schedule network analysis technique that modifies the project schedule to account for limited resources. [PMBOK Page 423] [Project Time Management]

23.   C - The correct option is to inform your company's HR department. This is a disciplinary matter and the project manager needs to let the company guidelines handle the situation. [Prof. Responsibility]

24.   C - Team Development Activities should take place throughout the project life cycle, but have greater benefit when conducted early in the project life cycle. [Project Human Resource Management]

25.   A - Planned Value is the budgeted cost of the work scheduled to be completed on an activity or WBS component up to a given point in time. [PMBOK Page 182] [Project Cost Management]

26.   A - All activities listed are planning activities. PMBOK Pg. 43 [Project Framework]

27.   D - The probability and impact matrix chart prioritizes risks according to their potential implication for having an effect on the project's objectives and is done in the planning phase. PMBOK Pg. 281 [Project Framework]

28.   D - It is possible to identify both positive and negative stakeholders at any time during a project. [Project Framework]

29.   D - All the three listed choices are inputs to the Develop Project Charter process. Contract is a specific input in the Develop Charter process when a project is being done for an external customer. [Project Integration Management]

30.   D - The project management plan defines how the project is executed, monitored and controlled, and closed.

[PMBOK Page 78] [Project Integration Management]

31. A - When dealing with a virtual team, Communications Planning becomes increasingly important and is a key activity in ensuring project success. Additional time may be need to set clear expectations, develop protocols for confronting conflict, including people in decision-making and in sharing credit in successes. [Project Human Resource Management]

32. A - Grade is a category or rank used to distinguish items that have the same functional use; Quality indicates the degree to which items have meet requirements. [Page 428 / 437] [Project Quality Management]

33. B - Inspection includes activities such as measuring, examining, and verifying to determine whether work and deliverables meet requirements and product acceptance criteria. [Page 123] [Project Scope Management]

34. C - In a RACI chart, the names of roles are documented as Responsible, Accountable, Consult and Inform [Project Human Resource Management]

35. C - Breaking down the schedule activity into smaller components and then rolling up the estimates for each smaller activity is an example of Bottom Up Estimating. PMBOK Pg. 144 [Project Time Management]

36. A - Schedule compressing is the technique of shortening the project schedule duration without reducing scope. [PMBOK Page 439] [Project Time Management]

37. A - The cumulative CPI is used to forecast project costs at completion. CPIC= EVC/ACC. [PMBOK Page 183] [Project Cost Management]

38. D - If the project is terminated early, the Close Project or Phase process should establish and document the level and extent of completion.[Page 133] [Project Scope Management]

39. C - Integrated change control includes maintaining the integrity of baselines by releasing only approved changes for incorporation into project products or services, and maintaining their related configuration and planning documentation. [PMBOK Page 93] [Project Integration Management]

40. C - The Direct and Manage Project Execution process requires the project manager and the project team to perform multiple actions to execute the project management plan to accomplish the work defined in the project scope statement. [PMBOK

Page 83] [Project Integration Management]

41. A - The Make-or-Buy analysis is not a valid technique in the Conduct Procurements process. All the other three choices are valid techniques. [Project Procurement Management]

42. B - The best option is to inform the necessary authorities about the report so that the right decision can be taken, even if it means the project will be cancelled. [Prof. Responsibility]

43. D - Upper level WBS components are decomposed into more easily managed elements, and can be process or product oriented. [PMBOK Page 118 / 120] [Project Scope Management]

44. B - This represents a linear scale since the values are uniformly spaced [Project Risk Management]

45. B - The business case to justify a project typically contains the business need and the cost-benefit analysis. The business case provides the necessary information to determine whether or not the project is worth the required investment. [Project Framework]

46. B - Control diagrams is not a valid response. [Project Risk Management]

47. A - Quality costs are the total costs incurred by investment in preventing nonconformance to requirements, appraising the product or service for conformance to requirements, and failing to meet requirements (rework). [PMBOK Page 195] [Project Quality Management]

48. A - A CPI value of less than 1.0 indicates a cost overrun of the estimates. A CPI value greater than 1.0 indicates a cost underrun of the estimates. [PMBOK Page 183] [Project Cost Management]

49. A - Knowing if stakeholders, vendors, etc. are risk aversive or risk tolerance it will help the project rank the risks. [Project Risk Management]

50. A - The response 'Theta distribution' is the right answer since it is not a valid distribution. Continuous probability distributions represent the uncertainty in values, such as durations of schedule activities and costs of project components. Triangular, Beta, Logarithmic, Normal and Uniform distributions are other examples of commonly used distributions. [Project Risk Management]

51. D - Project performance measurements are used to assess the magnitude of variation. Important aspects of project scope control include determining the cause of variance relative to the scope baseline. [PMBOK Page 127] [Project Scope Management]

PMP Lite Mock Exam 9
Practice Questions

Test Name: PMP Lite Mock Exam 9
Total Questions: 50
Correct Answers Needed to Pass:
35 (70.00%)
Time Allowed: 60 Minutes

Test Description

This is a cumulative PMP Mock Exam which can be used as a benchmark for your PMP aptitude. This practice test includes questions from all PMBOK knowledge areas, including the five basic project management process groups.

Test Questions

1. A project was estimated to cost $ 100,000 with a timeline of 5 months. Due to certain atypical causes, the schedule was delayed. At the end of the third month, the project manager reviews the project and finds that the project is 40% complete and Actual Costs are $ 60,000. The Estimate to complete (ETC) for the project would now be:

    A. $40,000

    B. $120,000

    C. $90,000

    D. $60,000

2. You have been assigned as project manager of a software development project. One of the requirements is to use a remote team and you find that that the remote team has limited technical communications capabilities. This is an example of:

    A. An assumption

    B. A hindrance

    C. A show-stopper

    D. A constraint

3. A project manager presented Earned value analysis data in a tabular format while providing a performance report. An alternative way in which the project manager could have presented the Earned value analysis data is by using:

    A. A linear graph

    B. An S-curve

    C. A logarithmic curve

    D. An Epsilon graph

4. Which of the following endeavors is unlikely to be a project?

    A. A research paper on "The next generation of high-speed internet connectivity"

    B. Updating of data in an HR database.

    C. A new business function to support production.

    D. A new model of a laser printer.

5. Santa Rosa Valley Farms is conducting a project to install new packing equipment in one of its California farms. One month into the project, Santa Rosa Valley Farms conducts a review to determine how well the installer selected for this project is meeting goals for scope, quality, cost, and schedule. This is an example of _____.

    A. A procurement performance review

    B. Capacity planning

    C. A project review meeting

    D. An audit

6. An issue log or action-item log is a tool that can be used to document and monitor the resolution of issues. At a minimum, the issue log should contain:

    A. A target resolution date.

    B. An owner name.

    C. An owner name and a target resolution date.

    D. An owner name, a target resolution date, financial impact on the project, impact on schedule.

7. As the project manager of a large project, you have just completed the Estimate Costs process. As you begin the Determine Budget process, which of the following would you require as inputs?

    A. Activity cost estimates, Basis of estimates

    B. Activity cost estimates, Changes to activity cost estimates

    C. Resource breakdown structure and Cost aggregation

    D. Activity cost estimates, Staff management plan

8. A major construction project has included in the project budget the cost of the construction loans taken out to finance the work, and this will be accounted for on a monthly basis. The project manager will factor in these cost estimates into the project during which process?

A. Estimate Project Cost

B. Estimate Activity Resources

C. Estimate Activity Durations

D. Estimate Activity Costs

9. A project manager is trying to plan for a contingency reserve as part of the cost estimates for the project. Which of these would be an incorrect way to plan for contingency reserves?

A. Start with a zero value for contingency reserve.

B. Plan for contingency reserve as a fixed number.

C. Plan for contingency reserve as a percentage of the estimated cost.

D. Use quantitative analysis methods to arrive at the contingency reserve.

10. An asphalt company is demanding a code change to a software module your team is creating for them to generate Safety Data Sheets. The change will only add one week to the critical path. What is your next step, as the project manager?

A. Compress the schedule to make up the week lost

B. Modify the scope of the project

C. Consult with the Sponsor

D. Advise the client of the change

11. A collection of formally documented procedures that define how project deliverables and documentation are controlled, changed and approved is called:

A. An authorization system

B. Project documentation

C. A change control board

D. A change control system

12. A cost, time, quality, technical or resource value is used as a parameter and included in product specifications. Crossing this value triggers some action such as an exception report. This value would be called:

A. A turning-point

B. A threshold

C. An exception-point

D. A trigger

13. The costs on a project are typically classified as direct and indirect costs. The cost of electric utilities for the office would be considered as:

A. An indirect cost

B. An operational cost

C. A specific cost

D. A direct cost

14. Which option is NOT an objective of the kick-off meeting?

A. An opportunity to define the scope and provide cost estimates

B. An opportunity to receive commitment from the project stakeholders about specific deliverables

C. An opportunity for project team members to share lessons learned from similar projects

D. An opportunity to introduce project team members to one another

15. What BEST describes an input to the Manage Stakeholder Expectations process?

A. Communications Management Plan

B. WBS

C. Issue Log

D. Approved Change Requests

16. Which of the following is considered an output from the Direct and Manage Project Execution process?

A. Budgeted costs

B. Project charter

C. Work performance information

D. Execution plan

17. Long hours to meet a looming deadline and immense pressure for

success from management is causing a downturn in team morale. Occasionally there are conflicts between team members over priorities and resources. How should these non-disruptive conflicts be handled?

A. Use of disciplinary actions

B. When the differences become a negative factor, project team members are initially responsible for resolving their own conflicts.

C. Escalation to senior management

D. Arbitration

18. One of the senior team members, who is the best performer in your project plays 'favorites' and a few of the team members who work closely with him, have got very good appraisal reports in the past, even though they may not have deserved it. As the project manager, what would you need to proactively do?

A. Ask all the members of your team who are appraisers of other team-members, to be liberal in their appraisals. This will help compensate for the appraisals done by the senior team member.

B. Speak to the senior team member and ask for appraisals to be done fairly, in accordance with the appraisal guidelines.

C. Ignore the matter since you would otherwise lose a senior team member who is key to your project.

D. Ensure that the senior team member does not get to appraise anybody.

19. Which type of risk analysis ranks risks for future action or analysis by evaluating their probability of occurrence and impact?

A. RBS

B. Assumptions analysis

C. Qualitative analysis

D. Quantitative analysis

20. Lessons learned documentation focuses on identifying project successes and project failures, and includes recommendations to improve future performance on projects. Lessons learned are compiled, formalized and stored:

A. At the end of the project

B. At the start of the project.

C. Through the duration of the project

D. At the start, midway and at the end of the project.

A. be mitigated

B. remain neutral

C. decrease

D. increase

21. A project manager from a buyer organization is invited to lunch by the manager of a seller organization. The project manager's organization does not permit receipt of gifts from vendors. The project manager should:

A. Go out for lunch and refrain from informing his / her managers about the lunch.

B. Avoid going out to lunch with anyone from the seller organization.

C. Insist on paying for his / her lunch.

D. Permit the manager from the seller organization pay for his / her lunch since it has a very small value.

22. The accuracy of estimates of the cost of a project will _____ over the life of a project.

23. The development of requirements in the Collect Requirements process begins with an analysis of the information contained in the _____ and _____.

A. Project charter, Stakeholder register

B. Scope baseline, Requirements traceability matrix

C. Scope baseline, Stakeholder register

D. Project charter, Project scope statement

24. What do buyers and seller have in common with regards to Administer Procurements?

A. Each party ensures that both it and the other party meet their contractual obligations and that their own legal rights are protected.

B. Both parties have specific resources that can be idle.

C. Both parties have a contract change management plan.

D. Each party has its own project plan and legal team

25. You are a project manager for a computer security project and have gathered your team to begin looking at identifying risks for your current project. All of the following are methods that you can use to gather information for this purpose EXCEPT:

   A. Brainstorming

   B. Risk Register

   C. Interviewing

   D. Delphi technique

26. Melissa is managing a hardware deployment project, and is creating a risk management plan. Which of the following would NOT be included in this plan?

   A. Exposure

   B. Risk Categories

C. Budgeting

D. Methodology

27. You are decomposing your WBS into smaller pieces of work. What is one item that does NOT describe how far the work should be decomposed?

   A. Until it can be realistically estimated

   B. Can't be subdivided any further

   C. Until a meaningful conclusion

   D. Until it can be done by one person

28. A fellow project manager is retiring and moving to the mountains, you will be taking over his project. Before he leaves he tells you the project is on schedule, but only because he has had to "put the hammer down" on his project team and push them relentlessly. What should be the first thing you do on this project?

   A. Develop a management strategy

   B. Check the CPI

   C. Meet with the team and review your expectations

D. Check the SPI

29. A technique which enhances brainstorming with a voting process used to rank the most useful ideas so that they can be taken up for further brainstorming is:

A. Six thinking hats

B. Nominal group technique

C. Affinity diagram

D. Mind mapping

30. Identifying, communicating, and remediating a serious omission or error made during execution of a project task is mandated by what PMI code?

A. Code of Practitioner Ethics

B. Code of Ethics and Professional Conduct

C. Code of Honorable Conduct

D. Code of Ethical Standards.

31. Which one of the following tools and techniques is NOT part of the Develop Project Team process?

A. Co-location

B. Recognition and Rewards

C. Conflict management

D. Ground rules

32. Which of the following have the highest priority for a project manager?

A. Completing the project as per the defined scope.

B. Completing the project with zero defects.

C. Completing the project on time.

D. Completing the project within the budgeted cost.

33. Which method of conflict resolution is NOT a long term solution?

A. Problem Solving

B. Forcing

C. Smoothing

D. Compromise

34. You are the project manager for a Fortune 100 IT company and you are currently engaged in an important project. You want to choose the best contractor for a specialized task. What should you do to evaluate potential contractors?

A. Create a lessons learned document

B. Conduct a performance review

C. Evaluate proposals

D. Perform a Make-or-Buy analysis

35. Joanne is attempting to quantify possible outcomes for her project and the probability of achieving specific project objectives. Which of the following techniques could she use?

A. Monte Carlo simulation

B. Quantification tabling

C. Delphi technique

D. Control Room method

36. A project manager is performing Reserve Analysis as a technique in one of the project management process that he is currently working on. Which of these is likely to be that process?

A. Estimate Reserves

B. Report Costs

C. Estimate Costs

D. Plan Costs

37. You are forming a virtual project team that includes members from four different countries around the world. What is NOT an obstacle that you must overcome to build an effective team?

A. Different time zones

B. Disparate tools and technologies

C. Cultural differences

D. Members wanting to work from home

38. Joe is attempting to calculate the financial impact of a specific outcome scenario. What method could he use?

A. Sensitivity analysis

B. Earned value analysis

C. Decision tree analysis

D. Expected monetary value analysis

39. A RAM diagram shows the relationship between _____ and _____ in a tabular format.

A. Cause and effect

B. Risks and mitigation plans

C. Deliverables and costs

D. Work packages and project team members

40. You took over a project from an individual who was let go. You are reading the project documentation and found the project charter was signed by five managers. What should be your primary concern at this time?

A. Determining reporting structure

B. Communicating in a matrix organization

C. Getting a single sponsor

D. Identifying who can represent the project for change control

41. As part of Define Activities, you are looking at dependencies used to define the sequence among the activities. Which of these is not a valid type of dependency?

A. Linked dependency

B. External dependency

C. Discretionary dependency

D. Mandatory dependency

42. A company is looking for an experienced project manager to manage a large construction project. You meet all of the requirements for the position except for one. The organization is looking for a certified PMP with five years of experience and you have four years of experience managing similar projects. What is the BEST way to fill out your application?

A. Show how you meet the requirements but include your actual years of experience

B. Do not fill out that particular section.

C. Explain why years of experience should not matter.

D. Since you have plenty of experience, embellish your actual years of experience.

43. Hillbrand Dairies is structured so project managers share responsibility with the functional managers for assigning priorities and directing the work of persons assigned to the project. This is an example of a _____organization.

A. Dotted line

B. Hierarchical

C. Traditional

D. Matrix

44. When are risk identification activities performed?

A. During the Perform Qualitative Risk Analysis process

B. During the Plan Risk Management process

C. During the Perform Quantitative Risk Analysis process

D. Ongoing throughout the project

45. Bill is the project manager of a software project that is originally estimated for 12 months. 2 months into the project, it is discovered that the original estimating assumptions were fundamentally flawed. The Estimate at Completion (EAC) in such a project will be:

A. EAC = AC + ETC where EAC = Estimate at Completion AC = Actual Cost to date ETC = Estimate to Complete based on a new estimate

B. EAC = BAC where EAC = Estimate at Completion BAC = Budget at Completion

C. EAC = AC + [BAC - EV]/CPI where EAC = Estimate at Completion AC = Actual Cost to date BAC = Budget at Completion EV = Earned value. CPI = Cost performance index.

D. EAC = AC + BAC - EV where EAC = Estimate at Completion AC = Actual Cost to date BAC = Budget at Completion EV = Earned value.

46. The formula for forecasting EAC using remaining budget is:

A. EAC=ACC+((BAC-EV)/CPIC)

B. EAC= BAC-EV

C. EAC=ACC+BAC-EV

D. EAC=(BAC-EV)*CPIC

47. A project consists of multiple phases. Which of the following is a valid statement and applies to each phase of the project?

   A. Each phase is generally concluded with a review of the work accomplished and a decision authorizing the next phase of the project.

   B. Each phase of the project is considered complete when the project sponsor signs off on that phase of the project.

   C. Each phase of the project is generally concluded with a review of the work accomplished and deliverables to determine acceptance and whether the phase should be considered closed.

   D. Each phase is generally concluded with a review of the work accomplished. A phase is never considered complete until the end of the project when the entire project can be deemed complete.

48. Which of the following is an example of data that may be presented in a performance report?

   A. Earned value

   B. Quality metrics

   C. Schedule variance

   D. All of the above

49. Risks may be identified during the entire lifecycle of a project. Identify Risks is what type of process?

   A. Qualitative

   B. Effort driven

   C. Never ending

   D. Iterative

50. The most effective method of resolving conflict or other issues with stakeholders is_____.

   A. electronic information exchange.

   B. binding arbitration.

   C. a face to face meeting.

   D. a facilitated discussion group.

PMP Lite Mock Exam 9
Answer Key and Explanations

1. D - The Budget at completion (BAC) = $100,000 (given) The Actual Cost (AC) = $ 60,000 (given) The Earned value (EV) = (40/100) * 100,000 since 40% of the project is complete. Hence, Earned Value (EV) = $ 40,000. This is an instance of an atypical cause of variance in the project. Hence, the calculation used for Estimate to Complete ETC is: ETC = BAC - EV = 100,000 - 40,000 = 60,000 [Project Cost Management]

2. D - This is an example of a constraint. Constraints are factors that limit a project management team's options. Examples of constraints include team members situated in different geographical locations, incompatible communication software versions or limited technical communications capabilities. [Project Communications Management]

3. B - The correct response is 'S-curve'. Both S-curves and Tabular formats can be used to represent Earned value analysis data. This analysis is often included as part of performance reporting. [Project Communications Management]

4. B - The endeavor "Updating of an HR database" is not likely to have been a project. It is part of ongoing operations in the HR department. The other three - writing of a research paper, creation of a new business function and development of a new laser printer, are likely to have been projects. Projects can create a product or artifact, a capability to perform a service or a result such as documents from research. [Project Framework]

5. A - A procurement performance review is a structured review of the seller's progress to deliver project scope and quality, within cost and on schedule, as compared to the contract. [PMBOK- Page 338] [Project Procurement Management]

6. C - An issue log should at a minimum contain the owner name and a target resolution date. An issues should be clarified in a way that it can be resolved. Unresolved issues can be a major source of conflict and project delays. Having just the owner name or target resolution date leaves the issue log incomplete. Providing additional details such as financial impact on the project, impact on schedule, number of days the issue is unresolved etc are 'nice-to-have's beyond the minimum requirement of just the owner name and target resolution date. [Project Communications Management]

7. A - Activity Cost estimates are quantitative assessments of the

probable costs required to complete project work. The Basis of estimates consists of additional details supporting the cost estimate. These include documentation of the basis for the estimate, documentation of all assumptions, documentation of any known constraints and indication of the range of possible estimates. These form inputs to the Develop Budget process. [Project Cost Management]

8. C - Activity Duration Estimates will affect cost estimates on any project where the project budget includes an allowance for the cost of financing, including interest charges, and where resources are applied per unit of time for the duration of the schedule activity. [PMBOK- Page 170] [Project Cost Management]

9. A - It would be incorrect to start with a zero value for contingency reserves. One of the three methods listed could be used to arrive at a contingency reserve number. As more precise information about the project is available, the contingency reserve may be used, reduced or eliminated. [Project Cost Management]

10. C - Your first step should always be to communicate any requested changes with the sponsor to asses the next steps. [Project Integration Management]

11. D - The correct response is 'change control system'. A collection of formally documented procedures that define how project deliverables and documentation are controlled, changed and approved is called a change control system. This is a subsystem of the configuration management system. [Project Integration Management]

12. B - This is called a threshold. It is a cost, time, quality, technical or resource value used as a parameter and may be included in product specifications. Crossing the threshold generally triggers an action such as generating an exception report which can get appropriately escalated. [Project Quality Management]

13. A - The cost of electric utilities for the office would be considered as an indirect cost. Indirect costs are also known as overhead and general and administrative costs. They are the costs allocated by the project team as a cost of doing business. Ex: Salaries of management indirectly involved in the project, cost of electric utilities etc. [Project Procurement Management]

14. A - The kickoff meeting is the first opportunity to bring the project team together. Team members, key stakeholders, senior management, the sponsor, and the customer usually

attend the kickoff meeting. This is where project team members are introduced to one another and lessons learned can be shared from similar projects. By the end of the kickoff meeting, the goal is to have commitment from the project stakeholders about specific deliverables and objectives. At the kickoff meeting, specific details are not discussed like a detailed scope or cost estimates. [Project Integration Management]

15. C - Considered an input to the Manage Stakeholder Expectations process, an issue log is a written log that documents points or matters that are in dispute or in question within the project. As issues come about the log can be used to document who is responsible for resolving issues and by what date. PMBOK Pg. 263 [Project Communications Management]

16. C - The Direct and Manage Project Execution process involves the management of the direction of the planned project activities. Work Performance Information is routinely collected as part of this process. [PMBOK Page 87] [Project Integration Management]

17. B - When managed properly, differences of opinion are healthy and can lead to increased creativity and

better decision-making. When the differences become a negative factor, however, project team members are initially responsible for resolving their own conflicts. [PMBOK- Page 239] [Project Human Resource Management]

18. B - As project manager, you would need to proactively speak to the senior team member and ask for all appraisals to be done in an objective manner. The other options are incorrect. Ignoring the matter will not help solve it. Likewise the other two options are impractical. [Prof. Responsibility]

19. C - Qualitative analysis examines risks from the risk register and analyzes its probability of occurrence and the impact it would have on the project deliverables if it did occur. PMBOK Pg. 289 [Project Risk Management]

20. C - The correct response is that lessons learned are compiled, formalized and stored through the project's duration. The focus of lessons learned meetings can vary. In some cases, the focus in on strong technical or product development processes, while in other cases the focus is on the processes that aided or hindered performance of the work. [Project Communications Management]

21. C - The correct action is for the project manager to insist on paying for his / her lunch. Avoiding going out to lunch with anyone from the seller organization is drastic as it may be an opportunity to build relationships and to understand the seller's position for a project, better. Going out for lunch and not informing his / her managers about the lunch is unethical. Allowing the seller organization to pay for the lunch since it is a small value may be okay in certain organizations. For example some organizations have a limit on the nature of "gifts" that may be received by their employees and permit gifts not exceeding a certain value (ex: $ 50). In such a case, a lunch may be within limits. However, in the current situation, the data only reflects that the buyer organization does not permit its employees to receive any gifts. Hence this option is not acceptable. [Prof. Responsibility]

22. D - The accuracy of a project estimate will increase as the project progresses through the project lifecycle. In the initiation phase, a project could have a rough order of magnitude estimate in the range of -50% to +50%. Later as more information is known, estimates could narrow to a range of -10% to +10%. [PMBOK- Page 168] [Project Cost Management]

23. A - Collect Requirements is the process of defining and documenting stakeholders' needs to meet project objectives. The development of requirements begins with an analysis of the information in the project charter and the stakeholder register. [Project Scope Management]

24. A - Both the buyer and the seller administer the contract for similar purposes. Each party ensures that both it and the other party meet their contractual obligations and that their own legal rights are protected. [PMBOK- Page 335] [Project Procurement Management]

25. B - The risk register is not an information gathering technique used for identifying risks. It is a repository for information gathered during risk identification PMBOK Pg. 286 [Project Risk Management]

26. A - The risk management plan describes how risk management will be structured and performed on the project. It does not identify individual risks or the probability of their occurrence. [PMBOK-Page 279/280] [Project Risk Management]

27. D - You are decomposing into work packages which can be performed by more than one person. PMBOK Pg. 118 / 120 [Project Scope Management]

28. A - By developing a management plan it will dictate the rest of your actions, such as meeting with your team. You will also need a management plan if the CPI and/or SPI are askew. [Project Integration Management]

29. B - The nominal group technique enhances brainstorming with a voting process. This then allows the most useful ideas to be prioritized and taken up for further brainstorming. [Project Scope Management]

30. B - When we make errors or omissions, we take ownership and make corrections promptly. When we discover errors or omissions caused by others, we communicate them to the appropriate body as soon they are discovered. [Project Management Institute Code of Ethics and Professional Conduct Section 2.2.4] [Prof. Responsibility]

31. C - Conflict management is a tool and technique used in Human Resource Management; however, it is associated with the Manage Project Team process, not with the Develop Project Team process. PMBOK 232, 233, 234 [Project Human Resource Management]

32. A - The primary responsibility of a project manager is to ensure that the project creates the necessary work products as per the defined scope. The other choices are also important, but do not represent the primary objective of the project and project manager. [Prof. Responsibility]

33. C - Smoothing is a temporary means of conflict resolution which involves trying to minimize the severity of conflict. While this method is good for relationships between the disagreeing parties, smoothing does not lead to a permanent solution. In the future both parties will realize that a problem still exists and the conflict will return. [Project Human Resource Management]

34. C - An input to the Conduct Procurements process, seller proposals are prepared by sellers in response to a procurement document package. These are then evaluated by the buyer to perform source selection. PMBOK Pg. 330/331 [Project Procurement Management]

35. A - Perform Quantitative Risk Analysis analyzes the effect of risk events and assigns a numerical rating to those risks. It also presents a quantitative approach to making decisions in the presence of uncertainty. This process uses techniques such as Monte Carlo simulation and decision tree analysis. [PMBOK- Page 299] [Project Risk Management]

36. C - Many cost estimators include reserves (also called contingency allowances), as costs in their schedule activity cost estimates. Contingency reserves are estimated costs to be used at the discretion of the project manager to deal with anticipated but not certain events. These events are "known unknowns" and are part of the project scope and cost baselines. [Project Cost Management]

37. D - Virtual teams share a common project goal but share little time in a traditional, face-to-face business environment. The virtual team concept is made possible with electronic communication and one of the benefits of such teams is the ability of members to work from home. PMBOK Pg. 228 [Project Human Resource Management]

38. D - Expected monetary value (EMV) analysis is a statistical concept that calculates the average outcome when the future includes scenarios that may or may not happen. The EMV of opportunities will generally be positive values, while risks will result in negative values. [PMBOK- Page 298] [Project Risk Management]

39. D - A responsibility assignment matrix (RAM) chart is used to illustrate the connections between work packages and project team members. [PMBOK- Page 221] [Project Human Resource Management]

40. C - A charter should be issued, signed and updated by one individual. Your immediate concern should be find a single sponsor for the project. Note though, that the sponsor can be a single person or group. PMBOK Pg. 74 [Project Integration Management]

41. A - Linked dependency is not a valid example of a dependency. The other three choices are valid examples of dependencies. Mandatory dependencies are inherent to the nature of the work being done and may often have physical limitations. Discretionary dependencies are usually established based on the knowledge of best practices within a particular application area. External dependencies are those that involve a relationship between project activities and non-project activities. [Project Time Management]

42. A - For project management professionals, honesty is the best policy. You should never mislead others in regard to your experience in the field and your knowledge of the project management processes. [Prof. Responsibility]

43. D - In a matrix organization, the project manager shares responsibility

with the functional managers for assigning priorities and for directing the work of persons assigned to the project. [PMBOK- Page 430] [Project Human Resource Management]

44. D - Identify Risks is the process of determining what risks can affect the project. Many different stakeholders usually participate in the Identify Risks process. The process of Identify Risks is iterative because unknown risks can be discovered throughout the life cycle of the project. PMBOK Pg. 282 [Project Risk Management]

45. A - The correct response is: EAC = AC + ETC where EAC = Estimate at Completion AC = Actual Cost to date ETC = Estimate to Complete based on a new estimate This approach is used because the original assumptions are fundamentally flawed and the estimate would require to be recalculated based on the new estimate. [Project Cost Management]

46. C - EAC equals ACC plus the budget required to complete the remaining work, which is the budget at completion (BAC) minus the earned value (EV). [PMBOK- Page 184] [Project Cost Management]

47. C - A project phase is generally concluded with a review of the work accomplished and the deliverables to

determine acceptance, whether extra work is still required and to decide whether the phase should be considered closed. The other options are not valid. Formal phase completion does not include authorizing the next phase of the project. [Project Framework]

48. D - Performance reports present the result of any analysis as compared to the performance measurement baseline. [PMBOK- Page 270] [Project Communications Management]

49. D - Identify Risks is an iterative process because new risks may become known as the project progresses through its lifecycle. [PMBOK- Page 282] [Project Risk Management]

50. C - Face to face meetings are the most effective means for communicating and resolving issues with stakeholders. When face to face meetings are not warranted or practical, telephone calls, email, or other electronic tools are useful for exchanging information and dialoguing. [Project Communications Management]

Knowledge Area Quiz
Project Communications Management
Practice Questions

Test Name: Knowledge Area Test: Project Communications Management
Total Questions: 10
Correct Answers Needed to Pass: 7 (70.00%)
Time Allowed: 15 Minutes

Test Description

This practice quiz specifically targets your knowledge of the Project Communications Management knowledge area.

Test Questions

1. You are holding a kick off meeting for the build out of a new data center. This will be the largest, most costly and most complex project you have worked on in your career. You have counted up the number of stakeholders, vendors and project team members to be 52. In order to stress to the group how important and difficult communication will be on the project you want to tell them how many channels of communication exist on the project. What would you tell them?

A. 2625 channels exist on the project

B. 52 channels exist on the project

C. 2704 channels exist on the project

D. 1326 channels exist on the project

2. A communications management plan should include all of the following, EXCEPT:

A. Glossary   of   Common Terminology

B. Escalation List/Contacts

C. Person that will issue weekly reports

D. Risk Register

3. You are working on a project with a fixed fee contract, therefore communications should tend toward?

A. Formal Verbal Communication

B. Informal Written Communication

C. Formal Written Communication

D. Informal Verbal Communication

4. A project initially starts out with 3 stakeholders but the number increases to 7 during the course of the project. How many channels does the project manager now need to manage?

    A. 18 channels

    B. 10 channels

    C. 21 channels

    D. 7 channels

5. You are the project manager and are responsible for the development of a mall. As with any construction project, there will be multiple iterations of blueprints and engineering drawings, so you have decided to create an online database that can be used to query the documents by name, type, date, etc. This is an example of what type of communication tool?

    A. Information Distribution Tool

    B. Lessons Learned

    C. Project Records

    D. Information Presentation Tool

6. You are working on a project where all the team members are located in geographically different areas, therefore all the communication is done via e-mail and chat. It is sometimes hard to get the true meaning of these messages because you can't see facial expression or hear tone of voice, this is an example of?

    A. Encoding

    B. Medium

    C. Decoding

    D. Noise

7. You are reviewing a project with Tom, a new project manager. While discussing the communication requirements with Tom, you find that he has an impression that a project with 'n' number of stakeholders has 'n' communication channels. You are aware that this is wrong. What is the right answer?

    A. No of channels = $n(n+1)/2$ where n = number of stakeholders

    B. No of channels = $n2(n2-1)/2$ where n = number of stakeholders

C. No of channels = n(n-1)/2n where n = number of stakeholders

D. No of channels = n(n-1)/2 where n = number of stakeholders

8. Your project calls for communication with a very large audience. What communication method would be appropriate under such circumstances?

A. Pull communication

B. Interactive communication

C. Two-way communication

D. Push communication

9. You are looking at various techniques to help you in performance reporting for your project. Which of these choices will not help you do this?

A. Bar charts

B. Resource Activity Matrices

C. S-curves

D. Tabular reports

10. Successful project managers generally spend an inordinate of time, doing what?

A. Updating the Project Management Plan

B. Communicating

C. Working Scheduled Activities

D. Managing Risks

Knowledge Area Quiz
Project Communications
Management
Answer Key and Explanations

1. D - Communication Channel formula is: $n(n-1)/2$. N=Number of people involved on the project. $52(52-1)/2$ $52*51=2652$ $2652/2=1326$ PMBOK Pg. 253 [Project Communications Management]

2. D - The Risk Register is part of Risk Management and should not be included in the Communication Management Plan. PMBOK Pg. 257 [Project Communications Management]

3. C - Anytime contracts are involved in a project, the project manager/team should err on the side of formality with their communication. [Project Communications Management]

4. C - The correct answer is 21. The number of channels = $n(n-1)/2$ where n is the number of stakeholders. Since there are 7 stakeholders now, the number of channels is 7 X 6 / 2 = 21 [Project Communications Management]

5. A - The online database is an example of an Information Distribution Tool. PMBOK Pg. 260 [Project Communications Management]

6. D - Anything that interferes with the meaning of a message is considered noise. PMBOK Pg. 255 [Project Communications Management]

7. D - The correct response is $n(n-1)/2$ where n = number of stakeholders. A key component of planning the project's communications is to determine and limit who will communicate with whom and who will receive what information. [Project Communications Management]

8. A - The situation in the project would call for pull communication. This is suited for very large audiences and would allow them to access information content at their own discretion. [Project Communications Management]

9. B - Resource Activity Matrices (RAMs) illustrate the connection between work to be done and team members. They do not help in performance reporting. Performance reports organize and summarize the information gathered and present the results of any analysis as compared to the performance measurement baseline. [Project Communications Management]

10. B - Most projects fail because of poor communication. Successful project managers spend a great deal of time

communicating. PMBOK Pg. 243 [Project Communications Management]

PMP Lite Mock Exam 10
Practice Questions

Test Name: PMP Lite Mock Exam 10
Total Questions: 50
Correct Answers Needed to Pass:
35 (70.00%)
Time Allowed: 60 Minutes

Test Description

This is a cumulative PMP Mock Exam which can be used as a benchmark for your PMP aptitude. This practice test includes questions from all PMBOK knowledge areas, including the five basic project management process groups.

Test Questions

1. The total cost incurred by investment in preventing nonconformance to requirements, appraising the product or service for conformance to requirements and failing to meet requirements (rework) is called:

    A. Cost of Quality (COQ)

    B. Cost of Conformance (CoC)

    C. Embedded costs

    D. Cost of Poor Quality (CoPQ)

2. The key components of the basic model of communication between two parties are:

    A. Encode, message, medium, noise, decode

    B. Encode, send, receive, acknowledge, reply

    C. Encode, send, receive, translate, respond

    D. Encode, send, interference, response, acknowledgment

3. Which of the following methods of forecasting EAC and ETC is the most accurate?

    A. ETC based on atypical variances

    B. Earned Value

    C. ETC based on typical variances

    D. ETC based on new estimate

4. Your team has built an exotic sports car for a wealthy client, and now the project manager is reviewing the car to ensure it meets the specifications of the client, as agreed to in the project plan. What project

management process is represented here?

A. Closing

B. Monitoring and Controlling

C. Planning

D. Execution

5. You are the project manager for Fast Cars Inc. and you and your team members are using facilitated workshops as part of the Collect Requirements phase to define product requirements. Which other process also uses this technique?

A. Develop Scope

B. Develop Project Charter

C. Define Scope

D. Create WBS

6. Skills such as empathy, influence, creativity, and group facilitation are valuable assets when managing the project team. These skills are often referred to as _____.

A. Effort based management

B. Feedback based skills

C. Team development skills

D. Soft skills

7. The cost of running a project management office is an example of what type of cost?

A. Reimbursable

B. Fixed

C. Direct

D. Indirect

8. Gary is a project manager wrapping up the construction of a new office building. He creates several documents during this process. Which of the following are documents that he could create for the Close Procurements process?

A. Lessons learned documentation

B. Formal written notice of acceptance of deliverables

C. Closed contracts

D. All of the above

9. A project risk manager distributes anonymous questionnaires to project team members to help identify risks. This is called _____.

A. Game Theory

B. The Consensus Method

C. Interviewing

D. The Delphi Technique.

10. The project management team determines which dependencies are discretionary during the process of establishing the sequence of activities. They are fully documented since they can create arbitrary float values and can later limit scheduling options. Discretionary dependencies are also referred to as:

A. Preferential logic

B. Hard logic

C. Linked logic

D. Referential logic

11. Tim is the project manager of a project that has a timeline of 18 months. Tim has planned for daily status reports to be sent out to all stakeholders. After receiving two such reports, the project sponsor informs Tim that she would only like to have fortnightly reports. Tim had done an analysis of communications requirements and considered various attributes for the communications management plan. What aspect has he missed out, which resulted in a daily status report being sent out instead of fortnightly status reports?

A. He has not considered the frequency of information distribution.

B. He has not considered the purpose for distribution of information.

C. He has not considered the timeline of the project.

D. He has not considered the start/end dates of distribution of information

12. A software development project team has determined the best way to mitigate the risk of not having the computational resources to complete all bug testing on schedule is to add 3 more servers to the test bed. However, the network may not have enough capacity to handle the extra load of those three servers and could fail. This type of risk is called a _____ risk.

A. Secondary

B. Simulation

C. Bottleneck

D. Hidden

13. Which of the following enterprise environmental factors will influence the Develop Human Resource Plan process?

    A. Organizational culture and structure

    B. Existing human resources

    C. Personnel administration policies

    D. All of the above

14. As part of the Quality control in your project, you are looking at a technique which shows the history and pattern of variation. This is a line graph which shows data points plotted in the order in which they occurred. You are most likely looking at a:

    A. Run chart

    B. Pareto diagram

    C. Histogram

D. Cause and effect diagram

15. A team member who worked with you on certain projects earlier has tailored his project experience and is applying for PMP certification. You are aware that he has sent in his application and does not meet the eligibility criteria. You should:

    A. Ignore the matter since you feel that the team-member cannot clear the PMP exam.

    B. Inform PMI of this matter.

    C. Ignore the matter until PMI contacts you about it.

    D. Ignore the matter and certify that the team-member meets requirements when PMI contacts you.

16. The manager of a project to deploy a new ERP system is working to determine what information the stakeholders want, what format it should take, and how often they should be given updates. This is called_____.

    A. Report Project Status

    B. Manage Stakeholder Expectations

C. Plan Communications

D. Distribute Information

17. You are a PMP reviewing project files to help you write a lessons learned document on a software project you are finishing. What option is MOST likely contained in the project files?

A. Information on minimizing negative events and maximizing positive events

B. Information on the project's failures

C. Information on the project's successes

D. Information on the activities of the project

18. Which of the following processes gives the project management team insights into the health of the project?

A. Perform Quality Assurance

B. Perform Integrated Change Control

C. Monitor and Control project work

D. Report Performance

19. Which of the following are organizational process assets that can influence the project team with the Develop Human Resource Plan process?

A. Organizational standard processes

B. Historical information on organizational structures

C. Templates for organizational charts

D. All of the above

20. A project manager is using some information gathering techniques to identify risk. Which of these is not an information gathering technique used in identifying risk?

A. Simulation

B. Interviewing

C. Brainstorming

D. Strengths, weaknesses, opportunities and threats (SWOT) analysis.

21. The project manager in charge of a new credit card software project has asked the product manager to create a checklist to assist with the identification of risks. A risk checklist can be created from which of the following sources?

A. A SWOT analysis

B. The lowest level of the Risk Breakdown Structure

C. Ishikawa diagrams

D. All of the above

22. A planning technique used to provide products, services and results that truly reflect customer requirements by translating those customer requirements into the appropriate technical requirements for each phase of project product development is called:

A. Total Quality Management

B. PCM-CMMi

C. Voice of the Customer

D. ISO-9001

23. You have utilized 360-degree feedback techniques for your information gathering and are in the process of giving formal feedback to team members. You will be setting specific goals for employees for the remainder of the project. Which technique are you utilizing?

A. Project Performance Appraisals

B. Co-location

C. Issue Log

D. Observation and Conversation

24. You are a project manager who is in charge of an important project for your company. The project includes producing widgets for your customer. Data has been collected to help identify the greatest causes of defects in the overall process. Which technique should you use to determine the greatest source of defects?

A. Statistical sampling

B. Defect repair review

C. Pareto charting

D. Kaizen

25. A small project team has been assembled to develop a new retail store concept. The project manager wants to document the project's organization and position descriptions. Which of the following formats could he use?

A. Matrix based chart

B. Hierarchical chart

C. Text oriented format

D. All of the above

26. In a sender-receiver model for communication, information is sent and received between two parties, defined as the sender and the receiver. In such a model, anything that interferes with the transmission and understanding of the message is called:

A. Noise

B. Constraint

C. Medium

D. Barrier

27. Which of the following is not an appropriate method for dealing with a negative risk?

A. Avoid

B. Exploit

C. Transfer

D. Mitigate

28. Statistical sampling involves choosing part of a population for inspection. Appropriate sampling can often _____the cost of quality control.

A. neutralize

B. reduce

C. increase

D. mitigate

29. A risk with a positive outcome is called an _____.

A. Unlikely risk

B. Objective risk

C. Opportunity

D. Obsolete risk

30. Variance thresholds for monitoring cost performance are typically expressed as _____ from the baseline plan.

A. Positive deviation

B. Percentage deviation

C. Average deviation

D. Negative deviation

31. You are an inexperienced project manager who has been appointed to manage a project in a matrix organization. Because of this you can expect the communication in this project to be:

A. Open and Accurate

B. Easy to Automate

C. Simple

D. Complex

32. Predicting future performance based on historical events is called _____.

A. Historical analysis

B. Trend analysis

C. Parametric analysis

D. Pareto analysis

33. Which of the following estimating techniques will cost less, but is also generally less accurate?

A. Parametric Estimating

B. Analogous Estimating

C. Resource cost based Estimating

D. Bottom-up Estimating

34. A project manager is using a Risk Diagramming technique that is a graphical representation of situations showing causal influences, time ordering of events and other relationships among variables and outcomes. This would be:

A. A System flow chart

B. An Influence Diagram

C. Pareto chart

D. Risk flow diagram

35. Herzberg's Motivation-Hygiene theory includes which of the following concepts?

A. There are two ways to categorize people in the workplace.

B. Greater financial reward brings greater motivation.

C. People are always in a state of need.

D. Hygiene factors do not act as motivators by themselves.

36. The 80/ 20 rule, where 80% of the problems are caused by 20% of the causes, is also called:

A. Percentage of Defective Causes

B. Interactive analysis

C. Pareto's Law

D. Murphy's Law

37. You are a project manager for Enormous Co. and are currently engaged in a highly visible project. The company is about to implement an independent review to ensure that the project work is continuing to comply with the project's policies, processes, and procedures. During which process would this review occur?

A. Report Performance

B. Perform Quality Control

C. Monitor and Control Risks

D. Perform Quality Assurance

38. A project comprises of a virtual team with team members located in different offices in the same city as well as across different cities. The project manager wishes to built trust and good working relationships. One of the best ways to do this is:

A. To use team-building strategies.

B. Write a memo to the team, detailing out the need for good working relationships.

C. Plan for job-rotation on a weekly basis.

D. To encourage the use of telephonic conversations as much as possible.

39. Which process group corresponds to the "do" component of the plan-do-check-act cycle?

A. Monitoring and Controlling

B. Executing

C. Planning

D. Initiating

40. Which option is NOT representative of the inputs, tools and techniques, and outputs of Direct and Manage Project Execution?

    A. PMIS, Project Management Plan, and Deliverables

    B. Deliverables, Approved Change Requests, and Project Management Methodology

    C. Approved Change Requests, Recommended Defect Repair, and PMIS

    D. Approved Corrective Actions, Project Management Methodology, and Implemented Preventive Actions

41. As part of the Risk Response planning for your project, you are trying to come up with a strategy to deal with negative risks or threats. In order to eliminate the impact of a particular risk, you relax the objective that is in jeopardy by extending the project schedule. This is an example of

    A. Transference

    B. Mitigation

    C. Avoidance

    D. Postponement

42. You are the project manager for the production of an exotic car. You have completed the Define Scope process for your project. Which of the following may be generated through this process?

    A. Project scope statement, Project charter

    B. Project scope statement, Updates to Requirements traceability matrix

    C. WBS, Updates to Requirements traceability matrix

    D. Project scope statement, WBS

43. Perform Qualitative analysis of a risk is a quick way to prioritize how a project team will respond to risks. It is based on risk _____ and _____.

    A. Probability and exposure

    B. Probability and impact

    C. Probability and focus

    D. Exposure and cost

44. A project manager was assigned to a project as the project charter was being developed. Which of the following is an input that the project manager will utilize to develop the project charter?

   A. Make-or-Buy analysis

   B. Organizational Process Assets

   C. Project Acceptance Criteria

   D. Project Scope Statement

45. The Work Breakdown Structure (WBS) is a deliverable-oriented hierarchical decomposition of the work to be executed by the project team, to accomplish the project objectives and create required deliverables. The 'Create WBS' is a process under which Knowledge Area?

   A. Project Time Management

   B. Project Integration Management.

   C. Project Scope Management

   D. Project Cost Management

46. Gene is the project manager of a large highway expansion project. He has a number of stakeholders with competing priorities and agendas, and often has to resolve conflicts between stakeholders. Which knowledge area includes the Manage Stakeholder Expectations process?

   A. Project Quality Management

   B. Project Scope Management

   C. Project Communications Management

   D. Project Human Resource Management

47. There are 10 stakeholders in Megamart's ERP deployment project. How many potential communications channels are there?

   A. 25

   B. 10

   C. 45

   D. 30

48. Which of the following is NOT considered a method in the Distribute Information process?

   A. Speaking, Writing, Listening

B. E-mail, Fax, Voice Mail, Telephone

C. Project Meetings

D. Project Management Software

C. Project Quality Management

D. Project Integration Management

49. At a Project Management conference, the speaker refers to a "triple constraint" in project management. The speaker elaborates on how the project quality is balanced by the three factors involved and the relationship between these three factors being such that if any one of the factors changes, at least one other factor is likely to change. The speaker is referring to:

A. Project scope, time and cost.

B. Project schedule, cost and resources

C. Project Scope, cost and resources

D. Project scope, time and quality

50. Reporting information about scope to stakeholders is a process within which knowledge area?

A. Project Communications Management

B. Project Scope Management

PMP Lite Mock Exam 10
Answer Key and Explanations

1.   A - The total cost incurred by investment in preventing nonconformance to requirements, appraising the product or service for conformance to requirements and failing to meet requirements (rework) is called Cost of Quality (CoQ). Cost of Poor Quality refers to failure costs, which may categorized as internal and external.   [Project Quality Management]

2.   A - A basic model of communication demonstrates how ideas or information is sent and received between two parties, defined as the sender and the receiver. The key components of the model include encode, message, medium, noise, and decode. [PMBOK- Page 255] [Project Communications Management]

3.   D - ETC equals the revised estimate for the work remaining. This is typically done by the project manager and project team and will be a bottom-up manual summation. [PMBOK- Page 184] [Project Cost Management]

4.   A - The question is asking about PRODUCT verification, which occurs during the closing PMBOK Pg. 99 [Project Framework]

5.   C - Facilitated workshops are also used in the Define Scope process as a means of bringing key cross-functional stakeholders together. [Project Integration Management]

6.   D - Interpersonal skills, sometimes known as "soft skills" are particularly important to team development. By understanding the sentiments of project team members, anticipating their actions, acknowledging their concerns, and following up on their issues, the project management team can greatly reduce problems and increase cooperation. [PMBOK-Page 232] [Project Human Resource Management]

7.   D - Indirect costs are those costs that cannot be directly traced to a specific project. These costs are accumulated and allocated equitably over multiple projects by an approved and documented accounting procedure. [PMBOK- Page 169] [Project Procurement Management]

8.   D - Contract closure outputs include closed contracts, and organizational process assets, such as contract file, notice of deliverable acceptance, and lessons learned analysis and process improvement recommendations. [PMBOK- Page 344] [Project Procurement Management]

9.   D - The Delphi Technique is a way to reach a consensus of experts. Participants indicate their ideas about the important project risks on an anonymous questionnaire. The responses are summarized and are then recirculated to the experts for further comment. Consensus may be reached in a few rounds of the process. This techniques helps reduce bias in the data and keeps any one person from having undue influence on the outcome. [PMBOK- Page 286] [Project Risk Management]

10.   A - Discretionary dependencies are sometimes referred to as preferred logic, preferential logic or soft logic. They are usually established based on knowledge of best practices within a specific application area or some unusual aspect of the project where a specific sequence is required even though there are other acceptable sequences.   [Project   Time Management]

11.   A - Tim has most likely not considered the frequency of distribution of information. He should have analyzed the stakeholder requirements and planned for distribution of the status report accordingly. It is unlikely that on an 18 month project, the project sponsor would want to receive daily status reports. It is possible that at the end of the project, with a few days or weeks to go, the project sponsor might request for daily reports, in order to monitor the project closely, or in case there are issues with the project. Hence Tim should have considered stakeholder requirements and planned the frequency of the status report accordingly. The other choices are incorrect. The choice that Tim has not considered the timeline of the project may be one of the factors which influence the frequency of information distribution, but is not a complete response by itself. [Project Communications Management]

12.   A - A secondary risk arises as a direct result of implementing a risk response. [PMBOK-Page 441] [Project Risk Management]

13.   D - All the choices listed are Enterprise Environmental factors that influence the Develop Human Resource Plan process. [Project Human Resource Management]

14.   A - This is most likely to be a run chart. A run chart shows the trends in a process over a period of time. Trend analysis is performed using run charts since they show the history and pattern of variation. [Project Quality Management]

15.   B - The code of ethics and professional responsibility requires that you inform PMI that this team-

member does not meet the eligibility criteria, at least to the extent of the projects he has worked under you. You may do this only since you are you are absolutely certain that he has applied to PMI with false information. [Prof. Responsibility]

16. C - Identifying the informational needs of the stakeholders and determining a suitable means of meeting those needs is an important factor for project success. The Plan Communications Process determines the information and communications needs of the stakeholders; for example, who needs what information, when they will need it, how it will be given to them, and by whom. [PMBOK- Page 252] [Project Communications Management]

17. D - Project files generally record information on the activities of the project. They can be reviewed to help generate a lessons learned document. However, lessons learned documents will contain information on the project's successes, failures, and recommendations on minimizing negative events and maximizing positive events. [Project Integration Management]

18. C - The correct response is 'Monitor and Control Project Work'. This is the process necessary for collecting, measuring, and disseminating

performance information and assessing measurements and trends to effect process improvements. This process includes risk monitoring to ensure that risks are identified early, their status is reported, and appropriate risk plans are being executed. Monitoring includes status reporting, progress measurement, and forecasting. [Project Integration Management]

19. D - All the choices listed are Organizational Process Assets that influence the Develop Human Resource Plan process. [Project Human Resource Management]

20. A - Simulation is not a valid information gathering technique. Brainstorming is performed by the project management team along with a set of experts who are not necessarily part of the team. Interviewing experienced project participants, stakeholders and subject matter experts can identify risks. The Strengths, Weaknesses, Opportunities and Threats (SWOT) analysis ensures examination of the project from each of the SWOT perspectives. [Project Risk Management]

21. D - The lowest level of the RBS can be used as a risk checklist. Care should be taken to explore items that do not appear on the checklist,

however.   [PMBOK- Page 287] [Project Risk Management]

22.   C - The correct response is 'Voice of the Customer'. This is one of the non-proprietary approaches to quality management. In this planning technique, the customer's requirements are exactly met in the finished product during each phase of the project.   [Project Quality Management]

23.   A - Project Performance Appraisals are a technique of the Manage Project Team process. In a Project Performance Appraisal team members get feedback from project work supervisors. The supervisors can gather information from those who interact with the team member using 360-degree feedback principles. The term 360 feedback principles, simply means that information is gathered from multiple sources such as the workers supervisors, peers, and subordinates. PMBOK Pg. 238 [Project Human Resource Management]

24.   C - Pareto charts are used to analyze information that has already been collected and focus on identifying the problem areas that cause the greatest negative effect on the process. PMBOK Pg. 210 / 211 [Project Quality Management]

25.   D - Various formats exist to document team member roles and responsibilities. Most of the formats fall into one of three types: hierarchical, matrix, and text-oriented. [PMBOK- Page 220 / 221] [Project Human Resource Management]

26.   A - In a sender-receiver model, the key components include encoding of thoughts or ideas, a message as the output of encoding, a medium to convey the message and decoding the message back into meaningful thoughts or ideas. Anything that interferes with the transmission and understanding of the message is termed as noise (for example: distance). [Project Communications Management]

27.   B - Exploitative strategies are selected for risks with positive impacts where the organization wishes to ensure the opportunity is realized. This strategy seeks to eliminate the uncertainty associated with a particular upside risk by making the opportunity happen. [PMBOK- Page 303/304] [Project Risk Management]

28.   B - Appropriate sampling can often reduce the cost of the quality control. In some application areas, it may be necessary for the project management team to be familiar with a variety of sampling techniques. [Project Quality Management]

29.   C - Risks can pose a threat or an opportunity to a project. [PMBOK-Page 303] [Project Risk Management]

30.   B - Variance thresholds for monitoring cost performance are usually expressed as percentage deviations from the baseline plan. [PMBOK page 166] [Project Cost Management]

31.   D - Matrix organizations have don't have linear communications lines (e.g., top-down), therefore communication goes across many different "silos" [Project Framework]

32.   B - Trend analysis is an analytical technique that uses mathematical models to forecast future outcomes based on historical results. It is a method of determining the variance from a baseline of a parameter by using prior progress reporting periods' data and projecting how much that parameter's variance from baseline might be at some future point in the project if no changes are made in executing the project. [PMBOK- Page 443] [Project Quality Management]

33.   B - Analogous cost estimating is generally less costly than other cost techniques, but is also generally less accurate. It uses the actual cost of previous, similar projects as the basis for estimating the cost of the current project. It is more reliable when the previous projects are similar in fact, and not just in appearance, and the persons estimating have the needed expertise. [Project Cost Management]

34.   B - A Diagramming technique that is a graphical representation of situations showing causal influences, time-ordering of events and other relationships among variables and outcomes is known as an Influence Diagram. The Cause-and-effect diagram also identifies the causes of risk, but does not have the time-ordering of events [Project Risk Management]

35.   D - Herzberg's Motivation-Hygiene theory includes the concept that Hygiene factors do not act as motivators by themselves. Hygiene factors fall into a category of factors that if absent will make a person unsatisfied. Hygiene factors by themselves do not make a person satisfied. Motivation factors do just that, they motivate. Some examples of Hygiene factors include: salary, status, supervision, and personal life. Some examples of Motivation factors include: advancement, growth, and responsibility. [Project Human Resource Management]

36.   C - Pareto's Law holds that a relatively small number of causes will typically produce a large majority of the problems or defects. [PMBOK-Page 210 / 211] [Project Quality Management]

37. D - Quality audits are performed during the Perform Quality Assurance process. PMBOK Pg. 204 [Project Quality Management]

38. A - Use of team-building activities helps in building trust and establishing good working relationships. Among the other choices - encouraging the use of telephone calls can also help in building relationships, especially in distributed teams. However, this cannot be an alternative to email communication. Job-rotation within the team may also help team-morale, however doing it on a weekly basis may be counter-productive and inefficient. [Project Human Resource Management]

39. B - The Executing process group is contained within the "do" component of the plan-do-check-act cycle. The plan-do-check-act cycle was created by Shewhart and modified by Deming to illustrate how different results from one cycle become an input to another cycle. [Project Integration Management]

40. C - Recommended Defect Repair is not an input, tools and technique, or

output for the Direct and Manage Project Execution process. PMBOK Pg. 93 [Project Integration Management]

41. C - This is an example of avoidance. It involves changing the project management plan to eliminate the threat posed by an adverse risk, isolating the project objectives from the risk's impacts or to relax the objective that is in jeopardy, such as extending the schedule or reducing scope. Transference involves shifting the negative impact of a threat along with the ownership of the response. Mitigation implies a reduction in the probability and/or impact of an adverse risk. Postponement is not a valid strategy since it does not address the risk. [Project Risk Management]

42. B - The Define Scope process will result in development of the Project Scope statement and updates to project documents such as stakeholder register, requirements documentation and the requirements traceability matrix. [Project Scope Management]

43. B - Perform Qualitative risk analysis is usually a rapid and cost-effective means of establishing priorities for Plan Risk Responses. [PMBOK- Page 289] [Project Risk Management]

44. B - When developing the project charter, the project manager can draw from the assets that are part of the organizational process assets. There may be formal / informal policies, procedures, plans, and guidelines whose effects must be considered. Organizational process assets also represent the organization's learning from previous projects such as completed schedules, risk data and earned value data. These are invaluable in developing the project charter. [Project Integration Management]

45. C - The Work Breakdown Structure (WBS) is a deliverable-oriented hierarchical decomposition of the work to be executed by the project team, to accomplish the project objectives and create required deliverables. The 'Create WBS' is a process under the 'Project Scope Management' Knowledge Area. The WBS subdivides the project into smaller, more manageable pieces of work, with each descending level of the WBS representing an increasingly detailed definition of the project work. [Project Scope Management]

46. C - Manage Stakeholder Expectations refers to managing communications to satisfy the needs of and resolve issues with project stakeholders. Actively managing stakeholders increases the likelihood that the project will not veer off the track due to unresolved stakeholder issues and limits disruptions during the project. The project manager is usually responsible for stakeholder management. [PMBOK- Page 261] [Project Communications Management]

47. C - The total number of communications channels is n(n-1)/2, where n=number of stakeholders. [PMBOK- Page 253] [Project Communications Management]

48. A - Distribute Information is the execution of the communications management plan. Its main purpose is to gather and distribute project information to stakeholders throughout the life of the project to keep them updated. This process must be flexible enough to respond to unplanned requests from stakeholders. Speaking, Writing, and Listening are considered to be Communications Skills, not distribution methods. PMBOK Pg. 260 [Project Communications Management]

49. A - The "triple constraint" refers to project scope, time and cost. High quality projects deliver the required product, service or result within scope, on time and within budget. The relationship among these three factors is such that if any one of the factors changes, at least one other factor is likely to be affected. [Project Framework]

50.   A - The Report Performance process involves the collection of all baseline data and distribution of performance information to stakeholders. Performance reporting should generally provide information on scope, schedule, cost, and quality. [PMBOK- Page 266] [Project Communications Management]

PMP Lite Mock Exam 11
Practice Questions

Test Name: PMP Lite Mock Exam 11
Total Questions: 50
Correct Answers Needed to Pass:
35 (70.00%)
Time Allowed: 60 Minutes

Test Description

This is a cumulative PMP Mock Exam which can be used as a benchmark for your PMP aptitude. This practice test includes questions from all PMBOK knowledge areas, including the five basic project management process groups.

Test Questions

1. The State Board of Education is reviewing RFPs for deployment of its new HR system. An outside consultant has been hired to provide an independent estimate of the same work. This will be used as a_____.

   A. Procurement verification

   B. Benchmark estimate

   C. Prospective estimate

   D. Second opinion

2. A team of engineers is reviewing the architecture diagram for a new ERP system being deployed at a large accounting firm. The engineers are discussing the impact of the failure of each node in the diagram on overall availability of the final product. The intent of the discussion is to minimize the likelihood of failure and the effects of any failure. What is this called?

   A. SWOT Analysis

   B. Quantitative Analysis

   C. Failure Mode and Effect Analysis

   D. Deming Cycle

3. As a project manager based at the customer location for a performing organization, you strike up a rapport with a customer manager. As the project progresses, the manager asks you to make certain changes to the project scope and wants this to be handled on an informal basis. You should:

   A. Contact your manager in your organization and ask for this work to be done without payment, as a goodwill gesture.

B. Comply with the manager's request. It is important to continue to maintain a good relationship with the manager.

C. Refuse to take up any changes since the manager has asked you to do it informally.

D. Explain to the manager that you would need to formally document these as part of project scope change and put it through the change management process.

4. You are in the midst of a major code roll out for a new software module. However, it has come to your attention that the resources promised for the roll out are not going to be available. As the project manager, what is the BEST thing to do?

A. Explain the impact of the lost resources to the project schedule

B. Replan the project without the resources

C. Have the current staff work extra hours

D. Fast Track the schedule

5. What strategy should a project manager follow during the early stage

of a conflict between two of his team members?

A. Use a formal procedure to resolve the conflict

B. Address the two team-members in a team meeting and warn them.

C. Allow the team members to resolve their conflict

D. Use disciplinary action to resolve the conflict

6. The project management team performed activities such as measuring examining and verifying to determine whether work and deliverables met requirements and product acceptance criteria. Which of the following choices refers to a different set of activities than the ones just mentioned?

A. Walkthroughs

B. Prevention

C. Inspection

D. Reviews

7. _____ is performed on risks that have been prioritized by the Perform Qualitative Risk Analysis

process as potentially and substantially impacting the project.

A. Perform Risk Cost Analysis

B. Perform Risk Exposure Analysis

C. Perform Quantitative Risk Analysis

D. Perform Risk Outcome Analysis

8. Which of the following documents will help trace the requirements to product design?

A. Requirements traceability matrix

B. Design traceability matrix

C. Project scope statement

D. Product traceability matrix

9. As the project manager for Midway Carnival Rides, you are starting off on the Define Scope process. Which of the following is a key input to the process?

A. Risk Management Plan

B. Quality Management Plan

C. Project Charter

D. Staffing Management Plan

10. You are the project manager for a project. You are aware that cost and schedule risks are prevalent in your project. You want to compare the planned project performance with its actual performance. What should you perform to provide this information?

A. Variance and trend analysis

B. Reserve analysis

C. Risk audit

D. Risk reassessment

11. A key output of Develop Human Resources Plan is a list of project roles and responsibilities. What should this document include?

A. Role, Effort, Authority, Duties

B. Role, Responsibility, Authority, Title

C. Role, Title, Resource Cost, Responsibility

D. Role, Authority, Responsibility, Competency

12. What is the best way to show, at a glance, all the work packages or project activities assigned to a specific project resource?

  A. Organizational Breakdown Structure

  B. Authority Vesting Diagram

  C. Work Breakdown Structure

  D. Roles and Responsibilities Chart

13. RACI stands for_____, _____, _____, _____.

  A. Review, Analyze, Calculate, Implement

  B. Responsible, Actual, Complete, Informative

  C. Roles, Activities, Costs, Instructions

  D. Responsible, Accountable, Consult, Inform

14. As the project manager of a high-visibility project, you are in the process of Identifying risks. You are concerned that the data you collect might be biased. A technique that helps keep the bias out of the data

and keeps any one person from having undue influence on the outcome is:

  A. Interviewing

  B. Round-robin technique

  C. Ishikawa technique

  D. Delphi technique

15. A software team tracing the root cause of an application failure can use this to help determine the cause(s) of the failure:

  A. Ishikawa diagram

  B. Rummler-Brache swimlane diagram

  C. Threading analysis

  D. Deming chart

16. You are a project manager working on a project to create high efficiency electric motors for a company introducing a new electric golf cart. Your company's president is keenly interested in the project and requests a chart that shows the number of defects by type ordered by their frequency of occurrence. Which type of chart would BEST meet this request?

A. Pareto chart

B. Control chart

C. Statistical sampling

D. Scatter diagram

17. What term defines the work needed to complete a product, service, or result?

A. Product scope

B. Scope baseline

C. Scope verification

D. Project scope

18. During a weekly status meeting a team member suggests adding a component to the project . As the project manager, you indicate that all focus should be put on the current scope and don't worry about any enhancements. This is an example of?

A. Gold plating

B. Scope verification

C. Scope management

D. Change control

19. What type of method can be used to eliminate personal bias during the process of selecting a seller?

A. Independent estimates

B. Weighting

C. Vendor rankings

D. Screening

20. Which of these is an example of a facilitated workshop technique to determine critical characteristics for new product development?

A. Total Quality Management (TQM)

B. Voice of the User (VOU)

C. Internal Quality Deployment (IQD)

D. Quality Function Deployment (QFD)

21. A project manager is tracking the failure rate of a specific component used in the project, to determine if the quality level is within acceptable

limits for that project. What tool will help with this?

A. Control charts

B. Ishikawa diagram

C. Six Sigma

D. Quality control

22. You are planning a storage device migration in a data center. During this phase of the project, who should be controlling the project?

A. Project manager

B. SME's

C. Sponsor

D. Management

23. As project manager, you find you are constantly dealing with conflict amongst your team members. Everyone argues over sharing available project resources so you plan to use a conflict resolution method to alleviate the tension between team members. What conflict resolution method is NOT recognized by the Project Management Institute?

A. Forcing

B. Withdrawal

C. Elaboration

D. Smoothing

24. In a project that was yet to begin, many of the project team members were known in advance. This is called:

A. Proactive-planning

B. Skill-matching

C. Pre-assignment

D. Staffing-assignment

25. You are working on a mainframe upgrade, however the charter is constantly changing. Who has the responsibility to determine if these changes are necessary.

A. Project manager

B. Project Team

C. Stakeholders

D. Sponsor

26. All of the following are components of an effective change control system, EXCEPT:

    A. Lessons Learned

    B. Standard Reports

    C. Procedures

    D. Meetings

27. What similarity exists between a cost-reimbursable contract and a time and material contract?

    A. They have no definitive end.

    B. The closure date is part of the contract.

    C. They have fixed bonus rates.

    D. They can never grow in value.

28. Failure Mode and Effect Analysis (FMEA) is a non-proprietary approach to Quality Management. This is an analytical procedure in which:

    A. The effect of varying the various parameters that make up a process is determined by trying out various combinations of the parameters.

    B. Each potential failure mode in every component of a product is analyzed to determine its effect on the reliability of that component and, by itself or in combination with other possible failure modes, on the reliability of the product.

    C. A set of experts are asked to provide inputs on the reasons for failure of a product and corrective action is then taken.

    D. A list of historical causes for failure of a similar product is analyzed to determine the possible failure modes.

29. A team of engineers is reviewing a scatter diagram to determine how the changes in two variables in a new type of automobile tire are related. The closer points on the diagram are to a diagonal line, _____.

    A. the more likely a control group will be required

    B. the more closely they are related

    C. the less likely they are to be related

    D. the less likely a control group will be required

30. You are a project manager who is in charge of a technical documentation project. The project is 30% complete after 2 months and has cost $53,000. The budget for the project is $90,000 and is scheduled to last 6 months. How is the project performing?

A. The project is ahead of schedule and over budget.

B. The project is ahead of schedule and under budget

C. The project is behind schedule and under budget.

D. The project is behind schedule and over budget.

31. You are a project manager who is in charge of an important project for your company. The project is 40% complete after 3 months and has cost $350,000. The budget for the project is $950,000 and is scheduled to last 8 months. How is the project performing?

A. The project is behind schedule and over budget.

B. The project is ahead of schedule and under budget

C. The project is behind schedule and under budget.

D. The project is ahead of schedule and over budget

32. How will an organization with a weak matrix organization structure affect the Develop Human Resource Plan process?

A. The project manager will report directly to senior management.

B. The project manager will have a stronger role.

C. The project manager will have a relatively weaker role.

D. The project manager will have relatively more authority.

33. Product scope is measured against the product requirements whereas project scope is measured against:

A. The project charter, the project scope statement and the WBS.

B. The project management plan, the project scope statement and its associated WBS and WBS dictionary

C. The project requirements and WBS.

D. The acceptance criteria

34. In the procurement process, the seller may be viewed initially as a bidder, then as the selected source and then as the contracted supplier. The seller will typically manage the work as a project. In such an instance, which of the following is not true?

A. The Buyer becomes the customer and is thus a key project stakeholder for the seller.

B. Terms and conditions of the contract become key inputs to many of the seller's management processes. (ex: major deliverables, key milestones, cost objectives)

C. There need not be a contractual relationship between the buyer and the seller

D. The Seller's project management team is concerned with all the processes of project management and not just Procurement management.

35. A project manager found that unnecessary management time was being spent in a project. In addition, the resources were being used ineffectively and there was decreased efficiency in performing the work. The likely problem is that:

A. The team is likely to be an inexperienced one with the result that the project is running inefficiently.

B. The team is not working in a cohesive manner and requires some team-building activities to help improve efficiencies.

C. Decomposition of the deliverables into smaller more manageable components has been done excessively.

D. The project is a tough one and hence the processes are inefficient.

36. Lori is managing a project in a Functional organization. In this organization, she can expect to find that:

A. She wields considerable authority and can make independent decisions related to the project.

B. Management systems are designed to support projects and project management is easy.

C. Management systems are not designed to support project needs efficiently, and project management is difficult.

D. There are no barriers to communication between cross-functional teams. She is able to easily reach out to other teams without needing to go through the Functional manager.

37. Tom is a project manager who is assigned to a foreign country to manage a project. The project is a large one and comprises of smaller sub-teams, contributing to the entire project. As part of rewards and recognition within the project, Tom plans for a team award for the best sub-team. Later, one of the team-members meets Tom and tells him that he is unhappy with the format of the award and feels his contribution is not being recognized by the team award. What is your analysis of this situation?

A. This is a genuine lapse in recognition of an individuals efforts. Tom should institute a special award for the individual and recognize his efforts.

B. It is likely that Tom did not consider cultural differences in the foreign country. It is difficult

to develop appropriate team rewards in a culture that encourages individualism.

C. This is a matter which needs to be reported to HR for necessary disciplinary action.

D. This is an instance of a disgruntled team member. Tom should ignore the matter in the larger interests of the team.

38. A first-time project manager was assigned to a project that had a duration of 3 months. In order to gain a head start in the project, she took an older, completed project and incorporated all the tools, techniques and checklists from that project in their entirety into the current one. The older project had been completed in 14 months' time and was very similar in nature. The most appropriate comment on this would be:

A. This is an excellent example of re-use of artifacts from prior projects.

B. This may be unnecessary. The project management team needs to decide what is appropriate for the project.

C. This is not the correct procedure. The project manager should always create processes and documents afresh for new projects.

D. This is not correct. The project manager is violating copyright and intellectual property rights of the organization's prior customers.

39. A first-time project manager decided that he would have a 'perfect project'. He informed the customer that this project would not accept change requests of any kind and the scope would need to be detailed out accurately right at the start of the project. The customer agreed to this request. What would your comment on this situation be?

A. The is a good example of how the project management team can decide what is and what is not necessary for the project. Not allowing changes is a good way of ensuring that the project meets requirements as detailed out in project scope.

B. This is unrealistic and impractical. Change is inevitable and rather than look at a 'no change' project, it would be more in the project interests to plan for a robust change control process.

C. This indicates that the project manager is very aggressive and is likely to take the project to successful completion. Since he has announced the 'no change requests' policy, the customer manager can no longer request changes.

D. This is unrealistic and impractical. The project manager should not have announced his intentions to the customer. He should have had an unofficial policy of rejecting all change requests.

40. What is the MOST applicable responsibility of a Project Sponsor?

A. To ensure the project is within the budget, schedule, scope and quality standards

B. To achieve the project objectives

C. To be ultimately responsible for the project's success

D. To perform the project work

41. You have identified a risk that will negatively affect your security project. You and your team have decided to use an older encryption technology because of the high risk associated with the new technology. What type of risk strategy are you using?

A. Mitigation

B. Exploitation

C. Avoidance

D. Transfer

42. A project is contracted as a Cost-Plus-Fixed-Fee (CPFF) type of contract. The targeted cost is US$ 200,000 with a fee of US$ 30,000. If the project comes in at US$ 170,000, what would be the cost of the total contract?

A. US$ 195,500

B. US$ 230,000

C. US$ 200,000

D. US$ 170,000

43. A project is contracted as a Cost-Plus-Incentive-Fee (CPIF) type of contract. The project is negotiated such that if the final costs are less than expected costs, the sharing formula for cost savings is 80:20. The targeted cost is US$ 500,000 with a 10% fee. If the project comes in at

US$ 450,000, what would be the cost of the total contract?

A. US$ 495,000

B. US$ 510,000

C. US$ 505,000

D. US$ 550,000

44. A project is contracted as a Cost-Plus-Fixed-Fee (CPFF) type of contract with a fee of 10% of estimated costs. The estimated cost is US$ 50,000. If the project comes in at US$ 75,000 with no changes in project scope, what would be the total cost of the contract?

A. US$ 55,000

B. US$ 125,000

C. US$ 75,000

D. US$ 80,000

45. Creating a sense of community is a benefit of what type of strategy?

A. Group based management

B. Hoteling

C. Co-location

D. Virtual teams

46. You are fairly new to project management, but have been successfully managing a small project and now management has given you another project to manage, which you are excited about. However, the new project is growing exponentially everyday, you have also learned a project manager you work with managed a similar project last year. What should you do?

A. Wait to see if the scope of the project continues to grow

B. Get the project assigned to the PM who managed the similar project

C. Obtain Historical Records and get guidance from the PMO

D. Speak to the other project manager and get guidance

47. You are the project manager from a seller organization, based at the customer location. One of your team members is involved in certain unacceptable activities at the customer location. The HR manager of the customer team organizes a meeting between you, the team-member, your customer-manager and HR wherein the team member apologizes for his activities and agrees not to repeat them. You should:

A. Ignore the incident since the team member has agreed not repeat such activities.

B. Report this incident immediately to HR of your organization and to your managers.

C. Warn the team-member that this is the last opportunity and future incidents will lead to strict action.

D. Document the issue for your project records.

48. You have been asked by your project manager to help them create a chart that illustrates the project resources that will be working on each work package. What would be the best type of chart to use?

A. Milestone chart

B. RACI chart

C. Project organization chart

D. WBS

49. As the project manager of a development project, you are aware that there is a slight defect in the product developed, as a result of which it will fail to meet certain regulatory standards. This was due to faulty requirements. You are also aware that the product will continue to function properly even though it fails to meet that standard. Your customer manager asks you to certify that the product meets the necessary regulatory standards, stating that this will not be verified when the report is submitted to the necessary authorities, so there is no issue with your certifying. Your stance is that:

A. You certify the product. Regulations are anyway guidelines in the industry. Not meeting a regulation does not mean anything.

B. As a one-off instance, you will certify the product to make sure the project goes through successfully.

C. You will not certify that a product meets certain regulations when it does not, even though the product continues to function well.

D. You certify the product, but you document your conversation with your customer manager for future purposes.

50. The selection of life cycle for the project, the processes to be applied to each phase, and the results of the tailoring by the project management team are usually found in the:

A. Project scope statement

B. Project management plan

C. Project schedule

D. Project charter

PMP Lite Mock Exam 11
Answer Key and Explanations

1. B - For many procurement items, the procuring organization can either prepare its own independent estimates or have an independent estimate prepared as a check on proposed pricing. This independent estimate is used as a benchmark estimate. Significant differences from these cost estimates can be an indications that the procurement statement of work was not adequate, that the prospective seller either misunderstood or failed to respond fully to the procurement statement of work. [PMBOK- Page 332] [Project Procurement Management]

2. C - Failure Mode and Effect Analysis is an analytical procedure in which each potential failure mode in every component of a product is analyzed to determine its effect on the reliability of that component and the reliability of the product or system as a whole. [PMBOK- Page 427] [Project Risk Management]

3. D - The correct response is that you would explain to the manager that you would need to formally document these as part of project scope change and put it through the change management process. Complying with the manager's request is incorrect and violates the

code of ethics and professional responsibility that you have towards your organization. Refusing to take up changes may be too drastic a step. Contacting your manager in your organization may be considered after you have tried to get this formally included in the change management process. However, the decision to do work without payment involves financial considerations, and will be a more involved one. [Prof. Responsibility]

4. A - The first thing that should be done is to communicate the impact and then make decisions on the project from the feedback. [Project Integration Management]

5. C - During the early stages of a conflict between team members, it is best to allow them to resolve their own conflicts. [Project Communications Management]

6. B - The activities such as measuring examining and verifying to determine whether work and deliverables met requirements and product acceptance criteria are variously referred to as inspections, audits, reviews, product reviews, and walkthroughs. Prevention is not a valid term to describe these activities. [Project Scope Management]

7.   C - Perform Quantitative Risk Analysis is performed on risks that have been prioritized by the Perform Qualitative Risk Analysis process as potentially and substantially impacting the project's competing demands. Perform Quantitative Risk Analysis analyzes the effect of those risk events and assigns a numerical rating to those risks.[PMBOK- Page 294] [Project Risk Management]

8.   A - The requirement traceability matrix provides a structure to trace requirements to product design. [Project Framework]

9.   C - The Project Charter is the document that formalizes the project. It gives the project manager the authority to lead the project. It is a key input to the Define Scope process. PMBOK Pg. 112 [Project Scope Management]

10.   A - Variance and trend analysis are used to evaluate the differentials between planned and actual costs, schedules, and performance criteria. A variety of statistical techniques, such as Earned Value (EV) technique, are used to analyze these variances. PMBOK Pg. 186 [Project Cost Management]

11.   D - The following items should be addressed when listing the roles and responsibilities of team members needed to complete the project: role, authority, responsibility, competency. [PMBOK- Page 222 / 223] [Project Human Resource Management]

12.   A - The organizational breakdown structure (OBS) looks similar to the WBS, but instead of being arranged according to a breakdown of project deliverables, it is arranged according to an organization's existing departments, units, or teams. [PMBOK- Page 220] [Project Human Resource Management]

13.   D - RACI stands for Responsible, Accountable, Consult, Inform. [PMBOK- Page 221] [Project Human Resource Management]

14.   D - The Delphi technique is a way to reach a consensus of experts. Project risk experts participate in this technique anonymously. A facilitator uses a questionnaire to solicit ideas about the important project risks. The responses are summarized and then recirculated to the experts for further comment. Consensus may be reached after a few rounds of the process. Thus the Delphi technique helps reduce bias in the data and keeps out any one person from having undue influence on the outcome. [Project Risk Management]

15.   A - Cause and effect diagrams, also called Ishikawa diagrams, illustrate how various factors might be linked to potential problems or effects. [PMBOK- Page 208] [Project Quality Management]

16. A - A Pareto chart is a style of histogram used as a tool within the Perform Quality Control process. They display how many defects were produced by type or category of cause and ordered by their frequency. PMBOK Pg. 210 [Project Quality Management]

17. D - Project scope describes the work that must be performed to deliver a product, service, or result to the stakeholders. Product scope describes the features and functions that characterize a product, service, or result. PMBOK Pg. 103 [Project Scope Management]

18. C - This is an example of scope management. Gold plating would be if the team actually implemented the change. Scope verification is done during the closure of the project. PMBOK Pg. 103 [Project Scope Management]

19. B - A weighting system is a method for quantifying qualitative data to minimize the effect of personal prejudice on seller selection. [PMBOK- Page 328] [Project Procurement Management]

20. D - Quality Function Deployment (QFD) is a facilitated workshop technique to determine critical characteristics for new products. It begins with collecting customer needs, also known as Voice of the Customer (VOC). [Project Scope Management]

21. A - Control charts can be used to monitor any type of output variable. [PMBOK- Page 209] [Project Quality Management]

22. A - Once the project manager is assigned to the project they should be in control. However, it is the sponsor who ultimately has the responsibility to ensure the project is completed successfully. [Project Integration Management]

23. C - Elaboration is not one of the six conflict-resolving methods that are recognized and endorsed by the Project Management Institute (PMI). The six methods recognized and endorsed by PMI include Forcing, Smoothing, Compromising, Confronting, Collaborating and Withdrawing. [Project Communications Management]

24. C - This is known as pre-assignment. This situation can occur if the project is the result of specific people being promised as part of a competitive proposal, if the project is dependent on the expertise of particular persons,

or if some staff assignments are defined within the project charter. [Project Human Resource Management]

25. D - The project initiator or sponsor is responsible for authorizing and issuing the charter, and is responsible for determining if changes are needed and the subsequent updates. [Project Integration Management]

26. A - Lessons learned are reviews of procedures or past projects and are not part of a change control system. [Project Integration Management]

27. A - Time and material contracts resemble cost-reimbursable type arrangements in that they have no definitive end, because the full value of the arrangement is not defined at the time of the award. [PMBOK- Page 443] [Project Procurement Management]

28. B - Each potential failure mode in every component of a product is analyzed to determine its effect on the reliability of that component and, by itself or in combination with other possible failure modes, on the reliability of the product or system. For each potential failure, an estimate is made of its effect on the total system and of its impact. In addition, a review is undertaken of the action planned to minimize the probability

of failure and to minimize its effects. [Project Quality Management]

29. B - A scatter diagram shows the pattern of relationship between two variables. The closer the points are to a diagonal line, the more closely they are related. [PMBOK- Page 212] [Project Quality Management]

30. D - CPI=EV/AC
CPI=90,000*30%/53,000
CPI=27,000/53,000
CPI=.51(overbudget)   SPI=EV/PV
SPI=27,000/90,000x.33
SPI=27,000/29,970 SPI=.9 (behind schedule) PMBOK 182 & 183 [Project Cost Management]

31. B - CPI=EV/AC
CPI=950,00*40%/350,000
CPI=380,000/350,000
CPI=1.09(underbudget)
SPI=EV/PV
SPI=380,000/950,00x.375
SPI=380,000/36,250   SPI=1.07 (ahead of schedule) PMBOK Pg. 182 &183 [Project Cost Management]

32. C - An organization whose basic structure is a weak matrix means a relatively weaker role for the project manager. [Project Human Resource Management]

33. B - The correct response is that the completion of the project is measured against the project management plan, the project scope statement and its associated WBS and WBS dictionary. Project scope management needs to be well integrated with the various Knowledge Area processes, so that the work of the project will result in the delivery of the specified product scope. [Project Scope Management]

34. C - The statement that there need not be a contractual relationship between the buyer and the seller is incorrect. Whenever the seller is external to the organization, there needs to exist a contractual relationship between the buyer and the seller. [Project Procurement Management]

35. C - It is most likely that excessive decomposition was done. This typically leads to non-productive management effort, inefficient use of resources and decreased efficiency in performing the work. The project team needs to seek a balance between too little and too much in the level of WBS planning detail. [Project Scope Management]

36. C - Lori will find that the Functional organization in which she is managing the project will typically lack management systems to support project needs. The absence of a project-oriented system will make it difficult for her to run the project efficiently. She will need to spend considerable time on managing the

communications needs of the project. Communication will generally cascade upwards to the Functional manager who will then communicate with other Functional managers. They in turn cascade the communication down into their departments. The return communication follows the reverse path. [Project Framework]

37. B - The correct response is that it is likely Tom did not consider cultural differences in the foreign country. It is difficult to develop appropriate team rewards in a culture that encourages individualism. Hence rewards and recognition should consider cultural differences. [Project Human Resource Management]

38. B - The correct response is that this may be unnecessary. The project management team needs to decide what is appropriate for the project. Since the prior project had a duration of 14 months and the current one is of 3 months' duration, it is unlikely that the current project will have exactly the same processes applied. Some amount of tailoring will be required. The other responses are not valid. It cannot be said with certainty that the project manager will not be violating copyright and intellectual property rights of prior customers. Most organizations have very clear guidelines on what information can go into their organizational assets' database. [Project Framework]

39. B - The correct response is that this is unrealistic and impractical. Change is inevitable and rather than look at a 'no change' project, it would be more in the project interests to plan for a robust change control process thereby handling any uncontrolled changes. "Mandating" that there will be no changes will be ineffective. [Project Scope Management]

40. C - The project sponsor authorizes the project and is ultimately responsible for the project's success. The sponsor provides the financial resources for any project and can be the organization, a particular division or department of the organization, a senior manager, or an outside entity. [Project Integration Management]

41. C - In this scenario, you decided to avoid the risk by using an older technology because there is too high of a risk if you use the new technology. PMBOK Pg. 303 [Project Risk Management]

42. C - In a Cost-Plus-Fixed-Fee (CPFF) type of contract, the seller is reimbursed for allowable costs and receives a fixed fee payment calculated as a percentage of the estimated project costs. The fixed fee does not vary with actual costs unless

the project scope changes. In the current scenario, the fixed fee is fixed up as US$ 30,000. Although the actual project comes in at 170,000, the fixed fee remains the same. Hence the total cost to the project will be 170,000 + 30,000 = 200,000 [Project Procurement Management]

43. B - In a Cost-Plus-Incentive-Fee (CPIF) type of contract, the seller is reimbursed for allowable costs for performing the contract work and receives a predetermined fee. In some cases, if the final costs are less than the expected costs, then both the buyer and the seller benefit from the cost savings based on a pre-negotiated sharing formula. In the current situation, the predetermined fee is 10% of US$ 500,000 = US$ 50,000. Since the project came in at US$ 450,000, the savings is 500,000 - 450,000 = 50,000. The sharing formula is 80:20, hence the additional payout to the seller = (20/100) * 50,000 = 10,000. Hence the value of the total contract = 450,000 + 50,000 + 10,000 = US$ 510,000 [Project Procurement Management]

44. D - In the Cost-Plus-Fixed-Fee (CPFF) type of contract, the seller is reimbursed for allowable costs for performing the contract work and receives a fee calculated as an agreed-upon percentage of the costs. The costs vary depending on the actual

cost. The fee is based on estimated costs unless the scope of the project changes. For the current project, the agree-upon percentage of costs is 10%. The actual cost is US$ 75,000 even though the initial estimate was US$ 50,000. However, the fee is calculated as 10% of 50,000 = (10/100) X 50,000 = 5,000. The total cost of the contract is 75,000 + 5,000 = US$ 80,000. [Project Procurement Management]

45. C - Co-location involves placing many or all of the most active project team members in the same physical location to improve their ability to perform as a team. Co-location strategy can include a team meeting room, places to post schedules, and other conveniences that enhance communication and a sense of community. [PMBOK- Page 234] [Project Human Resource Management]

46. C - The historical records will give you an understanding of the past project; however you should also obtain guidance from the PMO. The project manager may not be experienced enough to provide you guidance. [Project Framework]

47. B - Unacceptable behavior is a disciplinary issue and the HR department of your organization needs to take the necessary action which could involve include recalling the team-member from the project, or any other disciplinary action. The other choices listed do not do not signify correct responses in this matter. [Prof. Responsibility]

48. B - RACI stands for responsible, accountable, consult, and inform. This is a type of responsibility assignment matrix that is used to illustrate the relationship between work that needs to be completed and team members. In a RACI chart, a matrix is created with work packages making up the rows, and team member roles in the columns. Typically, a RACI chart assumes that one person will be accountable for a work package and more than one person may be responsible for completing the work package. PMBOK Pg. 221 [Project Human Resource Management]

49. C - Your stance will be that you will not certify that a product meets certain regulations when it does not, even though the product continues to function well. It is possible that the customer manager might not be happy with this stance, however as a project manager, you have an obligation to uphold ethical practices and cannot certify a product that fails to meet the regulations. [Prof. Responsibility]

50.   B - Details of the life cycle, processes selected, and results of tailoring by the project management team are found in the project management plan. This plan integrates and consolidates all the subsidiary management plans from the planning processes. [Project Integration Management]

Knowledge Area Quiz
Project Risk Management
Practice Questions

Test Name: Knowledge Area Test: Project Risk Management
Total Questions: 10
Correct Answers Needed to Pass: 7 (70.00%)
Time Allowed: 15 Minutes

Test Description

This practice quiz specifically targets your knowledge of the Project Risk Management knowledge area.

Test Questions

1. Which of these is a valid response to negative risks and not positive risks?

   A. Exploit

   B. Mitigation

   C. Enhance

   D. Share

2. Which of these is accurate regarding risk management?

   A. Organizations are not likely to perceive risk as a threat to project success

   B. It has its origins in the uncertainty present in all projects

   C. The attitudes of individuals and organizations must not be a factor affecting risk management

   D. It is a passive activity in project management

3. As the project manager, of a project to construct a city park, you have identified 39 risks on the project, determined what would trigger the risks, rated them on a risk rating matrix, tested the assumptions and assessed the quality of the data used. You now plan to move to the next step of the risk management process. What have you missed?

   A. Overall risk ranking for the project

   B. Involvement of other stakeholders

   C. Risk Mitigation

   D. Simulation

4. Which of the following processes has risk register as the primary output?

    A. Plan Risk Management

    B. Perform Qualitative Risk Analysis

    C. Identify Risks

    D. Monitor and Control Risks

5. Which of these is an input of the Monitor and Control Risks process?

    A. Project management plan

    B. Risk register

    C. Work performance information

    D. All of the above

6. Which of the following is true about risks?

    A. The risk register documents all the risks in detail

    B. Risk impact should be considered, but probability of occurrence is not important

    C. Risks always have negative impact and not positive

D. Risk Response Plan is another name for Risk Management Plan.

7. During which stage of risk planning are risks prioritized based on probability and impact?

    A. Perform Qualitative risk analysis

    B. Identify Risks

    C. Perform Quantitative risk analysis

    D. Plan Risk Responses

8. If a project has a 60% chance of a U.S. $100,000 profit and a 40% chance of a U.S. $100,000 loss, the expected monetary value of the project is?

    A. $20,000 profit

    B. $40,000 loss

    C. $100,000 profit

    D. $60,000 loss

9. Which of these statements about Risk in a project is correct?

    A. Risks are always negative in nature and are threats that need to be managed well

B. A risk is always induced external to the project.

C. Risk responses reflect an organization's perceived balance between risk taking and risk avoidance

D. Risks need not be planned for in all projects

10.   An organization is using non-linear probability impact scales for Risk assessment (ex: 0.05, 0.1, 0.2, 0.4, 0.8). What would this indicate?

A. The organization is relatively inexperienced in handling risks and wishes to take a cautious approach in handling risk.

B. The organization perceives that negative risk is a higher possibility than positive risk.

C. The organization is highly experienced in handling risk and has factored this into a model.

D. The organization wishes to avoid high-impact threats or exploit high-impact opportunities even if they have relatively low probability.

Knowledge Area Quiz
Project Risk Management
Answer Key and Explanations

1. B - Risk mitigation is a valid response to negative risks. [Project Risk Management]

2. B - Risk management does indeed have its origins in the uncertainty present in all projects. [Project Risk Management]

3. B - The project manager is using a good process, however he/she should have involved the other stakeholders to help identify risks. [Project Risk Management]

4. C - The Risk Register is an output of the Identify Risks process. [Project Risk Management]

5. D - All of the stated options are inputs to the Monitor and Control Risks process. [PMBOK page 309] [Project Risk Management]

6. A - The risk register contains details of the risks. [Project Risk Management]

7. A - Perform Qualitative Risk Analysis assesses the impact and likelihood of identified risks. [Project Risk Management]

8. A - EMV=Probability x Impact .6 x $100,000=$60,000 ... .4 x ($100,000)=($40,000) ... $60,000-$40,000=$20,000 profit. [Project Risk Management]

9. C - Risk responses reflect an organization's perceived balance between risk taking and risk avoidance. The other choices are incorrect. Risks need not be induced only external to the project. For example, adopting a fast track schedule may be a conscious choice and result in some risks. This may however be in balance with the reward gained by taking the risk. Risks need not always be negative in nature. They may be positive as well. All projects need to plan for Risks. [Project Risk Management]

10. D - Use of non-linear values implies the organization wishes to avoid high-impact threats or exploit high-impact opportunities even if they have relatively low probability. In using non-linear values, it is important to understand what each of the numbers mean, their relationship to one another, how they were derived, and the effect they may have on different objectives of the project. [Project Risk Management]

PMP Lite Mock Exam 12
Practice Questions

Test Name: PMP Lite Mock Exam 12
Total Questions: 50
Correct Answers Needed to Pass:
35 (70.00%)
Time Allowed: 60 Minutes

Test Description

This is a cumulative PMP Mock Exam which can be used as a benchmark for your PMP aptitude. This practice test includes questions from all PMBOK knowledge areas, including the five basic project management process groups.

Test Questions

1. When your project first started, you had eight stakeholders. There have been changes made to the project and there are now 14 stakeholders. How many communication channels have been added to the project?

   A. 63

   B. 15

   C. 91

   D. 28

2. You are a project manager for a company that designs and develops automation systems for car companies. You are in the Close Project process for a project in which a new automation system has been designed and created for a car company located in Korea. You need to obtain formal acceptance for the new automation system. All of the following statements are true with respect to the final acceptance of the new system EXCEPT?

   A. Performance tests on the new automation system should be completed by the car company.

   B. A formal statement is issued indicating that the new automation system meets the terms of the contract.

   C. Final acceptance for the new automation system can be informal or formal.

   D. A checklist can be used to determine whether the new automation system meets the car company's specifications

3. Which of the following is NOT a valid statement regarding the critical path method?

A. The early start and finish dates and late start and finish dates are calculated without factoring in resource limitations.

B. A forward pass and backward pass are performed through the project network paths.

C. The resulting early and late start and finish dates will be the project schedule.

D. The flexibility of the schedule is measured by the difference between early and late dates.

4. You are the project manager of a large IT project. A manager from a company contracted to work on the project offers you free tickets to a local sporting event. The tickets are expensive but your organization has no formal policy regarding gifts. What is the BEST way to handle the offer?

A. Refuse the tickets and report the offer to your employer.

B. Accept the tickets but notify your employer.

C. Politely refuse the tickets.

D. Accept the tickets since there is no policy.

5. You are the project manager for a software engineering firm that creates customer tracking software for call centers. You are scheduling an instructor lead training session for your team to learn the newest features available for use in your development platform. Which statement BEST describes the tool or technique you are implementing?

A. Improving the skill set of your existing team members

B. Executing the staffing management plan

C. Identifying the skills required to complete product testing

D. Conducting a team building activity

6. As project manager, you scheduled a status update meeting. During the meeting, a problem developed and the group discussed it. The day after the meeting, Kevin approached you and expressed his concern that the problem was not really resolved. After thinking about it, he felt that his concerns were still valid and should be addressed. What conflict resolution method was used at the status meeting?

A. Smoothing

B. Forcing

C. Withdrawal

D. Confrontation

A. $ETC = (BAC - EV)/CPI$

B. $SV = EV - PV$

C. $CPI = EV/AC$

D. $EAC = AC + BAC - EV$

7. You are a project manager for your company. Part of the project requires producing 10,000 widgets, which your company will outsource. The company has agreed to pay all related costs and 5% of the estimated project costs. What type of contract has been negotiated?

    A. Cost-Plus-Incentive-Fee contract

    B. Cost-Plus-Fixed-Fee contract

    C. Time and Material contract

    D. Fixed-price contract

8. You are the project manager for JT's Lumber Yard. You are trying to forecast estimates for the last phase of the project you are currently working on. Based on the performance of the project to date, which formula can be used to estimate the total value of the project when completed assuming similar variances will not occur?

9. You work as an engineer for a large engineering firm. The last week you have been corresponding back and fourth with the supervisor of your department about the horizontal stabilizers required for the wings on a new aircraft you are designing. Which communication dimension does this represent?

    A. Horizontal

    B. Formal

    C. External

    D. Vertical

10. You are a member of a project team and the project manager frequently uses e-mail to provide you with details about how he feels your work on the project is progressing. What form of communication does this BEST describe?

    A. Formal verbal

B. Informal written

C. Informal verbal

D. Formal written

11. Which option correctly lists the stakeholders involved in approving the project management plan?

A. Executive management, project manager, project sponsor

B. Functional managers, suppliers, project sponsor

C. Functional managers, project manager, project sponsor

D. Executive management, functional managers, project manager

12. A measure taken to bring future results in line with the project plan BEST describes?

A. Implemented change request

B. Implemented preventive action

C. Documented corrective action

D. Recommended defect repair

13. With a clear contract statement of work, a seller completes work as specified, but the buyer is not pleased with the results. The contract is considered to be:

A. Null and Void

B. Complete

C. Waived

D. Incomplete

14. Which process is MOST responsible for updating and revising the schedule components of the Project Management Plan?

A. Develop Schedule

B. Perform Integrated Change Control

C. Develop Project Management Plan

D. Perform Quality Control

15. You are a project manager for Gleeson Associates. You are working together with a junior project manager on a project. You are currently discussing performance measurement analysis with her. You explain to her exactly the different

variables involved. You tell her all of the following statements are true about the cost variance EXCEPT?

A. It is calculated by the following formula: Cost Variance = Earned Value - Actual Cost.

B. It is used to determine whether or not the project is meeting the planned costs

C. It is always a positive value.

D. Its tendency is to decrease as the project is nearing the end.

16. Your project team works in two different buildings across the city from each other. The team has been struggling to perform effectively and has a difficult time resolving problems. What would be the BEST team development technique to resolve this issue?

A. Mediation

B. Rewards

C. Co-location

D. Training

17. You have been asked to create a graphical display of schedule-related information listing schedule activities on the left side of the chart, dates on the top, and activity durations as date-placed horizontal bars on the right side. What would such a chart be called?

A. PERT chart

B. Gantt chart

C. Hunt chart

D. GERT chart

18. Communication is an essential component of managing a project effectively. Which actions must be performed by a receiver for communication to be effective?

A. Perceiving, transmitting, encoding

B. Perceiving, decoding, understanding

C. Perceiving, encoding, understanding

D. Perceiving, transmitting, decoding

19. A complicated software project was authorized by a project sponsor. However, the users who were intended to use the product found it very difficult to articulate their

requirements. What technique can be employed to elicit requirements for such a project?

A. Job overlaying

B. Hidden participant

C. Job duplication

D. Job shadowing

20. You are a project manager who is in charge of an important project for your company. A number of changes and corrective actions have been recommended. The company uses a change control board to make decisions on its existing projects. Which of the following tools and techniques is used to determine which change requests should be approved?

A. Inspection

B. Expert judgment

C. Project management information system

D. Earned value technique

21. A project has several teams. Team C has repeatedly missed deadlines in the past. This has caused team D to have to crash the critical path several times.

As the team leader for team D, you receive word that the next deadline may also be missed. You should meet with the:

A. Project manager alone

B. Project manager and Management

C. Manager of Team D

D. Project manager and the leader of team C

22. A project manager would find team development to be the MOST difficult in which type of organization?

A. Weak matrix organization

B. Projectized organization

C. Composite Organization

D. Balanced matrix organization

23. Which tool is BEST used to display how a company structures itself departmentally?

A. WBS

B. BOM

C. OBS

D. RBS

24. Johan is a project manager working for a Norwegian accounting firm. To get results, Johan often tells team members that if deadlines are not met, he will have to discuss their performance with their functional managers. What type of power does Johan possess?

A. Coercive power

B. Referent power

C. Reward power

D. Expert power

25. You have recently been successful in passing the Project Management Professional exam. Others within the organization you work for are also pursuing the certification and have sought your assistance. They have requested that you provide them with a detailed list of the questions that you had on the exam. What is the FIRST course of action you should take?

A. Pretend that you do not recall any of the questions.

B. Indicate that you cannot disclose questions you saw on the exam.

C. Offer your coworkers a listing of all the questions you recall from the exam.

D. Report the violation to the PMI.

26. Which of the following is NOT a common name for one of the various types of procurement documents?

A. Request for quotation

B. Seller proposal

C. Invitation to bid

D. Tender notice

27. You are the project manager for a project and have just entered the third year of a scheduled four year project. You need to evaluate new risks that have emerged since the project began. What should you perform to provide this information?

A. Variance and trend analysis

B. Process Improvement Plan

C. Risk audit

D. Risk re-assessment

28. What is the BEST tool and technique that shows the intended cost of a project and helps identify significant variations from cost estimates?

A. Screening system

B. Bidder conferences

C. Independent estimates

D. Buyer-conducted performance review

29. Which of the following should be done FIRST during the Project Life Cycle?

A. List the key people and organizations that have a stake in the project.

B. Ascertain the stakeholder interests and expectations for the project.

C. Identify the key people and organizations that have a stake in the project.

D. Select and quantify the stakeholder interests and expectations for the project.

30. Smell is a company which specializes in computer sales, computer systems and network installation, computer

systems support and IT training. Smell is working with a company called MicroHard, to help decide which computer systems and networks to invest in. Smell has provided the executive, Bill Doors from MicroHard, with three possible solutions for this project. Bill Doors will use NPV as one selection method to determine which solution to choose. Solution A will have an initial investment of $1,700,000 with a total projected cash flow of $2,900,000 over 5 years. Solution B will have an initial investment of $3,500,000 with a total projected cash flow of $2,700,000 over 5 years. Solution C will have an initial investment of $6,500,000 with a total projected cash flow of $6,000,000 over 5 years. The total projected cash flow for each of the three projects is adjusted with a 7% interest rate over 5 years. If Bill Doors at MicroHard used NPV as the only selection method for choosing the solution, which solution would be the BEST choice?

A. Solution C with an NPV of ($500,000)

B. Solution B with an NPV of $800,000

C. Solution B with an NPV of $6,200,000

D. Solution A with an NPV of $1,200,000

31. You are the project manager for GeoThermal Systems. Which of the following must be done FIRST before proceeding with a new project?

A. Create the Project Scope Statement

B. Stakeholder analysis

C. Product analysis

D. Obtain Project Charter approval

32. You are a project manager for an automotive parts company. Your organization has been hired to produce clutches for an exotic car company which will involve the design and production of a custom clutches. During the course of the project you are reviewing a quality control statistics chart that examines every clutch produced for the month and notice several cases where the spring component of the clutch is expanding with too much force and is falling outside the upper control limit. Which type of Quality Control tool are you MOST LIKELY making use of?

A. Control charts

B. Statistical Sampling

C. Cause and Effect diagram

D. Precedence Diagramming Method

33. You are the project manager for Wicked Fast Cars, Corp. You are working on a project for the Human Resources department that is scheduled to take one year. After three months into the project, you calculate the EV at $35,000 and the PV at $45,000. Which option below represents the value for the SV?

A. ($10,000)

B. 1.29

C. 0.78

D. $10,000

34. You are a project manager creating the final project report. Which information would you NOT include in this report?

A. Team member recommendations

B. Performance of individual team members

C. Processes which yielded positive results

D. Techniques used to produce the results

35. Control charts exhibit all of the following characteristics EXCEPT?

A. The collected data shows whether the process is stable and predictable

B. It is a specialized type of run chart that plots a process variable over time

C. Control limits are statistically calculated to show variation in data below or above the highest value

D. It displays the limits of variation expected in the normal operation of a work process

36. Which statement is NOT true about the configuration management system?

A. The configuration management system is a sub-component of the overall change management system.

B. The configuration management system may include the proposed

change submission process, tracking systems, defined approval levels, and methodologies used to approve changes.

C. The configuration management system is a sub-component of the overall project management information system.

D. The configuration management system will define procedures to control any changes.

37. You are a PMP who is nearing the end of an important project. You have spent considerable energy on this project nurturing a cooperative relationship between your organization and the customer. What is the customer's MOST important role in bringing the project to a close?

A. The customer is delivered the last shipment of the product, service, or result

B. The customer acknowledges the delivery of the last shipment of the product, service, or result

C. The customer provides formal acceptance of the product, service, or result

D. The customer makes a final payment for the work completed on the project

38. All of the following statements are true about the cause and effect diagram EXCEPT?

A. A maximum of six causes are listed on the cause and effect diagram.

B. Ishikawa is another name for the cause and effect diagram.

C. The effect being studied is normally stated at the head of the diagram.

D. The cause and effect diagram is one tool that can be used for problem solving.

39. You are the project manager for Commodities, Inc. You are involved in a new project to create an internal web site for the employees of Commodities, Inc that will allow them to view events within the company. All of the following options listed are project constraints EXCEPT?

A. The project must be completed by December 31st of the current year.

B. There is a budget of $75,000 for the project.

C. The navigation menu for the website must be on the top of the page.

D. Only 3 employees are available to work on the project.

40. The sponsor and the project manager are discussing what type of contract the project manager plans to use on the project. The buyer points out that the performing organization spent a lot of money hiring a design team to come up with the design. The project manager is interested in seeing that the risk for the buyer be as small as possible. An advantage of a fixed price contract for the buyer is:

A. There is little risk

B. Risk is shared by all parties

C. Cost Risk is Lower

D. Cost Risk is Higher

41. What BEST describes the role of the project team members?

A. To perform the project work

B. To achieve the project objectives

C. To be ultimately responsible for the project's success

D. To authorize the project

42. What is the MAIN reason for controlling the project scope?

A. To enable scope creep

B. To prevent changes from affecting the project

C. To ensure deliverables are accepted by the stakeholders

D. To influence the impact of changes on the project

43. You are a project manager and are nearing the end of your project. You are now required to provide lessons learned documentation on the project. What is the MAIN purpose for preparing lessons learned documentation?

A. To identify the valued employees who improved efficiencies

B. To identify the problem employees who reduced efficiencies

C. To identify instances in which you positively affected the project

D. To identify improvements for managing similar future projects

44. Which strategy attempts to reduce the probability and/or the impact of a risk to the point where the risk can be accepted?

A. Mitigation

B. Avoidance

C. Acceptance

D. Transfer

45. You are a project manager for Groceries R' US, a supermarket chain, and are currently working on a project to build a new outlet. The planned values (PV) for the foundation and the frame are $150,000 and $500,000. After five months, you do a performance measurement analysis. You are currently not ahead of schedule. The actual costs for the foundation and frame were $175,000 and $650,000 up to this point where 100% of the foundation is complete and only 80% of the frame is complete. Which value represents the cost performance

index (CPI) to two decimal places at this point in the project?

A. 0.84

B. 1.5

C. 0.67

D. 1.19

46. Due to unforeseen circumstances your supplier has run out of the cement needed for your construction project. What is the BEST strategy for dealing with this issue?

A. Implement a workaround

B. Implement the contingency response strategy

C. Refer to the risk register

D. Transfer the risk

47. You are a project manager for a company that has a composite organization structure. The current project you are managing is coming to an end. There are a number of activities that need to be completed including releasing project resources. All of the following statements are examples or true statements related to

releasing project resources in this company EXCEPT?

A. Documenting the release date for project resources in the project management plan

B. Transferring project equipment to the regular operations of the company

C. Reassigning project team members to a new project within the company

D. Transferring the documented lessons learned into the lessons learned database

48. Which of the following is an output of the Conduct Procurements process?

A. Weighting Systems

B. Procurement Contract

C. Independent Estimates

D. Expert Judgment

49. Which technique is NOT commonly used to align the timing of activities with available resources?

A. Critical Path Method

B. Resource Leveling

C. Critical Chain Method

D. What-if Analysis

50. You have been asked to determine the logical relationships, leads, and lags for the activities that make up a project. What would be the BEST technique to use?

A. What-If Scenario Analysis

B. Critical Path Method

C. PERT

D. Resource Leveling

PMP Lite Mock Exam 12
Answer Key and Explanations

1. A - Communication Channel formula is: n(n-1)/2. N=Number of people involved on the project. PMBOK Pg. 253 [Project Communications Management]

2. C - Final acceptance for the product deliverables is formal; and must be formally signed off on by the customer or sponsor. [Project Integration Management]

3. C - The critical path method is a technique that calculates the earliest and latest possible start and finish times for work activities in a project. It uses the estimated duration of activities and the dependencies among them to determine limits for when each activity can be performed. PMBOK Pg. 154 / 155 [Project Time Management]

4. C - The best way to handle this type of offer is to politely reject the offer. Taking gifts can be viewed as personal gain and may affect your integrity as a project manager and open you and your organization to complaints of improper conduct. [Prof. Responsibility]

5. A - Improving the skill set of your existing team members is usually accomplished through training, which is a tool used in the Develop Project Team process. If project team members are weak in specific skills, those skills may be developed through formal or informal training. PMBOK Pg. 232 [Project Human Resource Management]

6. A - Smoothing is the method that was most likely used to resolve the conflict that arose at the status meeting. Smoothing is a temporary way to resolve conflict. [Project Human Resource Management]

7. B - This is an example of a Cost-Plus-Fixed-Fee contract. This type of contract determines the profit element as a fixed percentage of the estimated project cost. PMBOK Pg. 323 [Project Procurement Management]

8. D - The formula EAC = AC + BAC - EV is used to determine the total value of the project when completed assuming similar variances will not occur for the uncompleted project activities. EAC can also be used to estimate the total value of a WBS component or activity scheduled. PMBOK Pg. 184 / 185 [Project Cost Management]

9. D - In this case your communication is with your supervisor who would have a different level of responsibilities and authority. This is

an example of a vertical dimension with respect to communications. PMBOK Pg. 245 [Project Communications Management]

10.   B - E-mail messages are normally considered informal written communication. E-mail is a written form of communication. Another example of informal written communication could be memorandums. Informal verbal communication is characterized by the fact that it is frequently used within projects to communicate information. PMBOK Pg. 245 [Project Communications Management]

11.   C - The project management plan is a blue print of how the project is performed, controlled, and closed. Typically, the project manager, the project sponsor, and functional managers whose resources make up the project team approve the project plan. [Project Scope Management]

12.   C - A documented corrective action is anything that needs to be done to bring the project back on track. PMBOK Pg. 422 [Project Integration Management]

13.   B - If the seller completes work as specified in the contract statement of work, the contract is considered to be complete. It does not mean the same thing as contract closed. PMBOK Pg. 341 / 344 [Project Procurement Management]

14.   A - Develop Schedule uses resource and duration estimates to create an approved project schedule to be used as a progress baseline. This process provides updates to the Project Management Plan with respect to updated changes to managing the project schedule. PMBOK Pg. 152 [Project Time Management]

15.   C - The cost variance can be a negative value, zero, or a positive value depending on the earned value and actual costs. A negative cost variance indicates that the actual cost of the work was more than the amount of work being completed. PMBOK Pg. 182 [Project Cost Management]

16.   C - Co-location is an organizational placement strategy where the project team members are physically moved or placed next to one another to improve communication, working relationships, and productivity. PMBOK Pg. 234 [Project Human Resource Management]

17.   B - Such a chart would be called a Gantt chart. This is a popular representation of project schedule information. Activity start dates, end dates, durations, dependencies, and milestones are easily depicted on this chart in a graphical manner. [Project Time Management]

18.   B - A receiver of communication must perceive, decode, and understand. Once a message has been encoded by the sender and transmitted it to a receiver, the receiver must perceive it. In essence, the receiver must recognize that a message has been sent. Then the message must be decoded by converting the message into a form that can be interpreted. Finally, the message must be understood. If any of these processes fail, the message may be ignored or misinterpreted. PMBOK Pg. 255 [Project Communications Management]

19.   D - Job shadowing is a technique that can be employed in this case. It is done externally by an observer who views the user doing his or her job. This technique is also called observation. [Project Integration Management]

20.   B - Expert judgment involves the stakeholders on a change control board using past project experience to make decisions about whether to approve or reject requested changes. PMBOK Pg. 98 [Project Integration Management]

21.   D - Those having the problem should resolve the problem. Having had to crash the critical path several times implies that team D has already dealt with these problems. In this case, the two team leaders need to meet. The extent of this situation requires the project manager's involvement as well. [Project Human Resource Management]

22.   A - A project manager would find it most difficult to build a team in a weak matrix organization because the power rests with the functional manager. Weak matrices retain many of the characteristics of a functional organization and the project manager role is more that of a coordinator or expediter than that of a manager. PMBOK Pg. 28 [Project Framework]

23.   C - The Organizational Breakdown Structure (OBS) is a hierarchical organization chart that includes employees, department structures, and associated responsibilities. It is organized by the company's teams, or department breakdown. PMBOK Pg. 431 [Project Human Resource Management]

24.   A - Johan has coercive power because he influences others by telling them of the consequences of not working. Coercive power is based on fear. Behavior is influenced by the use of

threats and punishment. [Project Human Resource Management]

25.   B - The FIRST course of action is to indicate that you cannot disclose questions you saw on the exam. The PMI Code of Conduct states that it is the responsibility of candidates and those seeking certification to maintain and respect the confidentiality of the contents of the PMP examination. [Prof. Responsibility]

26.   B - The terms Invitation to bid, Tender notice and Request for quotation are various types of procurement documents. A seller proposal is prepared by a seller in response to a procurement document package. PMBOK Pg. 326 / 330 [Project Procurement Management]

27.   D - A risk re-assessment is a scheduled activity that involves re-evaluating project risks and identifying new risks that arise as the project moves forward. These risks are evaluated and placed in the risk register. PMBOK Pg. 310 [Project Risk Management]

28.   C - Independent estimates is a tool and technique for the Conduct Procurements process that shows the intended cost of a project. It helps identify significant variations from cost estimates. PMBOK Pg. 332 [Project Procurement Management]

29.   C - It is important to identify stakeholders, the key people and organizations that have a stake in the project, as early as possible in the Project Life Cycle so that they have a shared sense of ownership in the project and are more likely to accept the project deliverables. The "List the key people and organizations that have a stake in the project" option is incorrect. Before you can list the stakeholders, you need to identify them. [Project Framework]

30.   D - NPV is a capital budgeting technique that compares the projected cash flows to the costs of an investment. It uses the time value of money to evaluate these future cash flows at a particular point in time. If the NPV is less than zero, the solution should be rejected. A negative number signifies that the initial cash outlay will be more than what you can expect to receive in return. If the NPV is greater than or equal to zero and the solutions are of similar size and risk, you should select the one with the highest positive NPV. To calculate the NPV in this scenario, you simply subtract the initial investment from the total projected cash flow generated. For Solution A you would calculate NPV = $2,900,000 - $1,700,000 = $1,200,000. Since this NPV value is greater than 0 and is the largest value, this is the best choice. [Project Cost Management]

31. D - When managing a project, you must first make sure the Project Charter is signed and approved before proceeding. The Project Charter is the document that formalizes the project. It gives the project manager the authority to lead the project. The Project Charter is created first during the Initiating process. PMBOK Pg. 74 [Project Integration Management]

32. A - Control charts graphically display the interaction of process variables on a process. Control charts have three lines: a center line which gives the average of the process, an upper line designating the upper control limit (UCL) and showing the upper range of acceptable values, and a lower line designating the lower control limit (LCL) and showing the lower range of acceptable values. Points that fall outside of the UCL or LCL are evidence that the process is out of control. PMBOK Pg. 196 / 209 [Project Quality Management]

33. A - SV = Earned Value (EV) - Planned Value (PV) SV = $35,000-$45,000 SV = -$10,000 PMBOK Pg. 182 [Project Cost Management]

34. B - The performance of individual team members is not the type of information to be included in the final report. Individual team member performance is better documented in the reports for performance reviews. PMBOK Pg. 271, 237 [Project Integration Management]

35. C - Control limits are statistically calculated to show variation in data below or above the mean or average value from the set of data that has been collected. The highest data value is not used as the reference point for plotting the set of data on the control chart. PMBOK Pg. 196 /209 [Project Quality Management]

36. A - The configuration management system is a sub-component of the overall project management information system. This system may include the proposed change submission process, tracking systems, defined approval levels, and methodologies used to approve changes. PMBOK Pg. 82 [Project Integration Management]

37. C - It is important that the customer provides formal acceptance of the product, service, or result of the project. This should include a written statement that identifies that the company has fulfilled all the project requirements. This protects the organization and customer over confusion whether all terms within the project have been satisfactorily met. The project cannot be closed if a formal acceptance is not made. PMBOK Pg. 68 [Project Integration Management]

38.   A - While listing six causes is possible, there is no rule that states a maximum of six causes can be listed. You could list four or eight for example. PMBOK Pg. 208 [Project Quality Management]

39.   C - Constraints limit the project team's options. Predefined budgets, limits on the number of resources available, and imposed dates are project constraints. Positioning of the menu for the website is one of the requirements for the project and this is not considered a constraint. [PMBOK page 115] [Project Integration Management]

40.   C - In a fixed price contract the seller has the most cost risk and they buyer has lower risk. PMBOK Pg 322 [Project Procurement Management]

41.   A - Project team members are responsible for performing the actual project work. They work with the project manager to complete project activities and achieve the goals of the project. The project manager is assigned by an organization to achieve specific project objectives [Project Human Resource Management]

42.   D - The main reason for controlling the project scope is to influence the impact of changes on the project. This is done by managing approved changes and disregarding rejected changes. This ensures that the effect of approved changes can be clearly recognized to determine whether the desired results are produced. PMBOK Pg. 125 [Project Scope Management]

43.   D - Lessons learned documentation provides you or other project managers with relevant information for similar future projects. The lessons learned from this project can reduce risks by enlightening the reader of possible pitfalls. PMBOK Pg. 214 [Project Integration Management]

44.   A - Risk mitigation is a strategy that seeks to reduce the risk to a level that is acceptable. A project manager may add specific project tasks to the work of a project to reduce the level of risk. PMBOK Pg. 304 [Project Risk Management]

45.   C - Get the total for the actual costs by adding the $175,000 and $650,000 for the foundation and frame. The total is $825,000. Now calculate earned value. We need to identify all of the activities that have been completed or partially completed as of the measurement date. If partially completed, we calculate the fractional value of the budgeted cost for the activity by the percent completion. Add together the budgeted cost for completed or partially completed work activities, INCLUDING any work that has been performed ahead of schedule. We are told that we are not ahead of schedule. So there is nothing to include for the ahead of schedule category. 100% of the foundation is complete and only 80% of the frame is complete. So we add 100% of $150,000 and 80% of 500,000, which is $400,000, together to get a total earned value of $550,000. Now find the CPI by taking the total for EV $550,000 up to this point and dividing it by the total of the actual cost $825,000 for the same time period. The result for CPI is 0.67 [Project Time Management]

46. A - In this situation, you would need to come up with a workaround. A workaround is similar to a contingency response strategy, but differs in that the risk was unexpected and a response was not planned prior to the risk event. Contingent response strategy is a means to address specific identified risks through a formal process and provide resources to meet risk events if they occur. The question states the problem was unforeseen. PMBOK Pg. 445 [Project Risk Management]

47. D - Transferring the documented lessons learned into the lessons learned database does not involve the reassigning of project team members or transferring of project equipment at the end of the project. Lessons learned track project successes and failures, which would include factors that led to the project being cancelled. It's important to archive or transfer these records to a lessons learned knowledgebase for reference on future projects or for cancelled projects later reinstated. [Project Integration Management]

48. B - The procurement contract is an output of the Conduct Procurements process. PMBOK Pg. 333 [Project Procurement Management]

49. A - The critical path method is not a technique commonly used to align the timing of activities with available resources. The critical path method is a technique used to establish a rough timeline fitting the project's work activities within the deadlines defined in the scope statement. PMBOK Pg. 154 [Project Human Resource Management]

50. B - The critical path method is a technique that calculates the earliest and latest possible start and finish times for work activities in a project.

PMBOK Pg. 154 [Project Time Management]

Knowledge Area Quiz
Project Human Resource
Management
Practice Questions

Test Name: Knowledge Area Test: Project Human Resource Management
Total Questions: 10
Correct Answers Needed to Pass: 7 (70.00%)
Time Allowed: 15 Minutes

Test Description

This practice quiz specifically targets your knowledge of the Project Human Resource Management knowledge area.

Test Questions

1. Ken is managing a project where the morale of the team is very low. The team members have been on the project for more than a year and though the project is due to end in a few weeks' time, they do not know what is in store for them. What should Ken have planned better to avoid such a situation?

   A. Bonuses at the end of the project

   B. 360-degree feedback

   C. Job rotation within the project.

   D. Release criteria

2. You are the project manager of a project whose team has interacted with a number of stakeholders. You feel that in order to have a very objective project performance appraisal, you would like to obtain feedback for the project team members from all the people they have worked with, including superiors, peers and subordinates. This is called:

   A. Multi-point feedback

   B. All-round Analysis (A-square)

   C. 360-degree feedback

   D. 180-degree feedback

3. Which of the following is not a tool and technique of the Develop Human Resource Plan process?

   A. Matrix based org chart

   B. Networking

   C. RACI chart

   D. Rewards and Recognition

4. Which of these is not an Enterprise environmental factor that can influence the Develop Human Resource Plan process?

   A. Organizational culture

   B. Resource calendar

   C. Marketplace conditions

   D. Personnel administration policies

5. Which of the following does the communications management plan provide?

   A. Stakeholders communication requirements

   B. Frequency of communication

   C. Person responsible for communicating the information

   D. All of the above

6. You are managing a project and an audit team wants to know where they can find information on training plans for the team members and certification requirements. This would be found in the:

   A. Resource Breakdown Structure

   B. HR Management plan

   C. Staffing Management Plan

   D. Work Management plan

7. You are managing a project and find that you need to apply resource leveling to extend the length of the schedule. What would be a good choice of a tool to do this?

   A. Resource Assignment Matrix

   B. Network diagram

   C. Resource Histogram

   D. Resource Breakdown Structure

8. Which of the following is not among the processes of Project Communications Management?

   A. Report Performance

   B. Estimate Costs

   C. Plan Communications

   D. Manage stakeholders Expectations

9. Ground rules are established to set clear expectations regarding acceptable behavior by the project team members. Whose responsibility is it to enforce ground rules?

    A. The project manager

    B. All project team members share the responsibility for enforcing the rules once they are established

    C. The HR team

    D. The project manager and senior team members

10. Win-lose rewards that reward a limited number of project team members (ex: Team member of the month) have the following effect:

    A. They unfairly get bagged by the best of the team members

    B. They help in inculcating a healthy competition amongst the team.

    C. They positively impact team cohesiveness.

    D. They negatively impact team cohesiveness.

Knowledge Area Quiz
Project Human Resource
Management
Answer Key and Explanations

1. D - The correct response is Release Criteria. While job rotation is a good way of ensuring high morale within the team, it is more of an ongoing effort and within the project team. The project manager needs to determine the method and timing of releasing team members (release criteria). Smooth transitions to upcoming projects helps improve the morale. [Project Human Resource Management]

2. C - This is called 360-degree feedback. While it provides all-round feedback, care must be taken to ensure that the process is objective and does not result in biased results. [Project Human Resource Management]

3. D - Rewards and Recognition is a tool and technique used in the Develop Project Team process and not in the Develop Human Resource Plan process. [Project Human Resource Management]

4. B - A resource calendar is not an enterprise environmental factor used in the Develop Human Resource Plan process. It is an output of the Acquire Project Team process. [Project Human Resource Management]

5. D - The Communication Management Plan covers all of these items. [Project Human Resource Management]

6. C - The correct response is Staffing Management Plan. This lists the time periods that team members are expected to work on the project along with information such as training plans, certification requirements and compliance issues. [Project Human Resource Management]

7. C - The Resource Histogram is a tool for charting human resources and illustrates the number of hours that a person, department or entire project team will be needed each week or month over the course of the project. The chart can include a horizontal line that represents the maximum number of hours from a particular resource. This can be used for a resource leveling strategy. [Project Human Resource Management]

8. B - Estimate Costs is not one of the processes of Project Communications Management. [Project Human Resource Management]

9. B - All project team members share responsibility for enforcing the rules

once they are established. [Project Human Resource Management]

10.   D - Win-lose (zero sum) rewards that reward a limited number of project team members (ex: Team member of the month) have a negative effect on team cohesiveness. Rewarding win-win behavior that everyone can achieve, such as turning in project reports on times, tends to increase support among team members. [Project Human Resource Management]

PMP Lite Mock Exam 13
Practice Questions

Test Name: PMP Lite Mock Exam 13
Total Questions: 50
Correct Answers Needed to Pass:
35 (70.00%)
Time Allowed: 60 Minutes

Test Description

This is a cumulative PMP Mock Exam which can be used as a benchmark for your PMP aptitude. This practice test includes questions from all PMBOK knowledge areas, including the five basic project management process groups.

Test Questions

1. A project audit team discovered that a project did not have a risk register. Which phase under the Risk management knowledge area has likely been missed out or improperly done?

    A. Identify Risks

    B. Perform Risk Assessment

    C. Plan Risk Responses

    D. Plan Risk Management

2. Lois is a project manager managing a town-development project. She has set up a series of interviews with various stakeholders to gather some experiential and historical information on risks. Which phase is this likely to happen in?

    A. Perform Qualitative Risk Analysis

    B. Plan Risk Responses

    C. Understand Risks

    D. Perform Quantitative Risk Analysis

3. Which of the following models describes stakeholders based on their power, urgency and legitimacy?

    A. Influence / Impact grid

    B. Power / influence grid

    C. Power / Interest grid

    D. Salience model

4. A project was awarded based on a competitive proposal. Management made a commitment that a few key team members would be made posted on the project. When such

assignments happen, they are termed as:

A. Bargaining agreements

B. Pre-project assignments

C. Planned assignments

D. Pre-assignments

5. The Direct and Manage Project Execution phase requires implementation of approved changes covering all the following except:

A. Defect Repair

B. Corrective Action

C. Preventive action

D. Acceptance criteria

6. Various forecasting methods are used to predict future project performance. Which of these methods use the assumption that it is possible to identify the underlying factors that might influence the variable that is being forecasted?

A. Econometric methods

B. Probabilistic forecasting

C. Time series method

D. Judgmental methods

7. A project manager had scheduled a number of training programs for his team. However, he was aware that apart from planned training, unplanned training also took place in a number of ways. Which of these is not one of the ways in which unplanned training can happen?

A. Classroom

B. Observation

C. Project performance appraisals

D. Conversation

8. As part of the procurement process, the procuring organization elected to have an estimate of costs prepared by an outside professional estimator. The estimator came up with an estimate of $ 500,000. However, the cost estimates prepared by prospective sellers were in the range of $ 200,000. How can this be best interpreted?

A. The procurement statement of work was deficient and ambiguous.

B. The professional estimator has inflated the estimate of costs.

C. The prospective sellers do not have the required skills to do the project.

D. Prospective sellers are trying to underbid and win the project.

9. A project manager is working on the Perform QA phase of a project. He is looking for an iterative means to improve quality and eliminate activities that don't add value. Which of the following will help him do this?

A. Quality control measurements

B. Quality checklist

C. Continuous process improvement

D. Process improvement plan

10. For projects that have a product as a deliverable, it is very effective to perform product analysis. Which of these tools is not a product analysis technique?

A. Systems breakdown

B. Systems analysis

C. Systems engineering

D. Requirements analysis

11. A project manager included contingency reserves and management reserves in the total budget of a high-risk project. He also made certain earned value measurement calculations. Which of the following is incorrect?

A. Reserves are included as part of earned value measurement calculations.

B. Reserves are not part of the project cost baseline.

C. The project manager needs to get approval before spending management reserve.

D. Reserves are usually included in the total budget of a project.

12. Linda is a first-time project manager and is analyzing a project schedule. She intends to apply resource leveling and has been given the following guidelines on resource leveling. Which of these four statements is incorrect?

A. Resource Leveling can often cause the critical path to change.

B. Resource leveling is applied to a schedule before it has been analyzed by the critical path method.

C. Resource leveling is applied to keep resource usage at a constant level.

D. Resource leveling is necessary when resources have been over-allocated.

13. The Code of Ethics and Professional Conduct has as its foundation four values identified by practitioners from the global project management community. They are:

A. Respect, fairness, transparency and freedom.

B. Responsibility, transparency, fairness and honesty.

C. Respect, freedom, honesty and transparency.

D. Responsibility, respect, fairness and honesty

14. Risk identification checklists are usually developed based on historical information and knowledge accumulated from previous similar projects. Which of the following

statements about risk identification checklists is wrong?

A. It is impossible to build an exhaustive checklist.

B. The lowest level of the Risk Breakdown Structure (RBS) cannot be used as a risk checklist

C. Quick and simple risk checklists are the least effective ones.

D. Risk checklists should be reviewed during project closure.

15. Identify the incorrect statement about risk among the following:

A. Risk always has an adverse effect on the project

B. Unknown risks cannot be managed proactively.

C. Risk is an uncertain event or condition

D. Project risk is always in the future.

16. The list of identified risks is found in the risk register whereas the high-level risks are listed in the:

A. Scope statement

B. Requirement document

C. Project charter

D. Risk management plan

C. Cost Variance (CV)

D. To-Complete Performance Index (TCPI)

17. A number of identified risks occurred early in a project. As a result, most of the project objectives ended up in jeopardy. The project manager decided to present a case to management that the project be closed down. This is an example of:

A. Risk Acceptance

B. Risk Mitigation

C. Risk Avoidance

D. Risk Transfer

19. A project uses rounding of Activity Estimates data to the nearest $100, uses staff hours as the unit of measure for resources, and has a variance threshold of 10% deviation from the baseline plan. These would be typically documented in the:

A. Cost management plan

B. Scope Statement

C. WBS

D. Project charter

18. 20% of the work was completed in a project. At this stage the project manager determined that the budget at completion (BAC) was no longer viable and developed a forecasted estimate at completion (EAC). What index can the project manager use to look at the calculated projection of cost performance that must be achieved on the remaining work

A. Schedule Performance Index (SPI)

B. Cost Performance Index (CPI)

20. You are two days late on reporting status for a project that you are managing. The status report indicates that the project is lagging behind schedule. During the current week, you are confident of making up some of the lost time. How should you report project status?

A. Since the status report is already due, do nothing. Send out the status report next week when the project is back on track.

B. Since the status report is already 2 days overdue, you may communicate to stakeholders that you will send a consolidated status report next week. In this manner, you can avoid being untruthful or falsifying reports.

C. Send out a status report to all stakeholders indicating that the project is on track. Once this week goes by, things will be fine and the status reports will be back to normal from next week.

D. You should report project status exactly as it is. You may also mention that you expect to make up some of the lost ground, but will truthfully represent current status.

21. A project manager receives news that a strike at a vendor's factory is likely to cause a major delay in the arrival of a critical component required for her project. What would be her next course of action?

A. She would need to plan to crash the schedule. This will allow the impact of the delay to be mitigated.

B. She would need to perform schedule compression once the component is received. This will

ensure that the project end-date is maintained.

C. She should now apply the critical chain method and introduce buffers in the project to account for delays.

D. She would need to perform a what-if scenario analysis to assess the feasibility of the project schedule and mitigate the impact of the delay.

22. A project manager who is a PMP discovered that there had been an error in the estimation of a project. A certain cost had been double calculated with the result that the budget, which had already been approved, was now in excess by a figure of $ 25,000. She is aware that publicizing this information will cause her to receive a poor performance appraisal since her company is very fastidious about such matters. What should she do?

A. She does not need to do anything since this will have a positive impact on the project's spend and margins.

B. Since the excess funds won't be required, she can now use the funding to make additional investments for the project.

C. She should bring this to the notice of the appropriate stakeholders and have the necessary steps taken to decrease the budget.

D. She does not need to do anything since the budget has already been approved. This situation is okay as long as the extra funds are not spent.

23. Conformance to requirements and fitness for use are key concepts in quality management. Which of the following tools is used to capture unstated needs for a product?

A. Malcolm Baldrige model

B. Six Sigma

C. Voice of the customer

D. Total quality management (TQM)

24. A project manager uses a Power / Interest grid to identify stakeholders in the project and to manage their expectations. Identify which of the following statements is wrong in the context of a Power / Interest grid.

A. Stakeholders with lower power and lower interest need to be monitored.

B. Stakeholders with higher power and lower interest need to kept satisfied.

C. Stakeholders with lower power and higher interest need to be kept informed

D. Stakeholders with higher power and higher interest need the least attention.

25. A project involved team members situated in Arizona, Nebraska, New York and Ireland. Which of the following activities becomes very important in such a team environment?

A. Team-building

B. Status reporting

C. Conflict resolution

D. Communication planning

26. The total planned value (PV) for a project was $ 150,000. During the course of the project, the actual cost incurred turned out to be $ 275,000. What is the limit that the project

manager usually imposes on the actual cost (AC)?

A. The AC is usually limited to twice the planned value.

B. The AC will not have an upper limit.

C. The AC is usually limited to thrice the planned value.

D. The AC is usually limited to 1.5 times the planned value.

27. All team members had not yet been acquired for a project. However, the project manager went ahead with estimating activity durations, budgeting and other activities. What could likely happen to the activity durations?

A. The activity durations are likely to decrease.

B. The activity durations are likely to change.

C. The activity durations will remain the same.

D. The activity durations are likely to increase.

28. The senior analyst on a project came up with Activity Duration Estimates as follows:
Activity A: 10 days + a lag of 2 days
Activity B: 1 week + a lead of 3 days
The project manager who reviewed this came up with some objections to these estimates. What would they most likely be?

A. The analyst should have included % variance information while mentioning the Activity Duration Estimate. This would indicate a range of possible results.

B. Activity Duration Estimates should not include any lag or lead information.

C. It is advisable not to mix up units such as days and weeks while coming up with Activity Duration Estimates.

D. The Activity Duration Estimate should have also mentioned the predecessor or successor activity to which the lag or lead is attached.

29. A requesting organization for a project created a document that included the business need and the cost-benefit analysis. What would this document be termed as?

A. The project statement of work

B. The business case

C. The project charter

D. The contract

30. A seller was notified that they were one of the selected sellers based on their proposal. The seller immediately circulated an internal newsletter stating that they had just been awarded a large contract for a term of 5 years. Would the newsletter be factually correct?

A. The newsletter is likely to be factually incorrect. A selected seller is one whose proposal has been accepted and a contract has been completed pending signatures of the authorized parties.

B. It is likely that the newsletter is factually incorrect. While the seller has been selected for the work, it is unlikely that the term of the project would have been 5 years.

C. It is likely that the newsletter is factually incorrect. A selected seller is one whose proposal has been judged to be in a competitive range. It does not

mean they have been awarded the work.

D. The newsletter is likely to be factually correct. A selected seller is one who has been awarded a contract based on the procurement process.

31. Variance analysis refers to cost performance measurements used to assess the magnitude of variation in comparison to the original cost baseline. What is the trend on the percentage range of acceptable variances as the project progresses?

A. The percentage range of acceptable variances will tend to decrease as the project progresses.

B. The percentage range of acceptable variances will tend to increase as the project progresses.

C. The percentage range of acceptable variances will tend to decrease first and then increase as the project progresses beyond 50% completion.

D. The percentage range of acceptable variances remain the same as the project progresses.

32. Most organizations treat contract administration as an administrative function separate from the project organization. Who carries out the function of contract administration in a project?

    A. The project manager

    B. The Procurement advisor

    C. The Procurement administrator

    D. The Contract advisor

33. A project involved three performing organizations. Organization A had a well-defined quality policy, Organization B a lacked a formal quality policy and Organization C had a rudimentary quality policy. What should the project management team do?

    A. There is no action required by the project management team. Once the project has been awarded to a performing organization, the onus of execution rests with the performing organization.

    B. The project management team will need to ask Organization B and Organization C to come up with a formal quality policy.

    C. The project management team will need to ask Organization A to share its quality policy with Organization B and C.

    D. The project management team will need to develop a quality policy for the project that can be shared with all the three performing organizations.

34. A project was randomly picked up for a quality audit and a number of issues and non-conformances were found by the external auditor. The project manager lodged a protest with the quality department that this was incorrect procedure and he should have been given notice since an external auditor was involved. What is your view?

    A. The project manager is correct. Quality audits need to be scheduled when an external auditor is involved so that the project manager has time to prepare for them.

    B. The project manager is correct. All quality audits need to be scheduled and cannot be randomly done.

    C. The project manager has no case. Quality audits may be random and performed by internal or external auditors.

D. The project manager has no case. All quality audits need to be randomly planned and performed by external auditors.

35. As part of tracking a project, a project manager is validating the completion of project scope. She would measure this against:

    A. Requirements traceability matrix

    B. The project management plan

    C. The project charter

    D. The requirements management plan

36. During the procurement process, a contractual relationship gets established between a buyer and a seller. During the contract lifecycle, what is the correct sequence in which the following terminology is applied to a seller?
Vendor
Selected source
Bidder

    A. The seller is viewed first as a selected source, then as a bidder and then as a vendor.

    B. The seller is viewed first as a selected source, then as a bidder and then as a vendor.

    C. The seller is viewed first as a bidder, then as a selected source and then as a vendor.

    D. The seller is viewed first as a bidder, then as a vendor, then as a selected source.

37. A number of ethical issues came up in a large project consisting of 55 team members. The project manager explained to the sponsor that this was a common problem in larger teams. Whose responsibility is it to ensure that all team members maintain professionalism and follow ethical behavior?

    A. The project manager

    B. The sponsor

    C. The HR department

    D. The project management team

38. One of the stakeholders of a project initiated a change request which was then documented in the change control system. In general, who would be responsible for approving or rejecting the change request?

A. An authority within the project management team or external organization.

B. The sponsor.

C. The stakeholder who raised the change request.

D. The project manager.

39. A critical project rollout was delayed because one of the stakeholders did not receive necessary communication on time. On further analysis, the project manager discovered that communication had been sent out to the wrong teams. This would have happened because:

A. Communication broke down between the project team and the stakeholder.

B. The project manager failed to manage stakeholder expectations.

C. The stakeholder register was not updated properly to reflect the correct stakeholder information.

D. The stakeholder did not proactively ask for updates.

40. While sequencing activities for a project, the project management team of a project applied certain discretionary dependencies. This was based on their knowledge of best practices within the project application area. What is the potential risk involved in using such dependencies?

A. They can create fixed float values and create external dependencies.

B. They can create arbitrary float values and limit later scheduling options.

C. They can create arbitrary float values and create external dependencies.

D. They can create arbitrary float values and create mandatory dependencies

41. Activity attributes extend the description of the activity by identifying various components associated with the activity. Typically how many attributes are associated with each activity?

A. They should be between 5 and 10 in number

B. The number of attributes varies by application area.

C. They should be less than 5 in number

D. The number of attributes depends on the activity.

42. Due to a tight project schedule, a project manager did not document lessons learned all through the project. However, at the end of the project, he finally documented the lessons learned. Your comment on this would be:

A. This is ok. At a minimum, lessons learned should be documented at the end of the project.

B. This is not ok. Lessons learned need to be documented all through the project as well as at the end of the project.

C. This is not ok. Lessons learned need to be documented all through the project and must not be done at the end of the project.

D. This is correct. Lessons learned are intended to be documented only at the end of the project.

43. A project manager is preparing the WBS for a software project. The WBS includes all the product and project work but excludes the project management work. From the following choices, select a statement that correctly describes this situation.

A. This is incorrect. Product work and project management should be included as part of the WBS, but project work should be excluded.

B. This is incorrect. Project work and project management should be part of the WBS but product work should be excluded.

C. This is incorrect. Product work, project work and project management work should all be included in the WBS

D. This is correct. Product and project work should be included as part of the WBS, but project management work should be excluded.

44. As part of EVM, a project manager is calculating the to-complete performance index (TCPI) based on EAC. The data that he has is: the budget at completion for the project is $ 100,000. The earned value for the project is $ 25,000. The actual costs

to date are 40,000 and the estimate at completion is $ 115,000. What is the TCPI that he will obtain?

A. 1.1

B. 0.9

C. 1

D. 0

45. How can changes be made to a project management plan once it has been baselined by the project manager?

A. By generating a change request and having it approved through the Perform Integrated Change Control process.

B. This is typically done by using a version control system. The project manager creates a new version with the changes and baselines it as the new baseline.

C. This is done by maintaining a revision history or log. The project manager documents the changes in detail and then baselines it.

D. A project management plan cannot be changed once it has been baselined. An addendum has to be created to incorporate the changes.

46. The morale of the team members of a project was very low. Team members felt that they were not given opportunities to participate in team development activities and that they did not have opportunities to grow. Which of the following is a primary factor for this situation?

A. Use of zero-sum rewards in the project

B. A poorly defined resource calendar

C. Too many senior team members

D. Poor interpersonal skills in the team

47. Given multiple alternatives, the group decision method that allows the largest block in a group to decide (even if more than 50% of the members of the group do not support the decision) is called:

A. Commonality

B. Plurality

C. Unanimity

D. Majority

48. In a multi-phase project, the procurement team decided to close the procurements applicable to a particular phase of the project. What happens to unresolved claims?

A. Unresolved claims are usually resolved at the end of all phases of the project.

B. Unresolved claims are also closed when the procurements for that phase are closed.

C. Unresolved claims remain open for a period of 1 year from closure of procurements.

D. Unresolved claims may still be subject to litigation after closure.

49. During the Control Scope phase, analysis of the scope performance resulted in a change request to the scope baseline. This change request will be processed for review and disposition in the:

A. Perform Quality Control phase

B. Perform Integrated Change Control phase

C. Monitor and Control Project Work phase

D. Verify Scope phase

50. A project manager is informed that a limited number of resources are going to be available for his project. He creates a project schedule by adding buffers to the project to protect the target finish date. What type of schedule network analysis is he using?

A. What-if analysis

B. Critical path method

C. Critical chain method

D. Resource leveling.

PMP Lite Mock Exam 13
Answer Key and Explanations

1. A - The Risk register is an output of the Identify Risks process. It primarily contains a list of identified risks and responses to those risks. If a project does not have a Risk register, then either this process has not been done completely, or it has been missed out altogether.
[Refer PMBOK, 4th Edition, page 288] [Project Risk Management]

2. A - Such meetings or interviews are usually done as part of Qualitative Risk Analysis. This technique draws on experiential learning and historical data to quantify the impact of risks on project objectives.
[Refer PMBOK, 4th Edition, page 296] [Project Risk Management]

3. D - The Salience model describes stakeholders based on their power (ability to impose their will), urgency (need for immediate attention) and legitimacy (their involvement is appropriate). Based on this classification, the potential impact of each stakeholder is then assessed.
[Refer PMBOK, 4th Edition, page 249] [Project Communications Management]

4. D - When team members are assigned to projects in advance of the start of the project, they are termed as pre-assignments. Such assignments can happen when resources are promised as part of a competitive proposal, when projects are dependent on critical resources, or if some staff assignments have been defined in the project charter.
[Refer PMBOK, 4th Edition, page 227] [Project Human Resource Management]

5. D - The Direct and Manage Project Execution phase is the process of performing the work defined in the Project management plan to achieve the project's objectives. This includes corrective action, preventive action and defect repair. However, acceptance criteria are not part of this list. The project's deliverables are measured against the acceptance criteria, which do not typically change in the Direct and Manage Project Execution phase.
[Refer PMBOK, 4th Edition, page 83] [Project Integration Management]

6. A - Econometric (or causal) methods operate on the assumption that it is possible to identify factors that might influence the variable that is being forecasted. For example, if a particular product is associated with weather conditions, the expectation is that understanding the causes for weather conditions will allow them to be used in the forecast.

[Refer PMBOK, 4th Edition, page 269] [Project Communications Management]

7. A - Scheduled training occurs as stated in the Human Resource plan and could include online, classroom, on-the-job, etc. Unplanned training takes place through conversation, observation and project performance appraisals.
[Refer PMBOK, 4th Edition, page 232] [Project Human Resource Management]

8. A - When prospective bids are significantly different from the estimates prepared by a professional estimator, it likely means that the procurement statement of work (SOW) was deficient or that the prospective sellers have misunderstood the procurement SOW.
The other choices jump to conclusions without relevant data. It is possible that prospective sellers do not have the skills or are trying to underbid, but in this case, all of them are off by a large percentage. Hence it points to a deficient statement of work.
[Refer PMBOK, 4th Edition, page 332] [Project Procurement Management]

9. C - Continuous process improvement is an iterative means to improve the quality of all processes. It reduces waste and eliminates activities that don't add value. This allows processes to operate at increased levels of efficiency.
[Refer PMBOK, 4th Edition, page 202] [Project Quality Management]

10. A - Systems breakdown is an invalid technique and is not used for product analysis. Valid techniques are Product breakdown, systems analysis, requirements analysis, systems engineering, value engineering and value analysis.
[Refer PMBOK 4th Edition, page 114] [Project Scope Management]

11. A - Contingency reserves are for unplanned but required changes to a project from realized risks. Management reserves are for unplanned changes to project scope and cost. However, reserves are not included as part of earned value measurement calculations.
[Refer PMBOK 4th Edition, page 177] [Project Cost Management]

12. B - Resource leveling is a schedule network analysis technique. It is applied to a schedule that has already been analyzed by the critical path method.
[Refer PMBOK 4th Edition, page 156] [Project Time Management]

13. D - The values that practitioners from the global project management community have identified as being the most important are: responsibility, respect, fairness and honesty. These values form the foundation for the Code of Ethics and Professional Conduct.
[Refer Section 1.4, Chapter 1, Page 1, PMI code of ethics document] [Prof. Responsibility]

14. B - A Risk Breakdown Structure (RBS) lists identified project risks hierarchically by risk category and sub-category that identifies the various areas and causes of potential risks. The lowest level in the RBS can be used as a basic risk checklist to cover all identified risks.
The other statements are all true.
[Refer PMBOK, 4th Edition, page 287, 280] [Project Risk Management]

15. A - Risk need not always have an adverse effect on the project. It is an uncertain condition that has an effect on one of the project objectives. This can be positive too. For example, if limited design personnel are available and they finish the designs within time, this is a positive risk that will result in potential cost savings.
[Refer PMBOK 4th Edition, page 275] [Project Risk Management]

16. C - The project charter is a document that authorizes the project. Along with details such as the purpose of the project, project objectives, high-level requirements etc, it also contains the high-level risks which are used as a starting point later on while identifying risks in detail.
[Refer PMBOK, 4th Edition, page 77] [Project Integration Management]

17. C - Risk avoidance involves changing the project management plan to eliminate the risk entirely. Although an extreme situation, entirely shutting down a project constitutes a radical avoidance strategy.
[Refer PMBOK 4th Edition, page 303] [Project Risk Management]

18. D - The to-complete performance index (TCPI) is the calculated projection of cost performance that must be achieved on the remaining work to meet a specified goal such as the BAC or EAC. It is defined as the work remaining divided by the funds remaining.
[Refer PMBOK 4th Edition, page 185] [Project Cost Management]

19. A - Cost management processes and their associated tools and techniques are documented in the cost management plan. These include parameters such as the level of accuracy (how much rounding), units of measure (staff hours, weeks etc), and control thresholds (percentage deviation from baseline plan)

[Refer PMBOK 4th Edition, page 165, 166] [Project Cost Management]

20. D - As practitioners in the global project management community, it is our responsibility to be truthful in our communications and conduct. We need to provide accurate information even if it is not favorable to us.
[Refer PMI Code of Ethics section 5.2, page 4] [Prof. Responsibility]

21. D - Her next course of action would be to perform a what-if analysis. A what-if analysis is used to assess the feasibility of the project schedule under adverse conditions and to prepare contingency/response plans to overcome / mitigate the impact of such adverse situations.
[Refer PMBOK 4th Edition, page 163 / 156] [Project Time Management]

22. C - She needs to bring this discrepancy to the notice of management and the appropriate stakeholders so that corrective action can be taken. She needs to do this even at the cost of receiving a poor performance appraisal.
[Refer chapter 5 (Honesty) on Page 4, PMI code of ethics document] [Prof. Responsibility]

23. C - Voice of the customer is a non-proprietary approach to quality management and is used to elicit stated as well as unstated customer

needs (quality and requirements). [Project Quality Management]

24. D - A Power/Interest grid groups stakeholders based on their level of authority (power) and their level of concern (interest). Stakeholders with higher power and higher interest need to be managed closely and require the most attention.
[Refer PMBOK 4th Edition, page 249] [Project Communications Management]

25. D - Communication planning is increasingly important when virtual teams are involved. Often, lack of face-to-face interactions can cause misunderstandings and conflict. These need to be handled by proper communication planning.
[Refer PMBOK 4th Edition, page 228] [Project Human Resource Management]

26. B - The actual cost will not have an upper limit. Whatever is spent to achieve the earned value will be measured.
[Refer PMBOK 4th Edition, page 182] [Project Cost Management]

27. B - When estimating of activity durations is done when all team members have not been acquired, it is possible that the competency levels of the newer team members will be different from that planned. So, it can

only be said that the activity durations will likely change. Whether they will remain the same, increase or decrease, will depend on the competency levels of the new team members.
[Refer PMBOK, 4th Edition, page 216] [Project Human Resource Management]

28. B - Activity duration estimates are quantitative assessments of the likely work periods to complete an activity. They do not include any lag or lead information.
[Refer PMBOK 4th Edition, page 151] [Project Time Management]

29. B - The business case usually provides information from a business standpoint so that any investment in the project can be justified. Typically it would contain both the business need as well as the cost-benefit analysis.
[Refer PMBOK 4th Edition, page 75] [Project Integration Management]

30. C - The newsletter will likely be factually incorrect. A selected seller is one who has proposal has been judged to be in a competitive range based on bid evaluation. The seller would have negotiated a draft contract that can become the actual contract when the award is made.
[Refer PMBOK 4th Edition, page 333] [Project Procurement Management]

31. A - During the start of the project, larger percentage variances are allowed. However, as more work is accomplished, the percentage range of acceptable variances will tend to decrease.
[Refer PMBOK 4th Edition, page 187] [Project Cost Management]

32. C - In most organizations, a procurement administrator is responsible for ensuring that the procurement relationship is properly managed. The procurement administrator may be on the project team, but typically reports to a supervisor from a different department.
[Refer PMBOK, 4th Edition, page 335] [Project Procurement Management]

33. D - When multiple performing organizations are involved, it is the responsibility of the project management team to develop a quality policy for the project that can used by all the organizations involved.
[Refer PMBOK 4th Edition, page 194] [Project Quality Management]

34. C - The project manager has no case. Quality audits may be scheduled or random and may be conducted by internal or external auditors. It is the responsibility of the project manager and the project management to ensure that the project

documentation is kept up-to-date and available for any quality audit.
[Refer PMBOK 4th Edition, page 204]
[Project Quality Management]

35. B - Completion of project scope is measured against the project management plan. (In contrast, the product scope is measured against the product requirements).
[Refer PMBOK 4th Edition, page 105]
[Project Scope Management]

36. C - During the contract life cycle, the seller can be viewed first as a bidder, then as a selected source and then as the contracted supplier or vendor.
[Refer PMBOK 4th Edition, page 216]
[Project Procurement Management]

37. D - The project management team needs to be aware of, subscribe and ensure that all team members behave professionally and follow ethical behavior.
[Refer PMBOK 4th Edition, page 216]
[Project Human Resource Management]

38. A - In general, some authority within the project management team or an external organization would approve or reject the change request. However, on many projects the project manager is given authority to approve certain types of change requests.
[Refer PMBOK 4th Edition, page 94]
[Project Integration Management]

39. C - The stakeholder register is a list of all relevant stakeholders in the project. It is used to ensure that all stakeholders are included in project communications. Hence, it is likely that the stakeholder list did not contain the stakeholder's details. This resulted in their missing out on project communication.
[Refer PMBOK, 4th Edition, 250]
[Project Communications Management]

40. B - Discretionary dependencies are established based on the knowledge of best practices within a specific application area. This is done to achieve a specific sequence even though there are other options. The risk is that they may create arbitrary float values and later limit scheduling options because of the specific sequencing chosen.
[Refer PMBOK 4th Edition, page 140]
[Project Time Management]

41. B - Activity attributes generally vary by application area. Components for each activity evolve over time. Initially they may include Activity ID, WBS ID and Activity name. Later, they may include activity codes, activity description, predecessor activities, successor activities, logical relationships, leads, lags, resource requirements, imposed dates, constraints and assumptions.

[Refer PMBOK 4th Edition, page 136] [Project Time Management]

42. A - Lessons learned need to be documented throughout the project cycle, but at a minimum should be documented at the end of the project. Since the project manager was unable to do it during the course of the project, he has done it at the end of the project, which is the minimum requirement.
[Refer PMBOK, 4th Edition, page 214] [Project Quality Management]

43. C - The WBS is a deliverable-oriented decomposition of all the work to be done by the project team to accomplish project objectives. It organizes and defines the total scope of the project. Hence it includes product work, project work and the project management work required to complete the project.
[Refer PMBOK 4th Edition, pages 116, 121] [Project Scope Management]

44. C - TCPI based on EAC = (BAC-EV)/(EAC-AC)
= (100000 - 25000) / (115000 - 40000)
= 75000/75000
= 1
[Refer PMBOK 4th Edition, page 185] [Project Cost Management]

45. A - Once the project management plan has been baselined, it may be changed only when a change request

is generated and approved through the Perform Integrated Change Control process. In order to keep track of changes, a version control system or a revision log will also be maintained. However, the changed version can be baselined only after approval.
[Refer PMBOK 4th Edition, page 82] [Project Integration Management]

46. B - Resource calendars identify times when the project team members can participate in team development activities. If the team members are unable to find time for such activities, it is likely that the calendar has been poorly planned out.
[Refer PMBOK 4th Edition, page 231] [Project Human Resource Management]

47. B - This group decision making technique is called Plurality. Even if a majority (where more than 50 % of the members support the decision) is not achieved, the largest block in the group makes the decision.
[Refer PMBOK 4th Edition, page 108] [Project Scope Management]

48. D - In multi-phase projects, although the procurements for a particular phase may have been closed, the unresolved claims are still subject to litigation after closure.

[Refer PMBOK, 4th Edition, page 341] [Project Procurement Management]

49. B - Analysis of Scope performance is done as part of the Control Scope phase. Determining the cause and degree of variance relative to the scope baseline is an important aspect of this activity (called Variance Analysis).
Change requests that result from this activity are processed in the Perform Integrated Change Control phase.
[Refer PMBOK 4th Edition, pages 127, 128] [Project Scope Management]

50. C - Critical chain is a schedule network analysis technique that is used when a project schedule has to account for limited resources. In this technique, duration buffers that are non-work schedule activities are added to manage uncertainty.
[Refer PMBOK 4th Edition, page 155] [Project Time Management]

Knowledge Area Quiz
Project Scope Management
Practice Questions

Test Name: Knowledge Area Test:
Project Scope Management
Total Questions: 10
Correct Answers Needed to Pass:
7 (70.00%)
Time Allowed: 15 Minutes

Test Description

This practice quiz specifically targets your knowledge of the Project Scope Management knowledge area.

Test Questions

1. Which of the following is not a Group Creativity Technique used in the Collect Requirements process?

   A. Nominal group technique

   B. Idea diagram

   C. Mind mapping

   D. Affinity diagram

2. Linda is a project manager managing the 'Online Banking' project. The project has completed phase 1 and is moving into the next phase of the project. What is the process Linda has to plan for, to ensure that the project requirements have been met in phase 1 and the project can move to the next phase?

   A. Administer Procurements

   B. Verify Scope

   C. Perform Quality Assurance

   D. Close Procurements

3. Which of the following processes is not a part of Project Scope Management?

   A. Create WBS

   B. Perform Quality Control

   C. Control Scope

   D. Collect Requirements

4. The WBS is finalized by establishing control accounts for the work packages and a unique identifier from a code of accounts. This provides a structure for hierarchical summation of:

A. Schedule and requirements information

B. Cost and requirements information

C. Cost and resource information

D. Cost, schedule and resource information

5. Uncontrolled project scope changes are often referred to as _____ .

A. Scope creep

B. Scope verification

C. Value Added Scope

D. Scope control

6. While managing a project, you have included the product acceptance criteria in the Quality Management Plan. When reviewing your plan, a senior manager asks you look at this closely. You then realize that what you have done is incorrect. Where would you actually place the product acceptance criteria?

A. Project Charter

B. Project Management Plan

C. Project Scope Statement

D. Scope Verification Plan

7. Project Scope Management is primarily concerned with:

A. Defining the scope of work that is included in the project.

B. Defining and controlling what is and what is not included in the project.

C. The scope of work that is required during the initiation phase.

D. Defining the specifications and functionality of the work product

8. A project manager approaches you to understand the Work Breakdown Structure (WBS) in better detail. You tell him that:

A. The WBS is a detailed project plan and includes the effort, resources and dates on which the tasks for the project are completed.

B. The WBS is a task oriented decomposition of work that identifies each task and the resource required to accomplish the task.

C. The WBS is a deliverable oriented hierarchical decomposition of the work to be accomplished by the project team to accomplish project objectives.

D. The WBS is a Gantt chart which contains details about the project deliverables required to be done by the project team.

9. Why must the Verify Scope be completed in a project?

A. To obtain scope documents from recent similar projects for benchmarking

B. To determine if the scope is assigned the correct complexity level

C. To obtain formal acceptance of deliverables by the customer or sponsor

D. To ensure the project team is all aware of the scope

10. A project manager wants to use a group decision making technique to generate, classify and prioritize requirements. Which of these is not a valid group decision making technique?

A. Dictatorship

B. Singularity

C. Majority

D. Unanimity

Knowledge Area Quiz
Project Scope Management
Answer Key and Explanations

1. B - Idea diagram is an invalid Group Creativity Technique. The others are valid techniques. Additional techniques are Brainstorming and the Delphi Technique. [Project Scope Management]

2. B - Verify Scope is the process completed at the end of each phase, and that of each project to confirm that the project has met the requirements. It leads to a formal acceptance of the project deliverable. [Project Scope Management]

3. B - Perform Quality control is not a part of the Project Scope management process. [Project Scope Management]

4. D - The WBS is finalized by establishing control accounts for the work packages and a unique identifier from a code of accounts. This provides a structure for hierarchical summation of costs, schedule and resource information.[PMBOK page 121] [Project Scope Management]

5. A - Scope creep is often viewed negatively, but can be managed using a change control process. [PMBOK Page 125] [Project Scope Management]

6. C - The project scope statement documents and addresses the characteristics and boundaries of the project and its associated products and services, as well as product acceptance criteria and scope control. [Project Scope Management]

7. B - Project Scope Management includes the processes required to ensure that the project includes all the work required and only the work required to complete the project successfully. It is primarily concerned with defining and controlling what is included and what is not included in the project. [Project Scope Management]

8. C - The WBS is a deliverable oriented hierarchical decomposition of the work to be accomplished by the project team to accomplish project objectives. [Project Scope Management]

9. C - Verify Scope is the process of formalizing acceptance of the completed project deliverables by the customer or sponsor of the project [PMBOK Page 123] [Project Scope Management]

10. B - Singularity is not a valid method to reach a group decision. The other choices are valid methods to reach a

group   decision.   [Project   Scope
Management]

PMP Lite Mock Exam 14
Practice Questions

Test Name: PMP Lite Mock Exam 14
Total Questions: 50
Correct Answers Needed to Pass:
35 (70.00%)
Time Allowed: 60 Minutes

Test Description

This is a cumulative PMP Mock Exam which can be used as a benchmark for your PMP aptitude. This practice test includes questions from all PMBOK knowledge areas, including the five basic project management process groups.

Test Questions

1. Which of the following is an incorrect classification of work such as a feasibility study?

   A. A feasibility study may be considered as a stand-alone project.

   B. A feasibility study may be considered as pre-project work.

   C. A feasibility study may be considered as the first phase of a project.

   D. A feasibility study may be considered a program

2. A seller started out a project on the basis of a Time and Material contract. The initial contract amount based on the agreed-upon rates and effort was $ 100,000 over a 1 year period. However, when the project was completed, the total contract value turned out to be $ 350,000 over a 2 year period. What mechanism could the buyer have used to prevent this unlimited cost growth and schedule change?

   A. Use of a not-to-exceed value and a time limit on the contract.

   B. A service level agreement.

   C. A penalty based on the increased cost and timeline.

   D. Use of a fixed price contract.

3. The Budget at Completion (BAC) for a project is $ 50,000. The Actual Costs (AC) to date are $ 10,000. The Earned Value (EV) is $ 7,000. At this stage, the project management team did a manual bottom-up summation of costs and forecast an Estimate to Complete (ETC) of $ 50,000. What is the Estimate at Completion (EAC) for the project?

A. $ 57,000

B. $ 40,000

C. $ 60,000

D. $ 53,000

4. Projects, portfolios and programs are different entities in an organization. Which of the following choices states a correct relationship between them?

A. A portfolio consists of a collection of projects or programs that are grouped together to achieve strategic business objectives. The projects or programs need not be directly related.

B. A project is a collection of programs and portfolios that are grouped together to achieve the project objectives.

C. A program consists of a collection of projects or portfolios that are grouped together to achieve strategic business objectives.

D. A program is a collection of projects that are grouped together for convenience. It may include unrelated work if the work is under the same business division.

5. Which of the following choices is unlikely to be considered a project?

A. A project that creates a capability to perform a service.

B. A project involving publishing of 1 million copies of a book.

C. A project involving one person.

D. A project that involves different contractors.

6. The Risk Management plan will usually contain the definitions of risk probability and impact. Which of the following has the highest impact (negative) on a project?

A. A rating of 1.1 on the impact scale

B. A rating of 0.8 on the impact scale

C. A rating of 0 on the impact scale

D. A rating of 0.1 on the impact scale

7. You are the project manager of a project and are about to conduct a risk identification exercise in a few

days' time. You would like to proactively remind the participants in the exercise of the various sources from which risk may arise in the project. What could you use to help you do this?

A. A Risk Breakdown Structure (RBS)

B. A Risk Simulation Structure (RSS)

C. A Risk Register

D. An Impact Matrix

8. Ron is a project manager handling the "Alternate water-supply project". During a project performance review, he notices the following:

    i.   Activity A, on the critical path, is delayed by 4 days.

    ii. Activity B, not on the critical path, is delayed by 9 days.

    iii. Activity C, on the critical path is delayed by 2 days

    iv. Activity D, not on the critical path, is delayed by 5 days.

In what sequence should Run prioritize his efforts in addressing these delays?

A. Activity A, Activity B, Activity D, Activity C

B. Activity A, Activity C, Activity B, Activity D

C. Activity B, Activity D, Activity A, Activity C

D. Activity B, Activity A, Activity D, Activity C

9. Which of the following statements about products and projects is true?

A. Adding new functionality to an existing product cannot be considered as a project.

B. A product life cycle is usually contained within a project life cycle.

C. One product may have many projects associated with it.

D. The product life cycle usually consists of non-sequential phases whereas the project life cycle consists of sequential phases.

10. In order to build a quality product, the project management team invested in training of the project team members and in purchase of high-end equipment to perform testing. Such costs will be classified as:

   A. Failure costs

   B. Cost of Nonconformance

   C. Appraisal costs

   D. Prevention costs

11. An important aspect of project management is the handling of stakeholder expectations. Typically, at what level are the stakeholders with respect to the project manager.

   A. At higher levels and with greater authority

   B. At all levels and with varying degrees of authority.

   C. At higher levels but only the project sponsor has authority greater than the project manager.

   D. At the same level with varying degrees of authority.

12. Public recognition of good performance creates positive

reinforcement for the team members. When is the best time for a project manager to recognize team members' performance?

   A. During the lifecycle of the project

   B. At the end of every phase of the project

   C. At the end of the project

   D. As mandated by the HR department.

13. The requirements elicitation team has obtained a large number of ideas during sessions to gather product and project requirements. Which of the following techniques is best suited to have these ideas sorted into groups for review and analysis?

   A. Mind mapping

   B. Venn diagram

   C. Affinity diagram

   D. Brainstorming

14. One of the performance requirements of a Company Website development project is that the home page should load in 1 second. Such performance requirements are usually part of:

A. Customer requirements

B. Business requirements

C. Project requirements

D. Product requirements

15. During a conflict between two team members of your project, one of the team members verbally abuses the other. This is brought to your notice. However, you are aware that the team member who now faces disciplinary action is the son of a senior board member of your company. What should you do?

A. Play down the incident. This is not such a serious matter since no one has been physically hurt. Reporting this will bring unnecessary attention to your project.

B. Make a report, but state that both parties were equally responsible for the incident.

C. Call the concerned team member and warn him not to indulge in such behavior again.

D. Make a report to the HR department and senior management stating the facts exactly as they occurred.

16. A first-time project manager is trying to understand the difference between configuration control and change control. The difference is:

A. Configuration control is focused on the specification of both the deliverables and the process whereas change control is focused on identifying, documenting and controlling changes to the project.

B. Configuration control is focused on ensuring that all changes are documented whereas change control is focused on the approval process.

C. Change control is focused on the specification of both the deliverables and the process whereas configuration control is focused on identifying, documenting and controlling changes to the project.

D. Change control is focused on ensuring that approved changes are documented and controlled whereas configuration control is focused on ensuring that changes are properly identified and approved by the change control board.

17. The project management team expects that during the course of the project, there could be delays in component delivery, strikes, changes in the permitting processes or extensions of specific engineering durations. What analysis will help come up with contingency and response plans to mitigate these?

    A. Contingency analysis

    B. Variance analysis

    C. What-If scenario analysis.

    D. Schedule compression

18. In the earned value management technique, the cost performance baseline is referred to as:

    A. Cost Measurement Baseline (CMB)

    B. Performance Measurement Baseline (PMB)

    C. Performance Base Value (PBV)

    D. Performance Cost Baseline (PCB)

19. A seller entered into contract with a buyer. At the end of the project, the seller was reimbursed for the cost of the project, but received a very low fee based on certain subjective criteria that had been laid down in the contract. What type of contract is this likely to be?

    A. Cost Plus Fixed Fee (CPFF) contract

    B. Fixed Price Incentive Fee (FPIF) contract

    C. Cost Plus Incentive Fee (CPIF) contract

    D. Cost Plus Award Fee (CPAF) contract

20. The two key processes which happen early on in the project life cycle are:

    A. Define Scope and Identify Stakeholders

    B. Define Scope and Manage Stakeholder expectations.

    C. Develop Project Charter and Plan Communications

    D. Develop Project Charter and Identify Stakeholders

21. Progressive elaboration usually applies in all of the following processes except:

A. Create WBS

B. Control Schedule

C. Develop Schedule

D. Estimate Activity Durations

22. During a cost performance review with certain senior officers from the finance department, you discover that there are certain inconsistencies in the way cost performance reporting is done, and you obtain data that shows these officers are deliberately misleading senior management. What should you do?

A. Write an anonymous letter to senior management about these activities.

B. Bring this to the notice of senior management even though there are no formal policies in place for whistle-blowers.

C. Do nothing, but make sure that the data for your project is clean.

D. Do nothing. The corrupt behavior of the finance department officials has nothing to do with your project.

23. Your company is planning to bid on a project in an application area in which you have never worked before. You are aware that your company does not have any resources with the necessary expertise. Your management is pressurizing you to submit a bid. What should you do?

A. Refuse to do what your company management asks you to do since it violates the code of ethics and professionalism.

B. Do what your management asks you to do. Your loyalty needs to be with your company. As long as management has the confidence that the project can be done, you can go with the plan.

C. Do what your management asks you to do, but inform them that you would not like to be associated with the project since it violates the code of ethics and professionalism.

D. Explain the gaps to your management clearly and also explain that this will be a stretch assignment. You can further explain to them that it is best to reveal to the potential buyer that your company does not possess the necessary skills, but are confident of ramping up the necessary skills and delivering the project successfully, based on your company's track record.

24. Effectiveness and efficiency are two important aspects of communication for a project manager. Identify which of the listed choices is incorrect.

   A. Efficient communication means providing much more than the information needed

   B. Effective communication means providing information at the right time

   C. Efficient communication means providing only the information that is needed.

   D. Effective communication means providing information in the right format.

25. Eric, a project manager, is a certified PMP. He is responding to an RFP from a buyer and needs to fill in details on the financial performance of his company. His company has performed badly during the current quarter and the results will be published in 2 to 3 days' time. However, the company has done very well in the previous quarters. The RFP is due in 10 days' time and all the other information in the RFP is ready and filled out (except the financial information). What should Eric do?

   A. Eric should fill in the financial information for the previous quarter and send out the RFP response before the current quarter results are published.

   B. Eric should present the previous quarter's results as the latest results. This will give his company a better chance to win the project.

   C. Eric should fill in the information for the previous quarter and ignore the current quarter. This is an aberration and the company will eventually come out of the bad patch.

   D. Eric should wait until the current results are out and update the latest financial information before sending out the RFP response.

26. A project manager is trying to budget time for the various processes in the Project Time Management Knowledge Area. As project activities are being performed, in which of

these processes will the majority of effort occur?

A. Control Schedule

B. Estimate Activity Durations

C. Define Activities

D. Develop Schedule

27. A buyer and seller are looking at getting into a long-term relationship spanning over 10 years. Both parties would like to be protected from conditions beyond their control. What type of contract is appropriate for such a relationship?

A. Fixed Price Incentive Fee (FPIF)

B. Firm Fixed Price (FPP)

C. Time & Material (T&M)

D. Fixed Price with Economic Price Adjustment Contract (FP-EPA)

28. Which of the following quality control tools and techniques may not be used for root cause analysis?

A. Fishbone diagram

B. Scatter diagram

C. Why-why and how-how diagram

D. Cause and effect diagram

29. Midway through the Collect Requirements process, a project manager finds that there are lots of unresolved issues. Which of the following is usually the best way to discover and resolve issues?

A. Interviewing

B. Use of a stakeholder register

C. Focus groups

D. Facilitated workshops

30. The administration team for a buyer is drafting up a contract to award work to an external supplier. They would include verbiage that the contract can be terminated for all of the following reasons except:

A. For cause

B. For default

C. For convenience

D. For the purpose of the court

31. A project manager would like to resolve conflicts with a give-and-take attitude rather than using a one-sided approach. Which of these approaches is he likely to use?

    A. Forcing

    B. Problem-solving

    C. Smoothing

    D. Withdrawing

32. A small project with a limited budget is trying to curtail costs. Which of the following processes may be eliminated in such a project?

    A. Perform Qualitative Risk Analysis

    B. Perform Quantitative Risk Analysis

    C. Identify Risks

    D. Plan Risk Management

33. A number of deliverables were submitted to the buyer as part of a project. Where would the project manager find documentation on the requirements for formal deliverable acceptance and how non-conforming deliverables can be addressed?

    A. In the SOW

    B. In the lessons learned document

    C. In the deliverable release note.

    D. In the contract.

34. Late in the project cycle, it was discovered that some of the project human resources needed to have been trained on a specific methodology. Ideally, where should these training needs have first been documented?

    A. In the requirements documentation

    B. In the procurement contract

    C. In the project scope statement

    D. In the company HR policy

35. A project manager prepared quantitative assessments of the probable costs required to complete a project and came up with Activity cost estimates. She also prepared some supporting detail for these estimates. Which of the following would not be a supporting detail for cost estimates?

A. Indication of the range of possible estimates (ex: $ 5,000 +/- 5%).

B. Indication of the confidence level of the final estimate (ex: 90%)

C. Documentation of the basis of the estimates.

D. Indication of the profit margin that can be expected on the project.

36. While managing a large project, the project manager decided to include indirect costs as part of his cost estimate. If indirect costs are included in an estimate which of the following is true?

A. Indirect costs should be included at the activity level or higher.

B. Indirect costs should be included at the activity level or lower.

C. Indirect costs should only be included in earned value measurements and not in cost estimates.

D. Indirect costs should not be included in cost estimates.

37. Which of these is not a legitimate model used to identify stakeholders and their expectations?

A. Influence / impact grid

B. Power / influence grid

C. Sufficiency model

D. Salience model

38. A project manager analyzed the project's communication requirements and decided that 10 out of the 30 stakeholders in the project would only need voicemail updates of certain information. This type of communication method is called:

A. Push communication

B. Pull communication

C. Interactive communication

D. On-demand communication

39. A project involved development of a high speed hard disk drive. As part of its testing, the hard disk was subjected to continuous operation at a high speed and an elevated temperature. At the end of the test, the hard disk was destroyed beyond use. The cost of such testing is usually classified as:

A. Appraisal costs

B. Internal failure costs

C. Cost of nonconformance

D. Prevention costs

A. Econometric method

B. Judgmental method

C. Time series method

D. Composite forecast

40. Identification of new risks, reassessment of old risks and closing of outdated risks are done as part of the Monitor and Control Risks phase. How often should project risk reassessment be scheduled?

A. It depends on how the project progresses relative to its objectives.

B. It is left to the discretion of the project manager.

C. Reassessment needs to be done at the 25%, 50%, and 75% stages of project completion.

D. Reassessment needs to be done at the 20%, 40%, 60% and 80% stages of project completion.

41. Forecasting is an important tool and technique used to report performance of a project. The forecasting method which uses historical data as the basis of estimating future outcomes is:

42. Rick has just been assigned as the project manager of a project to develop a complex product. The project is in the Define Scope phase. Which of these tools / techniques will not be used by Rick in this phase?

A. Lateral thinking

B. Process analysis

C. Pair wise comparisons

D. Value engineering

43. Teams go through various stages of development. As per the Tuckman ladder of development, the stage during which the least amount of work gets done is usually the:

A. Storming phase

B. Forming phase

C. Norming phase

D. Performing phase

D. Plan Risk Management

44. A project manager has been asked to manage a research project. By its very nature, this type of project is not very clearly defined and involves a lot of uncertainty. What phase-to-phase relationship should the project manager use for this project?

A. Open-ended relationship

B. Overlapping relationship

C. Iterative relationship

D. Sequential relationship

45. A senior project manager advises a first-time project manager that identifying risks is just one step. On a continuous basis, new risks need to be identified, and existing risks need to be analyzed, tracked and their status reported. All this is done as part of what process?

A. Direct and Manage Project Execution

B. Monitor and Control Project Work

C. Perform Integrated Change Control

46. A project manager has decided to use a decision tree to make a build or upgrade analysis. The build requires an investment of $ 200 M (where M represents million). On the build decision branch, there is a 60% probability of strong demand (yielding a revenue of $ 400 M) and a 40% probability of weak demand (yielding a revenue of $150 M). What is the expected monetary value (EMV) of the build?

A. $ 100 M

B. $ 300 M

C. $ 140 M

D. $ 200 M

47. A project management team came up with certain metrics such as defect frequency, failure rate, availability and reliability. These are usually defined as an output of what process?

A. Plan Quality

B. Define Scope

C. Collect Requirements

D. Perform Quality Assurance

48. In order to keep costs down, a project management team decided to apply statistical sampling while inspecting some of the work products. They decided to select 10 out of 50 engineering drawings for inspection. During which process should the sample frequency and sample size be determined?

A. Collect Requirements

B. Plan Quality

C. Perform Quality Control

D. Perform Quality Assurance

49. A project manager prepared a presentation that included data on utilization of resources on her project, improvements in efficiency of the staff on the project, and the cost savings. She is doing this as part of what process?

A. Manage Stakeholder Expectations

B. Monitor and Control Project Work

C. Control Schedule

D. Perform Quality Control

50. A very critical resource is on another project team. It is very important you get his time for your project. You have contacted his team's manager multiple times, but have received a poor response. What should you consider doing next?

A. Plan for an alternate resource since this resource is not available.

B. Try to use management influence to obtain the resource's time.

C. Contact the manager once again to see if he can help.

D. Train another resource within your project.

PMP Lite Mock Exam 14
Answer Key and Explanations

1.   D - Organizations may classify projects differently depending on their internal policies and structures. Hence a feasibility study can be considered as pre-project work, the first phase of a project or a stand-alone project. However, it cannot be referred to as a program. A program will have much larger scope.
[Refer PMBOK, 4th Edition, page 19]
[Project Framework]

2.   A - Use of not-to-exceed values and time limits placed in T & M contracts help prevent unlimited cost growth or schedule changes.
Use of a fixed price contract is an option, but that is a decision prior to awarding the project and signing the contract.
[Refer PMBOK 4th Edition, page 324]
[Project Procurement Management]

3.   C - When a bottom-up manual forecasting has been done for the ETC, the calculation for EAC is given by:
EAC = AC + bottom-up ETC
Hence, EAC = 10,000 + 50,000 = $ 60,000.
Note that the BAC is no longer viable at this stage.
[Refer PMBOK 4th Edition, page 184]
[Project Cost Management]

4.   A - A portfolio is a collection of projects or programs that are grouped together to achieve a strategic business objective. Portfolio management focuses on ensuring that projects and programs are reviewed to prioritize resource allocation and the management of the portfolio is aligned with organizational strategies. The projects or programs need not be directly related.
A program is a collection of projects, but they need to have common objectives, so unrelated work cannot be grouped together under a program.
[Refer PMBOK, 4th Edition, page 8, 9] [Project Framework]

5.   B - A project is a temporary endeavor to produce a unique product, service or a result. Producing a million copies of a book cannot be considered a project since it does not produce a unique result. It is repetitive by the nature of the activity and will be considered an on-going work effort rather than a project.
Projects can consist of a single person, involve different contractors or create a capability to perform a service.
[Refer PMBOK 4th Edition, page 5] [Project Framework]

6.   B - The impact scale will contain the probabilities of certain risks occurring, and will contain values from 0 to 1. A value of 0 indicates non-occurrence of the risk while 1 is a certainty.

Hence, a risk impact of 0.8 represents the highest impact among the choices presented.

[Refer PMBOK, 4th Edition, page 281] [Project Risk Management]

7.   A - The Risk Breakdown Structure (RBS) is a hierarchically organized depiction of identified project risks arranged by risk category and subcategory. This may be based on a previously prepared categorization framework The RBS serves to remind participants in the risk identification exercise of the different sources from which risk may project arise.

[Refer PMBOK 4th Edition, page 280, figure 11-4] [Project Risk Management]

8.   B - An important part of schedule control is to decide if schedule variation requires corrective action. Activities on the critical path are given the first priority for immediate action. Larger delays on activities not on the critical path may not require immediate attention since they may not affect the overall project schedule. Hence Ron will first look into the delays on the critical path and then tackle the delays on the other paths.

[Refer PMBOK 4th Edition, page 162] [Project Time Management]

9.   C - When the output of a project is a product, a number of projects could be involved. For example: the development of a new product could be a project. Similarly, adding new functions or features could be a project. Other possibilities are conducting a feasibility study, conducting a product trial in the market, running an advertising campaign, etc.

[Refer PMBOK 4th Edition, page 18] [Project Framework]

10.   D - Investments in training, test equipment, and documentation of processes are called prevention costs. Appraisal costs include the actual testing, loss due to destructive testing and inspections. Collectively, these are called Cost of Conformance.

[Refer PMBOK 4th Edition, page 195] [Project Quality Management]

11.   B - Project stakeholders are persons and organizations having a stake in the project. They typically exist at different levels and have varying degree of authority. For example, the project sponsor will be at a higher level and have a greater authority than the project manager. In contrast, a team member may be at a lower level and have lesser authority.

[Refer PMBOK, 4th Edition, page 246] [Project Communications Management]

12.   A - A good strategy for project managers is to give the team all

possible recognition during the life cycle of the project rather than after the project is completed. This will keep the team members motivated through the duration of the project.
[Refer PMBOK 4th Edition, page 234] [Project Human Resource Management]

13. C - The affinity diagram allows large numbers of ideas to be sorted into groups for further review and analysis. It is a tool used in gathering of requirements.
[Refer PMBOK 4th Edition, page 108] [Project Scope Management]

14. D - Performance requirements such as the loading time of websites are usually considered as part of product requirements.
Project requirements include business requirements, project management requirements and delivery requirements whereas product requirements include technical, security, and performance requirements.
[Refer PMBOK 4th Edition, page 105] [Project Scope Management]

15. D - We need to be fair in our transactions and not be biased by the power or position of any of the team members. Hence, we need to report the incident exactly as it occurred.
[Refer PMI Code of Ethics chapter 4, page 3] [Prof. Responsibility]

16. A - Configuration control is focused on the specification of both the deliverables and the process whereas change control is focused on identifying, documenting and controlling changes to the project.
A configuration management system with integrated change control provides a standardized and effective way to centrally manage approved changes within the project.
[Refer PMBOK 4th Edition, page 94] [Project Integration Management]

17. C - What-If scenario analysis is used to assess the feasibility of the project schedule under adverse conditions. This in an analysis of the question "What if the situation represented by scenario 'X' happens?" It is used in preparing contingency and response plans to mitigate the impact of the unexpected conditions.
[Refer PMBOK 4th Edition, page 156] [Project Time Management]

18. B - The cost performance baseline is an authorized time-phased budget at completion (BAC). It is used measure, monitor, and control overall cost performance on the project. In the earned value management technique, it is referred to as the performance measurement baseline (PMB).
[Refer PMBOK 4th edition, page 178] [Project Cost Management]

19. D - This is likely to be a Cost Plus Award Fee (CPAF) contract. In such a contract, the seller is reimbursed for all legitimate costs, but the fee is based on the satisfaction of certain broad subjective performance criteria defined in the contract. It is generally not subject to appeals.
[Refer PMBOK, 4th Edition, page 324] [Project Procurement Management]

20. D - The two initiating processes are Develop project charter and Identify stakeholders. The chances of success of the project are enhanced if the project charter is well written and the appropriate stakeholders are identified early on, as part of the initiating process group.
[Refer PMBOK, 4th Edition, page 42, 246] [Project Communications Management]

21. B - Progressive elaboration applies when only a certain amount of information is available initially and additional information is obtained as the project or phase progresses. This is applicable in the case of Estimate Activity Durations, Develop Schedule and the Create WBS processes. It does not apply in case of the Control Schedule process.
[Refer PMBOK 4th Edition, pages 146,152,116] [Project Time Management]

22. B - As practitioners in the global project management community, it is our responsibility to report unethical or illegal conduct. We may recognize that it is difficult to report such happening since they may have negative consequences, yet we need to do so.
[Refer PMI Code of Ethics section 2.3.2, page 2] [Prof. Responsibility]

23. D - Since you are aware that your company lacks the necessary skills, you need to be truthful while bidding. Rather than outright refusing to do what your company management asks you to do, it is better to explain the reasons to them and ensure that all stakeholders involved are aware that this will be a stretch assignment but you and your company are willing to put in the necessary effort to make the project a success. The other choices are unethical.
[Refer PMI Code of Ethics section 2.2.2, page 2] [Prof. Responsibility]

24. A - Efficient communication means communicating ONLY the information that is needed. This ensures that the project manager does not waste time on communicating information that is not needed. On most projects communications planning is done very early, during project plan development.

[Refer PMBOK 4th Edition, page 252]
[Project Communications Management]

25. D - As a PMP, Eric cannot behave in a manner that will mislead the buyer. Hence, given that there are still a sufficient number of days available before the RFP is due, it is his responsibility to wait for the current quarter results to be published and truthfully provide this information in the RFP.
[Refer chapter 5 (Honesty) on Page 4, PMI code of ethics document] [Prof. Responsibility]

26. A - As project activities are being performed, the majority of effort in the Project Time Management Knowledge Area will occur in the Control Schedule process to ensure completion of project work in a timely manner.
[Refer PMBOK 4th Edition, page 130] [Project Time Management]

27. D - The FP-EPA contract is used whenever the buyer-seller relationship spans across years. It is a fixed price contract with a special provision allowing for pre-defined final adjustments to the contract price due to changed conditions. It is intended to protect both the buyer and the seller from external conditions beyond their control.

[Refer PMBOK, 4th Edition, page 323] [Project Procurement Management]

28. B - Of the tools listed, scatter diagram is used to study and identify the possible relationship between two variables. The others can be used for root-cause analysis.
[Refer PMBOK, 4th Edition, pages 208,212] [Project Quality Management]

29. D - Facilitated workshops bring key cross-functional stakeholders together to define product requirements. Because of their interactive nature, well-facilitated sessions lead to increased stakeholder consensus.
This ensures that issues can be discovered and resolved more quickly than in other forums.
[Refer PMBOK 4th Edition, page 107] [Project Scope Management]

30. D - The choice "for the purpose of the court" is not valid. Typical causes included for early termination of contracted work are:
For cause, for convenience or for default.
[Refer PMBOK 4th Edition, page 337] [Project Procurement Management]

31. B - Problem-solving involves treating conflict as a problem to be solved by examining alternatives. This requires a give-and-take attitude. In contrast the

other alternatives listed - smoothing, forcing and withdrawing are more one-sided.
[Refer PMBOK, 4th Edition, page 240] [Project Human Resource Management]

32. B - Availability of budget and time is a key factor that determines the need for the Perform Quantitative Risk Analysis process. A small project with a limited budget may decide to do away with this process if the project management team decides that quantitative statements about risk and impacts are not needed.
[Refer PMBOK, 4th Edition, page 295] [Project Risk Management]

33. D - Requirements for formal deliverable acceptance and how to address non-conforming deliverables are usually defined in the contract.
[Refer PMBOK 4th Edition, page 344] [Project Procurement Management]

34. A - Training requirements should ideally be documented in the requirements documentation. This will allow the project manager to keep track of them and plan for the appropriate training when this is further elaborated in the Human Resource Plan which is a part of the project management plan.
[Refer PMBOK 4th Edition, page 110, 225] [Project Scope Management]

35. D - Indication of the profit margin that can be achieved on the project is not a supporting detail. The focus of the Estimate Costs process is to perform a quantitative assessment of all probably costs required to accomplish the project work.
[Refer PMBOK 4th Edition, page 174] [Project Cost Management]

36. A - Activity cost estimates are quantitative assessments of the probable costs required to finish project work. If included in project estimates, indirect costs should be included at the activity level or higher.
[Refer PMBOK 4th Edition, page 174] [Project Cost Management]

37. C - The sufficiency model is not a valid model. The others are valid models used to identify stakeholders as part of stakeholder analysis.
[Refer PMBOK 4th Edition, page 249] [Project Communications Management]

38. A - Use of voice mails is push communication. In this communication, information is distributed to specific recipients who need to know the information. However, this method does not certify that it actually reached or was received by the intended audience.
[Refer PMBOK 4th Edition, page 256] [Project Communications Management]

39. A - This type of testing is called destructive testing and it is classified under appraisal costs. Along with other tests and inspections, they help in assessing the quality of the product. [Refer PMBOK 4th Edition, page 195] [Project Quality Management]

40. A - The number of project risk reassessments scheduled depends on the progress of the project relative to its objectives. [Refer PMBOK 4th Edition, page 310] [Project Risk Management]

41. C - Time series methods use historical data as the basis for estimating future outcomes. Examples of these methods are earned value, moving average, extrapolation, and growth curve. [Refer PMBOK 4th Edition, page 269] [Project Communications Management]

42. B - Process Analysis is a tool / technique used in the Perform Quality Assurance phase and not in the Define Scope phase. Process analysis follows the steps listed in the process improvement plan to identify needed improvements. [Refer PMBOK 4th Edition, pages 114, 204] [Project Scope Management]

43. B - The forming phase is the phase where the team gets to know each other and learns about the project. Teams are usually on their "best behavior" and little tangible work gets accomplished. The project manager needs to guide the team and move them through this phase into the performing phase. [Refer PMBOK 4th Edition, page 233] [Project Human Resource Management]

44. C - An iterative relationship is one where only one phase is carried out at any given time. Planning for the next phase is carried on as work progresses on the current phase. This type of relationship is suitable in case of projects with unclear scope or changing environments. Hence, in a research type of project, an iterative relationship is used. [Refer PMBOK 4th Edition, page 22] [Project Framework]

45. B - Identifying new risks, and analyzing, tracking and monitoring existing project risks is done in the Monitor and Control Project Work phase. This phase also makes sure the status of the risks is properly reported and appropriate risk response plans are executed. [Refer PMBOK, 4th Edition, page 89] [Project Integration Management]

46. A - The payoff for the strong demand scenario is:
$ 400 M - $ 200 M = $ 200 M

(since the initial investment is $ 200 M)

The payoff for the weak demand scenario is:

$ 150 M - $ 200 M = - $ 50 M

Hence the EMV is computed as:

(0.6 x 200) + (0.4 x -50) where 0.6 represents the 60% probability of the strong demand and 0.4 represents the 40% probability of the weak demand scenario.

= 120 - 20 = $ 100 M.

Hence the expected monetary value is $ 100 M.

[Refer PMBOK 4th Edition, page 299]
[Project Risk Management]

47. A - Quality metrics are operational definitions that describe a project or product attribute in very specific terms. They also define how the quality control process will measure it. These metrics are an output of the Plan Quality process.

[Refer PMBOK 4th Edition, page 200]
[Project Quality Management]

48. B - Sample frequency and sizes are determined during the Plan Quality process so that the cost of quality includes the number of tests, expected scrap etc.

[Refer PMBOK, 4th Edition, page 198] [Project Quality Management]

49. B - Activities such as project performance analysis and tracking are done as part of the Monitor and Control Project Work process. This involves tracking, reviewing and regulating the progress to meet performance objectives.

[Refer PMBOK 4th Edition, page 89]
[Project Integration Management]

50. B - Contacting the manager once again will not help since you have already had a poor response. The best option is to try and use management influence to obtain the resource's time for your project. Planning for an alternate resource or training another resource are steps that need to be done as last steps after all options have been exhausted. [Project Human Resource Management]

PMP Lite Mock Exam 15
Practice Questions

Test Name: PMP Lite Mock Exam 15
Total Questions: 50
Correct Answers Needed to Pass:
35 (70.00%)
Time Allowed: 60 Minutes

Test Description

This is a cumulative PMP Mock Exam which can be used as a benchmark for your PMP aptitude. This practice test includes questions from all PMBOK knowledge areas, including the five basic project management process groups.

Test Questions

1. A project manager is estimating activity durations for a project. Which of the following should he consider while performing this activity?

    A. While calculating the duration of schedule activities, differences in the capabilities of staff assigned should not be taken into consideration. All senior and junior staff should be given equal weightage.

    B. While calculating the duration of schedule activities, differences in the capabilities of staff assigned should be taken into

    consideration. Hence, a senior staff member will generally be expected to finish an activity in 80% of the time that a junior member would take.

    C. While calculating the duration of schedule activities, differences in the capabilities of staff assigned should be taken into consideration. Hence, a senior staff member will generally be expected to finish an activity in less time than a junior member.

    D. While calculating the duration of schedule activities, an average should be used and the actual differences in the capabilities of staff assigned should not be taken into consideration.

2. As part of a strategy to handle negative risk, a project manager decided to adopt less complex processes, conduct more tests and choose a more stable supplier. What strategy would this be classified as?

    A. Acceptance

    B. Transference

    C. Mitigation

    D. Avoidance

3. Bill is the project manager of an external project for a customer. The project is expected to take about a year to complete. Six months into the project, the customer informs Bill

that the project needs to be scrapped. During which of the following processes would procedures be developed to handle early termination of a project?

A. Develop Project Charter

B. Close Project or Phase

C. Define Scope

D. Close Procurements

4. During a discussion with the quality department, a project manager was given to understand that both prevention and inspection meant the same as applied to projects. However, he had a different understanding of the terms. What would you comment on this situation?

A. The project manager is correct. Prevention is about keeping errors out of the process whereas inspection is about keeping errors out of the hands of the customer.

B. The project manager is correct. Inspection is about keeping errors out of the process whereas prevention is about keeping errors out of the hands of the customer.

C. The project manager is wrong. Both inspection and prevention are about keeping errors out of the hands of the customer. They are used in different contexts.

D. The project manager is wrong. Both inspection and prevention

are about keeping errors out of the process. They are used in different contexts.

5. A project manager prepared a composite resource calendar. Which of the following is unlikely to be part of the resource calendar?

A. Availability of Human Resources

B. Skills of Human resources.

C. Cost of Human Resources

D. Capabilities of Human Resources

6. While preparing a human resource plan, a project manager documented that one of the senior programmers in the team would make decisions on whether the quality of deliverables from the project met the project's documented standards. Which of the following aspects of a human resource plan does this address?

A. Competency

B. Responsibility

C. Authority

D. Role

7. Prioritization matrices are an important quality planning tool. They provide a way of ranking a diverse set of problems and/or issues by order of importance. How is this list usually generated?

A. Through flowcharts

B. Through use of historical records.

C. Through brainstorming

D. Through lessons learned

8. Sally, a project manager was reconciling expenditure of funds with funding limits on the commitment of funds for the project. She found a large variance between the funding limits and planned expenditures. As a result, she decided to reschedule work to level out the rate of expenditures. This is known as:

A. Funding limit reconciliation

B. Funding limit constraints

C. Funding limit expenditure

D. Funding limit appropriation

9. A project manager used the services of a trained moderator during the Collect Requirements Phase. Which of the following is likely to have required the services of a trained moderator?

A. Interviews

B. Prototypes

C. Questionnaires

D. Focus groups

10. Which of the following allows a project management team to consistently communicate all approved and rejected changes to the stakeholders?

A. Configuration management system

B. Verification management system

C. Configuration status accounting

D. Change management board

11. As part of stakeholder analysis, a project manager drew up a power / interest grid. The project manager identified that a stakeholder could be classified low on the "interest" scale, and also as low on the "power" scale. What strategy should be used for such a stakeholder?

A. Monitor

B. Manage closely

C. Keep informed

D. Keep satisfied

12. Which of the following statements accurately describes how the completion of project scope and product scope is measured?

A. The completion of project scope and product scope are both measured against the product requirements.

B. The completion of project scope is measured against the project management plan whereas the completion of product scope is measured against the product requirements.

C. The completion of project scope is measured against the product requirements whereas the completion of product scope is measured against the project management plan.

D. The completion of project scope and product scope are both measured against the project management plan.

13. Bill and Jake are two team members in a project. They do not get on well, and are constantly involved in verbal fights. The project manager in steps to resolve the situation. As an experienced project manager, he understands the characteristics of conflict and the conflict management process. Which of the following is a not a characteristic of conflict?

A. Openness resolves conflict

B. Conflict is natural and forces a search for alternatives

C. Disciplinary action should not be taken to resolve conflict

D. Conflict is an individual related matter and not a team issue

14. The Iterate Risks project involves determining which risks may impact a project. It is considered an iterative process. What is the frequency of iteration?

A. Every month

B. Every fortnight

C. The frequency of iteration will vary based on the situation

D. Every week

15. The project manager of a large project used the autoregressive moving average (ARMA) method of regression analysis to forecast future project performance. Under what category can you classify this type of forecasting?

A. Time series method

B. Ensemble method

C. Causal / Econometric method

D. Judgmental method

16. A project manager manages a distributed team with team members located in five countries. Due to time-zone differences, he is unable to find a time that is acceptable to all team members. What strategy should he apply to resolve this matter?

A. Authority

B. Co-location

C. Coercion

D. Negotiation

17. Acceptance is a strategy adopted because it is not possible to eliminate all risks from a project. This strategy indicates that the project management team has decided not to change the project management plan to deal with a risk. What action does passive acceptance require?

A. Passive acceptance is no longer adopted in projects and is not an accepted strategy.

B. Passive acceptance requires no action except to document the strategy and come up with a risk management strategy.

C. Passive acceptance requires no action.

D. Passive acceptance requires no action except to document the strategy.

18. A buyer and seller fixed up the rates for junior engineers, senior engineers, architects, and other predefined roles. In what type of a contract would this be applicable?

A. Fixed price with economic price adjustment contract

B. Fixed price incentive contract

C. Fixed-price contract

D. Time and material contract

19. A project manager is estimating project costs and needs to decide whether the estimates will include only direct costs, or whether the estimates will also include indirect costs. In which of the following phases does this decision need to take place?

A. Define Scope

B. Estimate Costs

C. Plan Expenses

D. Determine Budgets

20. At the beginning of the project, a project manager identified that the technical expertise in the team was limited, and that this was a risk to the project. Halfway into the project, the project manager felt that this was no longer a risk and considered it outdated. As part of which process, would the risk reassessment be done?

A. Perform Qualitative Risk Analysis

B. Perform Quantitative Risk Analysis

C. Perform Risk Assessment

D. Monitor and Control Risks

21. During a project status meeting, a project manager presented sensitive information related to the project. However, this information was not intended to be available to the audience. Which of the following processes was incorrectly done resulting in the project manager communicating sensitive information to the wrong audience?

A. Report Performance

B. Manage Stakeholder Expectations

C. Plan Communications

D. Identify Stakeholders

22. A project manager drew up a resource histogram. On plotting the histogram, he found that some bars extended beyond the maximum available hours. What does this usually signify?

A. This means that the resources on those bars are being underutilized.

B. This means that a resource leveling strategy needs to be applied

C. This means that the resources are producing outputs at a rate faster than the average rate.

D. This means that resources need to be reduced from the project.

23. A project manager is planning out the availability of resources as part of the Acquire Project Team phase. He needs to acquire resources that report to a functional manager. What

technique will he likely use to obtain these resources?

A. Pre-assignment

B. Authority

C. Negotiation

D. Coercion

24. Which of the following statements about project teams is incorrect?

A. The project management team is usually a team external to the project team.

B. The project management team is a subset of the project team.

C. For smaller projects, the project management responsibilities can be shared by the entire team.

D. For smaller projects, the project management responsibilities can be administered solely by the project manger.

25. A new project to setup a power generation plant is likely to displace current residents who live in the vicinity of the plant. The project manager of this project decides to include the residents as part of his stakeholder list. What would he classify them as?

A. Repatriated stakeholders

B. Displaced stakeholders

C. Positive stakeholders

D. Negative stakeholders

26. Sheila has been assigned as the project manager of a project. After a detailed discussion with the project management team, she decides to come up with a quality management plan that is informal and broadly framed. What would your comment on this be?

A. This is incorrect. A quality management plan should be formal but broadly framed.

B. This is incorrect. A quality management plan should be formal and highly detailed.

C. This is fine. The style and detail of the quality management plan is determined by the requirements of the project.

D. This is incorrect. A quality management plan should be informal and highly detailed.

27. A project manager was involved in preparation of the project charter for an external project. One of the inputs to the project charter was a statement of work (SOW). The SOW may have been received from the customer as part of all of the following except:

A. As part of a request for information

B. As part of the business case

C. As part of a request for proposal

D. As part of a contract

28. A project manager is determining dependencies that will require a lead or a lag to accurately define the logical relationship. Which of the following correctly describes leads or lags?

A. A lead allows a successor activity to be delayed.

B. A lag directs a delay in the predecessor activity.

C. A lag allows an acceleration of the successor activity.

D. A lead allows an acceleration of the successor activity.

29. Which of the following scenarios is likely to occur in a project?

A. During the early phases of an engineering design project, the project pool of resources included both junior and senior engineers in large numbers. During later phases, the pool was limited to people who were knowledgeable about the project.

B. During the early phases of an engineering design project, the project pool of resources included only senior engineers. During later phases, the pool was limited to junior engineers.

C. During the early phases of an engineering design project, the project pool of resources included only junior engineers. During later phases, the pool was limited to senior engineers.

D. During all phases of an engineering design project, the project pool of resources had the same number of junior and senior engineers.

30. A project began and was in the Collect Requirements phase. The people that used the product were unable to articulate their requirements and had difficulty doing so. In this scenario, which of the following tools could help determine the requirements?

A. Prototypes

B. Observations

C. Surveys

D. Questionnaires

31. A project manager estimated that a project would require 4375 person hours of effort. The project ended up using 6250 person hours of effort. This effort could be broken down into 4 groups as follows:
Group 1: 550 hours
Group 2: 1200 hours
Group 3: 4100 hours
Group 4: 400 hours

Which of these groups of effort could be expected to include effort from the Perform Quality Assurance phase?

A. Group 3

B. Group 1

C. Group 4

D. Group 2

32. Projects can deliver products that vary in quality and grade. Which of the following people is responsible for managing the tradeoffs involved to deliver the required level of quality and grade?

A. The customer

B. The project sponsor

C. The quality team

D. The project manager

33. A project manager is considering risk in a project. When does risk come into play in a project?

A. During the SWOT (strengths, weaknesses, opportunities, and threats) analysis.

B. During the Identify Risks phase.

C. As soon as the Plan Risk Management phase begins

D. As soon as a project is conceived

34. The scope of work in a project could not be clearly defined. There was also a strong possibility that the scope would be altered during the course of the project. Which type of contract would suit this type of situation?

A. Fixed price with economic price adjustment contract

B. Fixed-price contract

C. Cost-reimbursable contract

D. Fixed price incentive contract

35. An experienced project manager was assigned a project of very small scope. Which of the following scenarios could be representative of the project?

A. Defining Activities, sequencing activities, estimating activity resources, and developing the schedule could be viewed as a single process

B. Estimating activity resources may be skipped for the project

C. Developing and Controlling the schedule could be viewed as a single process

D. Defining Activities, estimating activity resources, developing the schedule, and controlling the schedule could be viewed as a single process

36. Jackie is the project manager of large project. During the Determine Budget phase, she identifies that contingency reserves need to be made for unplanned but potentially required changes that could result from realized risks identified in the risk register. Which of the following is true about reserves?

A. Reserves are not a part of project cost baseline, but may be included in the total budget for the project

B. Reserves are not a part of project cost baseline, and will not be included in the total budget for the project

C. Reserves are a part of project cost baseline, but will not be included in the total budget for the project

D. Reserves are a part of project cost baseline, and will be included in the total budget for the project

37. The legal nature of the contractual relationship between a buyer and a seller requires that appropriate legal counsel be involved in the project, for specific activities. Which of the following phases requires legal counsel to be involved.

A. Administer procurements

B. Plan procurements

C. Conduct procurements

D. All the above phases

38. A project manager is looking at a make-or-buy analysis as part of the Plan Procurements phase. What type of costs should the project manager consider for this analysis?

A. Direct costs

B. Indirect costs

C. Out-of-pocket costs

D. Both direct as well as indirect costs

39. Abraham Maslow was a humanistic psychologist who came up with a theory called the 'Hierarchy theory of needs'. As per his theory, there are five basic needs, and people do not feel the need for subsequent needs until their earlier needs have been met. As per his theory, the five needs from lowest to highest are:

A. Psychological needs, needs of belongingness, safety needs, needs for esteem, and needs for self-actualization

B. Physiological needs, safety needs, needs of belongingness, needs for esteem, and needs for self-actualization

C. Safety needs, physiological needs, needs of belongingness, needs for esteem, and needs for self-actualization

D. Psychological needs, safety needs, needs of belongingness, needs for esteem, and needs for self-actualization

40. During the execution of a project, a large number of defects were discovered. The project manager ensured that the issues, defect resolution and action item results were logged into a defects database. What would the defect database be considered a part of?

A. Expert Judgment

B. Deliverables

C. Change Requests

D. Organizational Process Assets

41. The WBS structure can be created in a number of forms except which of the following?

A. Using project deliverables as the first level of decomposition, with the phases of the project life cycle inserted at the second level.

B. Using major deliverables as the first level of decomposition.

C. Using phases of the project life cycle as the first level of decomposition, with the project deliverables inserted at the second level.

D. Using subprojects which may be developed by organizations outside the project team, such as contracted work.

42. A project manager is addressing stakeholder concerns that have not become issues yet, and is also trying to anticipate future problems. Which process group is this likely be to done in?

    A. Distribute Information

    B. Identify Stakeholders

    C. Plan Communications

    D. Manage Stakeholder Expectations

43. Which of the following may not be considered an attribute of a project?

    A. Repetitive elements may be present in some project deliverables.

    B. The impact of a project usually ends when the project ends.

    C. A project can involve a single person.

    D. There is uncertainty about the product that the project creates.

44. Which of the following structures is helpful in tracking project costs and can be aligned with the organization's accounting system?

    A. Project breakdown structure (PBS)

    B. Matrix breakdown structure (MBS)

    C. Resource breakdown structure (RBS)

    D. Organizational breakdown structure (OBS)

45. A first-time project manager is advised by an experienced project manager that he needs to plan for cost of quality. The first-time project manager is not sure of what costs are included in the cost of quality. What would your advise be?

    A. Cost of quality only includes cost of nonconformance

    B. Cost of quality includes cost of conformance and cost of nonconformance

    C. Cost of quality only includes prevention costs and internal failure costs.

    D. Cost of quality only includes cost of conformance

46. Miranda is an experienced project manager. As part of the Collect Requirements phase, she decides to use a group creativity technique. This technique is expected to enhance brainstorming with a voting process, and can be used to rank the most useful ideas for further brainstorming or prioritization. Which of the following will she likely use?

A. Normal group technique

B. Minimal group technique

C. Unanimous group technique

D. Nominal group technique

47. In which of the following situations would it be better to avoid using Analogous Estimating?

A. When the project team members have the needed expertise

B. When an accurate estimate is required

C. When an inexpensive estimate is required

D. When the previous activities are similar in fact and not just appearance

48. A group of people were discussing multiple alternatives during the Collect Requirements process. One of the individuals in the group made the decision for the group. This method of reaching a group decision would be termed as:

A. One Thinking Hat

B. Dictatorship

C. Plurality

D. Autonomy

49. Which of the following processes will determine the correctness of deliverables?

A. Plan Quality Assurance

B. Plan Quality phase

C. Perform Quality Control

D. Perform Quality Assurance

50. All of the monitoring and control processes and many of the executing processes produce change requests as an output. Change requests include corrective action and preventive action. Which of the following are normally affected by corrective and preventive actions?

A. Defect repair

B. Regressive baselines

C. The project baselines

D. The performance against baselines

PMP Lite Mock Exam 15
Answer Key and Explanations

1. C - While calculating the duration of schedule activities, differences in the capabilities of staff assigned should be taken into consideration. Hence, a senior staff member will generally be expected to finish an activity in less time than a junior member. There is no generic rule that a senior resource will finish an activity in 80% of the time that a junior resource.
[Refer PMBOK 4th Edition, page 148] [Project Time Management]

2. C - Actions such as adopting less complex processes, more testing, or choosing a more stable supplier would be considered as mitigation. These actions reduce the probability and/or impact of risks.
[Refer PMBOK 4th Edition, page 304] [Project Risk Management]

3. B - The Close Project or Phase process establishes the procedures to investigate and document the reasons for actions taken if a project is terminated before completion.
[Refer PMBOK 4th Edition, page 100] [Project Integration Management]

4. A - The project manager is correct. Prevention is about keeping errors out of the process whereas inspection is about keeping errors out of the hands of the customer. This is an important that the project management team needs to be aware of.
[Refer PMBOK 4th Edition, page 206] [Project Quality Management]

5. C - A composite resource calendar does not usually contain cost information. The other choices are valid constituents of a resource calendar.
[Refer PMBOK 4th Edition, page 143] [Project Time Management]

6. C - Authority is the best choice. Authority is the right to apply project resources and make decisions within the project. These decisions could include quality acceptance, selection of the method for completing an activity, and how to respond to project variances.
[Refer PMBOK 4th Edition, page 223] [Project Human Resource Management]

7. C - Prioritization matrices provide a way of ranking a set of problems and/or issues that are usually generated through brainstorming.
[Refer PMBOK 4th Edition, page 200] [Project Quality Management]

8. A - This is known as Funding limit reconciliation. It can be accomplished by placing imposed date constraints for work.
[Refer PMBOK 4th Edition, page 178] [Project Cost Management]

9. D - Focus groups bring together prequalified stakeholders and subject matter experts to learn about their expectations and attitudes about a proposed product, service or result. Typically a trained moderator is used

to guide the group through an interactive discussion.
[Refer PMBOK 4th Edition, page 107] [Project Scope Management]

10. A - A configuration management system, including change control processes provides a mechanism for the project management team to consistently communicate all approved and rejected changes to the stakeholders.
[Refer PMBOK 4th Edition, page 94] [Project Integration Management]

11. A - Power/Interest grids are used to group stakeholders based on their level of authority ("power") and their level of concern ("interest") regarding project outcomes. A stakeholder classified as low on the "interest" scale, and low on the "power" scale will be classified in the "Monitor" quadrant. This involves minimum effort. In contrast, stakeholders classified as High/High on the Power/Interest scale will need to be managed closely.
[Refer PMBOK 4th Edition, page 249] [Project Communications Management]

12. B - The completion of project scope is measured against the project management plan whereas the completion of product scope is measured against the product requirements. The work of the project results in delivery of the specified product scope.
[Refer PMBOK 4th Edition, page 105] [Project Scope Management]

13. D - Conflict is usually inevitable in a project environment. When managed properly, it can lead to better productivity and decision making. Although conflict should be addressed early and in private, it is still considered a team issue since it could affect the morale / performance of the entire team.
[Refer PMBOK 4th Edition, page 239] [Project Human Resource Management]

14. C - Identify Risks is an iterative process as new risks evolve or become known in a project. The frequency of iteration, and who participates in each cycle, will vary by the situation.
[Refer PMBOK 4th Edition, page 282] [Project Risk Management]

15. C - Regression analysis using the autoregressive moving average (ARMA) method is classified as a causal / econometric method of forecasting. Such methods use the assumption that it is possible to identify the underlying factors that might influence the variable that is being forecasted.
[Refer PMBOK 4th Edition, page 269] [Project Communications Management]

16. A - In such a situation, the project manager needs to assert his authority to hold the project meetings at a time that is convenient to most people. Negotiation may be an option, but with the time-zone difference being an unavoidable aspect of the work, it may not result in a solution. Coercion

is too drastic a step, and Co-location is not a practical solution.
[Refer PMBOK 4th Edition, page 26, 256] [Project Communications Management]

17. D - Acceptance is a strategy adopted because it is not possible to eliminate all risks from a project. This strategy indicates that the project management team has decided not to change the project management plan to deal with a risk. It requires no action except to document the strategy.
[Refer PMBOK 4th Edition, page 304] [Project Risk Management]

18. D - Unit labor or material rates are usually fixed up between the buyer and seller in case of Time and Material contracts. Specific categories such as junior or senior engineers at specific hourly rates are agreed upon by both parties.
[Refer PMBOK 4th Edition, page 324] [Project Procurement Management]

19. B - This is done in the Estimate Costs phase. The project manager works in accordance with the organization's guidelines and decides whether the estimates will be limited to direct project costs only or whether the estimates will also include indirect costs. Indirect costs are those that cannot be traced to one specific project, and are usually allocated equitably over multiple projects.
[Refer PMBOK 4th Edition, page 169] [Project Cost Management]

20. D - Risk reassessment is done as part of the Monitor and Control Risks process. Such project risk reassessments should be regularly scheduled and may result in the closure of outdated risks.
[Refer PMBOK 4th Edition, page 310] [Project Risk Management]

21. C - Deciding what information is relevant to an audience is an activity done in the Plan Communications phase. Improper communication planning will lead to problems such as delay in message delivery or communication of sensitive information to the wrong audience.
[Refer PMBOK 4th Edition, page 252] [Project Communications Management]

22. B - If the bars in a resource histogram extend beyond the maximum available hours, it means that a resource leveling strategy needs to be applied, such as adding more resources or modifying the schedule.
[Refer PMBOK 4th Edition, page 225] [Project Human Resource Management]

23. C - Staff assignments are negotiated on many projects. The project manager will negotiate with functional managers to ensure that the project receives competent staff in the required time-frame.
[Refer PMBOK 4th Edition, page 227] [Project Human Resource Management]

24. A - The project management team is a subset of the project team and is responsible for the project management and leadership activities such as initiating, planning, executing,

monitoring, controlling, and closing the various project phases. For smaller projects, the responsibilities can be shared by the entire team, or taken up solely by the project manager.
[Refer PMBOK 4th Edition, page 215] [Project Human Resource Management]

25. D - Stakeholders who perceive a negative outcome from the success of a project are called negative stakeholders. Current residents, who live close to the area where the plant is going to be set up, are likely to be displaced by the project. They will be negatively impacted. Hence, the project manager needs to take them into consideration. Overlooking negative stakeholders results in an increased likelihood of failure. [Refer PMBOK 4th Edition, page 24] [Project Framework]

26. C - The quality management plan may be formal or informal, highly detailed or broadly framed. The style and detail is determined by the requirements of the project as defined by the project management team.
[Refer PMBOK 4th Edition, page 200] [Project Quality Management]

27. B - The statement of work (SOW) is a narrative description of products or services to be delivered by the project. For an external project, the SOW may be received as part of a bid document such as the request for proposal, request for information, request for bid or as part of a contract. It is usually not part of the business case.

[Refer PMBOK 4th Edition, page 75] [Project Integration Management]

28. D - The project management team determines dependencies that will require a lead or a lag to accurately define the logical relationship. A lead allows an acceleration of the successor activity.
[Refer PMBOK 4th Edition, page 140] [Project Time Management]

29. A - During the early phases of an engineering design project, the project pool of resources may include both junior and senior engineers in large numbers. During later phases, the pool is limited to people who are knowledgeable about the project. This is as a result of having worked on the earlier phases of the project.
The other scenarios mentioned are impractical.
[Refer PMBOK 4th Edition, page 143] [Project Time Management]

30. B - Observations provide a direct way of viewing individuals in their environment. It is an extremely useful tool when the people using a product are unable to articulate their requirements. It is often done to uncover hidden requirements.
[Refer PMBOK 4th Edition, page 109] [Project Scope Management]

31. A - Perform Quality Assurance is an Executing Process Group. This process group usually takes the largest effort in a project and corresponds to group 3. Hence, group 3 is the correct choice.
[Refer PMBOK 4th Edition, page 16 and 41] [Project Framework]

32. D - The project manager and the project management team are responsible for managing the tradeoffs involved to deliver the required level of quality and grade. [Refer PMBOK 4th Edition, page 190] [Project Quality Management]

33. D - Project risk exists in a project the moment the project is conceived. The risks are identified as part of specific processes, but the risk always exist. [Refer PMBOK 4th Edition, page 276] [Project Risk Management]

34. C - A cost-reimbursable contract gives the project flexibility to redirect a seller whenever the scope of work cannot be precisely determined at the start of the project and needs to be altered, or when high risks may exist in the effort. [Refer PMBOK 4th Edition, page 323] [Project Procurement Management]

35. A - On projects with small scope, defining Activities, sequencing activities, estimating activity resources, and developing the schedule are very tightly linked, and are often viewed as a single process. The other choices are incorrect. [Refer PMBOK 4th Edition, page 129] [Project Time Management]

36. A - Reserves are not a part of project cost baseline, but may be included in the total budget for the project. A project manager may require approval before spending reserves. [Refer PMBOK 4th Edition, page 177] [Project Cost Management]

37. D - The legal nature of the contractual relationship between a buyer and a seller makes it important that appropriate legal counsel is involved in the project for all the phases listed. Of these, it is likely that the Administer Procurements phase will require a greater involvement of legal counsel. [Refer PMBOK 4th Edition, page 315,335] [Project Procurement Management]

38. D - The make-or-buy analysis needs to be as comprehensive as possible. Hence it should consider all possible costs - both direct and indirect costs. [Refer PMBOK 4th Edition, page 321] [Project Procurement Management]

39. B - As per Abraham Maslow's theory of motivation, humans have needs in the order of physiological needs, safety needs, needs of belongingness, needs for esteem, and needs for self-actualization. [General HR theory, Wikipedia] [Project Human Resource Management]

40. D - Issue and defect management databases are considered part of the organizational process assets. They typically contains historical issue and defect status, control information, issue and defect resolution, and action item results. [Refer PMBOK 4th Edition, page 86] [Project Integration Management]

41. A - The WBS structure is not created using project deliverables as the first level of decomposition, with the

phases of the project life cycle inserted at the second level. The converse is true. The other three choices are valid forms in which the WBS structure may be created.
[Refer PMBOK 4th Edition, page 118] [Project Scope Management]

42. D - This is done in the Manage Stakeholder Expectations process. It involves communication activities directed towards stakeholders and addresses concerns that have not become issues yet, usually related to the anticipation of future problems.
[Refer PMBOK 4th Edition, page 252] [Project Communications Management]

43. B - The impact of a project may far outlast the project itself. The other choices are valid attributes of projects.
A project may involve a single person, a single organizational unit, or multiple organizational units.
Repetitive elements may be present in some project deliverables, but this does not change the fundamental uniqueness of the project work.
Additionally because of the unique nature of the work, there are usually uncertainties about the work involved.
[Refer PMBOK 4th Edition, page 5] [Project Framework]

44. C - The resource breakdown structure (RBS) is helpful in tracking project costs and can be aligned with the organization's accounting system. It can contain resource categories other than human resources.

[Refer PMBOK 4th Edition, page 220] [Project Human Resource Management]

45. B - Cost of quality (COQ) includes all costs incurred over the life of a product. It includes cost of conformance (prevention and appraisal costs) as well cost of nonconformance (internal and external failure costs). [Refer PMBOK 4th Edition, page 195] [Project Quality Management]

46. D - Miranda likely intends to use the Nominal group technique. This enhances brainstorming with a voting process to rank the most useful ideas for further brainstorming or prioritization.
[Refer PMBOK 4th Edition, page 108] [Project Scope Management]

47. B - Analogous estimating is generally less costly than other techniques and are generally less accurate. It is most reliable when previous activities are similar in fact, and the project team members have the needed expertise.
[Refer PMBOK 4th Edition, page 149] [Project Time Management]

48. B - The method where a single individual makes the decision on behalf of a group is termed as Dictatorship. Other group decision making techniques are Unanimity (everyone agrees on a course of action), Majority (Support from more than 50% of the members of the group) and plurality (The largest block in a group decides even if a majority is not achieved).

[Refer PMBOK 4th Edition, page 108] [Project Scope Management]

49.   C - An important goal of quality control is to determine the correctness of deliverables. The results of the execution of quality control processes are validated deliverables. These are then an input to the Verify Scope phase for formalized acceptance.
[Refer PMBOK 4th Edition, page 213] [Project Quality Management]

50.   D - Corrective and preventive actions do not normally affect the project baselines, only the performance against the baselines. [Refer PMBOK 4th Edition, page 97] [Project Integration Management]

PMP Lite Mock Exam 16
Practice Questions

Test Name: PMP Lite Mock Exam 16
Total Questions: 50
Correct Answers Needed to Pass:
35 (70.00%)
Time Allowed: 60 Minutes

Test Description

This is a cumulative PMP Mock Exam which can be used as a benchmark for your PMP aptitude. This practice test includes questions from all PMBOK knowledge areas, including the five basic project management process groups.

Test Questions

1. A project manager is analyzing the relationship between the consumption of project funds and the physical work being accomplished for such expenditures. In which project management process would this be done?

    A. Determine Budget

    B. Estimate Costs

    C. Control Costs

    D. Manage Costs

2. As part of the Estimate Costs phase, a project manager obtained access to certain commercially available databases to get resource cost rate information. What type of input is such published commercial information considered as?

    A. Enterprise environmental factor

    B. Historical information

    C. Organizational process asset

    D. HR Input

3. A project needed to monitor the technical performance of the project and capture data related to how many errors or defects had been identified, and how many remained uncorrected. Which of the following techniques should the project use?

    A. Scatter diagram

    B. Pareto chart

    C. Run chart

    D. Histogram

4. Which of the following is not an example of parametric estimating?

    A. Activity duration estimated based on the number of drawings multiplied by the number of labor hours per drawing.

B. Activity duration estimated based on the number of labor hours per meter for cable installation.

C. Activity duration estimated based on the square footage in construction.

D. Activity duration estimated based on the actual duration of a similar, previous project.

5. The quality cost of a project went up significantly during the course of a project. A post-mortem analysis of the increased cost revealed that this was due to poorly defined acceptance criteria. During which phase should the acceptance criteria have been properly captured?

A. Develop Project Charter phase

B. Define Scope phase

C. Manage Stakeholder Expectations phase

D. Plan Quality phase

6. A project manager is looking at tools and techniques to use in the Report Performance process. What communication method should he prefer to use for status reporting?

A. Need-based communication

B. Pull communication

C. Informal communication

D. Push communication

7. A project charter that formally authorized a project was created. The project charter documented the initial requirements to satisfy stakeholders' needs and expectations. How often should the project charter ideally be revised?

A. At the beginning, middle and end of a project.

B. Once a month

C. Never

D. As required by the PMO.

8. Kelly, the project manager of a large project, found that she did not have the necessary number of resources required for some activities in the project. To account for the limited resources, she decided to apply the critical chain method. Which of the following would she use to protect the critical chain from slippage along the feeding chains?

A. Feeding buffers

B. Standby buffers

C. Overflow buffers

D. Dependent buffers

9. A statement of work (SOW) is a narrative description of the products or services to be delivered by the

project. It usually references all of the following except:

A. The business case

B. The product scope description

C. The strategic plan

D. The business need

10. A project manager wanted to obtain early feedback on the project requirements. However, she was concerned that the abstract representations of the requirements might not elicit useful feedback. Which of the following tools and techniques might help her overcome this hurdle?

A. Focus groups

B. Prototypes

C. Interviews

D. Questionnaires

11. A project manager needed to shorten a project schedule. He decided to apply crashing, a schedule compression technique. Which of the following activities would not be an example of crashing?

A. Bringing in additional resources

B. Reducing project scope

C. Paying to expedite delivery activities

D. Approving overtime

12. A project can be authorized by any of the following except:

A. The project manager

B. The PMO

C. The sponsor

D. The portfolio steering committee

13. A research project needed to be carried out under largely undefined, uncertain and rapidly changing environmental conditions. If this project is carried out as a multi-phase project, which of the following phase-to-phase relationships best suits it?

A. Overlapping relationship

B. Sequential relationship

C. Iterative relationship

D. Boxed relationship

14. A first-time project manager created a Work Breakdown Structure (WBS) where the deliverables had different levels of decomposition. What would your comment on this be?

A. This is incorrect. All deliverables need to have the same level of decomposition.

B. This is incorrect. Only deliverables under different branches can have different levels of decomposition.

C. This is fine. Different deliverables can have different levels of decomposition depending on the work involved.

D. This is fine. The focus of the WBS is not the deliverables, but the tasks involved.

15. A project was plagued by many quality problems. The quality of the work products deviated considerably from specifications. The project manager decided to do a root cause analysis. What activities does a root cause analysis include?

A. Discovery of the underlying causes of a problem

B. Problem Identification and discovery of the underlying causes of a problem.

C. Identification of a problem.

D. Problem identification, discovery of the underlying causes of a problem, and development of preventive actions.

16. Decision tree analysis is used to calculate the average outcome when the future includes scenarios that may or may not happen. What is the input and output in a decision node?

A. Input: Cost of each decision
Output: Probability of occurrence

B. Input: Cost of each decision
Output: Decision made

C. Input: Scenario probability
Output: Expected Monetary Value (EMV)

D. Input: Cost of each decision
Output: Payoff

17. Sensitivity analysis helps to determine which risks have the most potential impact on the project. A project manager prepared a display chart of sensitivity analysis for his project. The diagram contained a series of bars with the length of the bars corresponding to the risk impact on the project. The longer the bars, the greater was the risk presented. Such a diagram is likely to be:

A. An assessment diagram

B. A triangular distribution

C. A tornado diagram

D. A funnel distribution

18. A project manager was keen to ensure that the information she provided was both effective and efficient. How should she differentiate between these two terms?

A. Efficient communication means that the information is provided in the right format, at the right time, and with the right impact. Effective communication means providing only the information that is needed.

B. Both, effective, and efficient communication, are interchangeable terms in the context of project management.

C. Effective communication means that the information is provided in written form in the right format.
Efficient communication means providing selective information.

D. Effective communication means that the information is provided in the right format, at the right time, and with the right impact.
Efficient communication means providing only the information that is needed.

19. As part of the Plan Risk Management process, a project manager is looking at the activity of preparing a risk management plan. Which of the following is true about risks?

A. A risk may have one or more causes and, if it occurs, may have one or more impacts.

B. A risk usually has a single cause and, if it occurs, may have one or more impacts.

C. A risk usually has a single cause and if it occurs usually has a single impact.

D. A risk usually has more than one cause, and if it occurs, may have one or more impacts.

20. Analysis of the scope performance resulted in a change request to the scope baseline. Change requests can include all of the following except:

A. Defect repairs

B. Supportive action

C. Corrective actions

D. Preventive actions

21. A seller organization was executing work for a project under a contract. During the course of the project, a number of disputes arose over the scope and quality of work. Which of the following is the preferred method of resolving these claims?

A. Alternative dispute resolution (ADR)

B. Claims court

C. Appeals court

D. Negotiation

22. Which of the following is incorrect regarding a bidders conference?

A. Questions from each seller should be handled confidentially and not shared with other sellers.

B. No bidders should receive preferential treatment, even if they are part of the company's existing list of approved suppliers.

C. Bidders conferences should not involve face-to-face meetings

D. All prospective sellers should be allowed to have a common understanding of the procurement.

23. The Actual Cost (AC) is the total cost actually incurred and recorded in accomplishing work performed for an activity or work breakdown structure component. What is the upper limit for the AC?

A. 50% over and above the Planned Value (PV)

B. The Actual Cost (AC) is limited to the Planned Value (PV).

C. 100% over and above the Planned Value (PV)

D. There is no upper limit for the Actual Cost (AC).

24. You are the project manager of a project executing work under a contract signed with a buyer organization. Just after the project has started, you notice that the buyer organization had made a mistake in the financial terms and your organization stands to benefit

considerably through this oversight. What should your stance be?

A. Do not take any action since a contract is a binding and legal document.

B. Discuss with your management on how you could gain a bonus due to the increased revenue your company stands to gain.

C. Informally check with your counterpart in the buyer organization to see if they have noticed this error.

D. Bring the error to the notice of the buyer organization and have an amendment made to the contract since this was in good faith.

25. A project manager uses precedence diagramming method (PDM) to constructing a project schedule network and draws up a network diagram for the purpose. He decides to use the most common type of precedence relationship for all activities. Which of the following relationships would he use?

A. Start-to-finish (SF)

B. Finish-to-finish (FF)

C. Start-to-start (SS)

D. Finish-to-start (FS)

26. A project manager wanted to ensure that he avoided any win-lose (zero sum) types of rewards in his project. Which of the following rewards and recognition mechanisms could be classified as zero sum?

A. Updating of defects data into the defects database on time.

B. Team member of the month award

C. Attendance at a weekly project team meeting

D. Submission of progress reports in time award

27. Sheila is a project manager managing a global project. She has stakeholders located in various parts of the globe. Due to the nature of the project, she also has large volumes of information that needs to be shared with the recipients. What type of communication method should she prefer for this purpose?

A. Pull communication

B. Push communication

C. Request based communication

D. Interactive communication

28. Dan is a project manager in an organization and conducts a workshop on project management. Which of the following statements

made by him about projects is incorrect?

A. Projects exist within an organization and operate as a closed system.

B. Project processes usually generate information that helps improve the management of future projects.

C. Successful project management includes meeting sponsor, customer, and other stakeholder requirements.

D. Project management is an integrative undertaking.

29. Rick, a project manager, is updating its status of his project. Based on the performance indices, he expects the project to finish a month ahead of its planned finish date. However, he expects the project to exceed budgeted costs. What can you say about the schedule performance index (SPI) of the project?

A. The SPI is less than 1.0.

B. The SPI equals the CPI.

C. The SPI is greater than 1.0.

D. The SPI is equal to 1.0.

30. Kelly is part of a project management office (PMO) Her office is responsible for the centralized and coordinated management of 18 projects. Each project has its own project manager. Which of the following will not typically be a responsibility of her office (PMO)?

A. Coaching, mentoring, training, and oversight.

B. Development of a detailed description of each project and the product it produces.

C. Managing shared resources across all the projects administered by the PMO.

D. Developing and managing project policies.

31. Variance Analysis is an important tool used in the Control Costs Process. Which of the following statements regarding variances is correct?

A. The percentage range of acceptable variances will tend to increase as more work is accomplished and the project nears completion

B. The percentage range of acceptable variances will tend to decrease as more work is accomplished and the project nears completion

C. The percentage range of acceptable variances is high at the start of a project, tends to decrease in the middle of a project, and then tends to increase as the project nears completion

D. The percentage range of acceptable variances is a constant all through the project

32. As part of risk planning, some responses are designed for use only if certain events occur. A project manager of a multi-year project decided to trigger one such set of responses during the Monitor and Control Risks phase. Which of the following is likely to have triggered the responses?

A. Late receipt of status reports

B. A key employee going on vacation for three days.

C. Errors found in a deliverable document

D. Missing an intermediate milestone

33. Stakeholder analysis is an important technique in the Identify Stakeholders process. One of the steps involved is to identify the potential impact of each stakeholder and classify them appropriately. Which of the following is not a valid model used for this purpose?

A. Salience model

B. Tolerance model

C. Power / interest grid

D. Influence / impact grid

34. A key project in an organization has been ignored due to high travel expenses associated with the movement of subject matter experts and other specialists across various project locations. Which of the following will permit such a project to be taken up in a cost-efficient manner?

    A. Management sign-off

    B. Negotiation

    C. Virtual teams

    D. Co-location

35. A new project manager has just taken over a project that is 50% complete. As part of the hand-over process, the outgoing project manager provided the new project manager with a list of stakeholders that needed to be managed. The list had been drawn up at the start of the project. Which of the following is true about stakeholders?

    A. Stakeholder identification is usually performed when there are problems with the project

    B. Stakeholder identification needs to happen at the start of each new phase of a project

    C. Stakeholder identification is a continuous process and needs to happen all through the project

    D. Stakeholder identification needs to happen at the start of the project

36. A project manager is performing a set of processes in the Initiating Process Group. Which of the following is likely to be part of the Initiating Process Group?

    A. Develop Project Management Plan

    B. Define Scope

    C. Develop Project Charter

    D. Plan Quality

37. During the course of the project, the project management team developed a forecast for the estimate at completion (EAC) based on the project performance. Which of the following statements about EAC is correct?

    A. Any of the above three approaches can be correct for any given project.

    B. The EAC forecast is best estimated using the estimate to complete (ETC) work performed considering both SPI and CPI factors.

    C. The EAC forecast is best estimated using the estimate to complete (ETC) work performed at the present CPI.

D. The EAC forecast is best estimated using the estimate to complete (ETC) work performed at the budgeted rate.

B. Survey

C. Prototypes

D. Affinity diagram

38. A project manager is confused about the perspective of the buyer-seller relationship in the context of project procurement management. How would your clarify this?

A. The buyer-seller relationship exists only between organizations external to the acquiring organization.

B. The buyer-seller relationship is only between organizations internal and external to the acquiring organization.

C. The buyer-seller relationship is applicable only when a performing organization is involved.

D. The buyer-seller relationship can exist at many levels on one project, and between organizations internal to and external to the acquiring organization.

39. It was found that there were a large number of hidden requirements to be uncovered in the Collect Requirements phase. Which of the following tools should a project manager use to identify them?

A. Participant observer

40. Stakeholder identification is a continuous process. Which of the following statements about stakeholders is incorrect?

A. Positive stakeholders benefit from the outcome of a project

B. A project manager needs to focus on the positive stakeholders since their needs are best served by the project

C. Overlooking negative stakeholders can result in an increased likelihood of failure

D. Stakeholders can have conflicting or differing objectives

41. Which of the following is not an enterprise environmental factor influencing the Develop Project Management Plan process?

A. Industry standards

B. Hiring and firing guidelines

C. Work performance information

D. Employee performance review

42. A project manager in a seller organization discovered that certain deliverables had been handed over to the buyer without undergoing proper testing. Recalling the deliverables will result in a cost overrun to the project. What should the project manager do in such a case?

A. Recall the deliverables even though there will be a cost overrun.

B. Terminate the project.

C. Approach management to obtain additional funding to handle the potential cost overrun.

D. Wait for the procuring organization to get back with their list of defects in the deliverables.

43. Matt is the project manager of a project that involves a buyer-seller relationship. If teaming agreements are a part of this project, to what process would they be an input?

A. Administer Procurements

B. Conduct Procurements

C. Close Procurements

D. Teaming agreements do not apply in the context of buyer-seller relationships.

44. A project manager is estimating the project duration and finds that the only information available to him is a previous project that was quite different from the current one.

However, some portions of the previous project were similar to the current one. Which of the following tools is the project manager likely to use?

A. Analogous estimating

B. Program Evaluation and Review Technique (PERT)

C. Three-point estimates

D. Parametric estimating

45. During the Conduct Procurements phase, the procuring organization found that there were significant differences in the pricing by different sellers. What is the best course of action in such a scenario?

A. Award the project to a supplier who is already on the procuring organization's preferred supplier list.

B. Cancel the procurement activity.

C. Investigate whether the project statement of work was defective or ambiguous.

D. Award the project to the highest bidder.

46. A first-time project manager was of the opinion that all training activities need to be planned. He discussed this with an experienced project manager, and understood that some training was necessarily unplanned. Which of

the following correctly lists examples of unplanned training?

A. Training by observation, conversation, and project management appraisals

B. Training by mentoring, on-the-job training, and online courses

C. Training by conversation, coaching, and classroom training

D. Training by mentoring, observation, and coaching

47. A project manager used a control chart to determine whether a process was stable or not, and to determine if its performance was predictable. He determined the upper and lower specification limits based on the contractual requirements. A set of eighteen data points were taken. Of these, 8 consecutive data points were above or below the mean. What can you say about such a process?

A. A process is considered as out of control if five consecutive data points are above or below the mean. Hence the process is out of control.

B. A process is considered as out of control if nine consecutive data points are above or below the mean. Hence the process is within control.

C. A process is considered as being within control if less than half the data points are above or below

the mean. Hence the process is within control.

D. A process is considered as out of control if seven consecutive data points are above or below the mean. Hence the process is out of control.

48. While analyzing the risk in a project, a project manager came up with a Risk Urgency Assessment document. In which process would this be done?

A. Close Risks

B. Monitor and Control Risks

C. Perform Qualitative Risk Analysis

D. Plan Risk Management

49. A project manager is looking at various classification methods to share information among project stakeholders. Which of the following correctly classifies the different methods used?

A. Pull communication - Meetings
Push communication - Newsletters
Interactive communication - E-learning repository

B. Interactive communication - Meetings
Push communication - E-learning repository
Pull communication - Newsletters

C. Push communication - Meetings
Pull communication - Newsletters

Interactive communication - E-learning repository

D. Interactive communication - Meetings
Push communication - Newsletters
Pull communication - E-learning repository

50. Which of the following roles in a project is more likely to be involved in negotiations on procurements during the Conduct Procurements phase?

A. Legal representative

B. Project team member

C. Project manager

D. Project sponsor

PMP Lite Mock Exam 16
Answer Key and Explanations

1. C - Control Costs is the process of monitoring the status of a project to update the project budget and managing changes to the cost baseline. Much of the effort of cost control involves analyzing the relationship between the consumption of project funds to the physical work being accomplished for such expenditures.
[Refer PMBOK 4th Edition, page 179] [Project Cost Management]

2. A - Such published commercial information is considered as part of enterprise environmental factors that influence the Estimate Costs process.
[Refer PMBOK 4th Edition, page 171] [Project Cost Management]

3. C - Trend analysis is performed using run charts and involves mathematical techniques to forecast future outcomes based on historical results. It is often used to monitor the technical performance of the project to capture data related to how many errors or defects have been identified, and how many remain uncorrected.
[Refer PMBOK 4th Edition, page 212] [Project Quality Management]

4. D - Activity duration estimated based on the actual duration of a similar, previous project is an instance of Analogous estimating. The other three choices are examples of parametric estimating.
[Refer PMBOK 4th Edition, page 149] [Project Time Management]

5. B - Acceptance criteria are documented in the project scope statement, developed during the Define Scope phase. Poorly defined acceptance criteria would then propagate to the Plan Quality phase used for planning quality. Poorly defined acceptance criteria can significantly increase or decrease costs in a project.
[Refer PMBOK 4th Edition, page 193] [Project Quality Management]

6. D - Status reports need to be sent only to specific recipients who need to know the information. This is done by push communication. Push communication ensures that the information is distributed but does not certify that it actually reached or was understood by the recipient.
[Refer PMBOK 4th Edition, page 256] [Project Communications Management]

7. C - The project charter is a high level document that authorizes a project. It documents a broad understanding of the project and usually does not need to be updated during the course of the project. [Project Integration Management]

8. A - In the critical chain method, additional buffers known as feeding buffers, are placed at each point that a chain of dependent tasks not on the critical chain feeds into the critical chain. These buffers protect the critical chain from slippage.
[Refer PMBOK 4th Edition, page 155] [Project Time Management]

9. A - The statement of work (SOW) usually does not reference the business case. The business case may contain cost sensitive information that may not be made available to a wider audience. Note that the business case also includes the business need.
[Refer PMBOK 4th Edition, page 75]
[Project Integration Management]

10. B - Prototypes are working models of the expected product before actually building it. The tangible nature of prototypes allows stakeholders to experiment with a model of their final product early in the cycle, and to come up with very clear feedback.
[Refer PMBOK 4th Edition, page 109] [Project Scope Management]

11. B - Schedule compression techniques such as crashing and fast tracking shorten the project schedule without changing the project scope. Approving overtime, bringing in additional resources and paying to expedite delivery activities are valid examples of crashing. Reducing project scope is not a valid example of crashing.
[Refer PMBOK 4th Edition, page 156-157] [Project Time Management]

12. A - Projects are authorized by someone external to the project such as a project sponsor, PMO or portfolio steering committee. A project manager does not authorize a project.
[Refer PMBOK 4th Edition, page 74]
[Project Integration Management]

13. C - An iterative relationship is best suited for projects to be carried out in uncertain conditions as may be the case in research. In this methodology, only one phase is carried on at any time, and the planning for the next phase is carried out as work progresses in the current phase. Sequential and overlapping relationships are not suitable for these types of projects. Boxed relationship is not a valid choice.
[Refer PMBOK 4th Edition, page 22]
[Project Framework]

14. C - This is fine. All deliverables need not have the same level of decomposition. This will depend on the work involved in coming up with the deliverable.
[Refer PMBOK 4th Edition, page 120] [Project Scope Management]

15. D - Root cause analysis includes all of the following - problem identification, discovery of the underlying causes of a problem, and development of preventive actions.
[Refer PMBOK 4th Edition, page 204] [Project Quality Management]

16. B - Decision tree analysis is used to calculate the average outcome when the future includes scenarios that may or may not happen. In a decision node, the input is the cost of each decision while the output is a decision made.
[Refer PMBOK 4th Edition, page 298, 299] [Project Risk Management]

17. C - The chart is likely to be a tornado diagram. Tornado diagrams are very useful for comparing relative

importance and impact of variables that have a high degree of uncertainty to those that are more stable. The charts are positioned vertically, with the bars running out horizontally. The longer bars are at the top of chart, and the shorter bars are the bottom. This appears like the shape of a tornado, and hence the name.
[Refer PMBOK 4th Edition, page 298] [Project Risk Management]

18. D - Effective communication means that the information is provided in the right format, at the right time, and with the right impact.
Efficient communication means providing only the information that is needed.
A communication plan will allow a project manager to document the strategy required to achieve this.
[Refer PMBOK 4th Edition, page 252] [Project Communications Management]

19. A - A project risk is an uncertain event or condition that, if it occurs, has an effect on the objectives of the project. A risk may have one or many causes and, if it occurs, may have one or more impacts.
[Refer PMBOK 4th Edition, page 275] [Project Risk Management]

20. B - Change requests can include preventive or corrective actions and defect repairs. Supportive action is not a valid choice.
[Refer PMBOK 4th Edition, page 128] [Project Scope Management]

21. D - When a buyer and seller enter into a dispute over the execution of work under the terms of a contract, negotiation is the preferred method of resolution of all claims and disputes.
[Refer PMBOK 4th Edition, page 339] [Project Procurement Management]

22. A - A key objective of a bidders conference is to ensure that all bidders have the same level of understanding of the procurements. Hence, in order to be completely fair, buyers must ensure that all sellers hear every question from any individual prospective seller and every answer from the buyer.
[Refer PMBOK 4th Edition, page 331] [Project Procurement Management]

23. D - There is no limit to the Actual Cost (AC). Whatever is spent to achieve the Earned Value (EV) is measured as the Actual Cost.
[Refer PMBOK 4th Edition, page 182] [Project Cost Management]

24. D - The correct thing to do would be to bring this to the notice of the buyer organization and have an amendment to the contract made.
[Refer PMI code of ethics and professional conduct] [Prof. Responsibility]

25. D - Finish-to-start (FS) is the most commonly used type of precedence relationship. In contrast, the start-to-finish (SF) relationship is rarely used.
[Refer PMBOK 4th Edition, page 138] [Project Time Management]

26. B - Rewards such as the team member of the month award hurt team cohesiveness, and are considered as win-lose (zero sum) rewards. The other choices listed are win-win.
[Refer PMBOK 4th Edition, page 234] [Project Human Resource Management]

27. A - Pull communication is suited for this purpose. It is used for very large volumes of information, or for very large audiences and requires the recipients to access communication content at their own discretion.
[Refer PMBOK 4th Edition, page 252] [Project Communications Management]

28. A - Projects exist within an organization and cannot operate as a closed system. They require input data from the organization and beyond, and deliver capabilities back to the organization.
[Refer PMBOK 4th Edition, page 38] [Project Framework]

29. C - In a project that is expected to complete ahead of its planned finish date the SPI is greater than 1.0 since it indicates that more work was completed than was planned.
[Refer PMBOK 4th Edition, page 183] [Project Cost Management]

30. B - The primary function of a PMO is to support project managers in a variety of ways. This may include developing and managing project policies, coaching, mentoring, training, and oversight. This may also include management of shared resources across the projects. However, development of a detailed description of each project would be a responsibility of the project manager handling a project, and not that of the PMO.
[Refer PMBOK 4th Edition, page 11] [Project Framework]

31. B - Variances assess the magnitude of variation to the original cost baseline. The percentage range of acceptable variances will tend to decrease as more work is accomplished and the project nears completion.
[Refer PMBOK 4th Edition, page 187] [Project Cost Management]

32. D - Responses designed for use only if certain events occur are known as contingent response strategies. These responses are triggered by events such as missing intermediate milestones. The other events listed may not warrant triggering of contingency responses.
[Refer PMBOK 4th Edition, page 305] [Project Risk Management]

33. B - Tolerance model is not a valid classification model. The other three models are valid approaches and classify stakeholders based on power / interest, influence / impact or power / urgency and legitimacy as in the case of salience model.
[Refer PMBOK 4th Edition, page 249] [Project Communications Management]

34. C - Virtual teams overcome the hurdle of high travel expenses by forming teams of people based in different geographical areas.

It might appear that management sign-off or co-location may also permit the project to take off. However, they will not be as cost-efficient as virtual teams.
[Refer PMBOK 4th Edition, page 228] [Project Human Resource Management]

35.   C - Stakeholder identification is a continuous process and is quite difficult. Failure to identify stakeholders can result in project overruns. The new project manager can use the list of stakeholders provided by the outgoing project manager as a starting point, but will need to perform his own analysis to identify stakeholders during the rest of the project.
[Refer PMBOK 4th Edition, page 23-24] [Project Framework]

36.   C - The Initiating Process Group consists of those processes performed to define a new project or phase. Develop Project Charter is part of this group and is the document that formally authorizes a project or a phase.
The other choices listed are part of the Planning Process Group.
[Refer PMBOK 4th Edition, page 43 / 104] [Project Integration Management]

37.   A - Any of the above three approaches can be correct for a given project, and will provide the project management team with an "early warning" signal if the EAC forecasts are not within acceptable tolerances.
[Refer PMBOK 4th Edition, page 185] [Project Cost Management]

38.   D - Project procurement management is usually looked at within the perspective of buyer-seller relationships. The buyer-seller relationship can exist at many levels on one project, and between organizations internal to and external to the acquiring organization.
[Refer PMBOK 4th Edition, page 315] [Project Procurement Management]

39.   A - This is done by a "participant observer" who actually performs a process or procedure to experience how it is done, to uncover hidden requirements.
[Refer PMBOK 4th Edition, page 109] [Project Scope Management]

40.   B - A project manager needs to take into consideration all types of stakeholders - positive and negative. Focusing only on positive stakeholders will increase the probability of failure of the project.
[Refer PMBOK 4th Edition, page 24] [Project Framework]

41.   C - Work performance information is an output of the Direct and Manage Project Execution process. It is not an enterprise environmental factor that influences the Develop Project Management Plan process.
Valid enterprise environmental factors are Governmental or industry standards, project management information systems, organizational structure and culture, infrastructure, and personnel administration such as hiring and firing guidelines, employee

performance reviews and training guidelines.
[Refer PMBOK 4th Edition, page 87]
[Project Integration Management]

42. A - It is the project manager's primary responsibility to ensure that deliverables are tested and have gone through the process outlined in the project management plan. Hence the project manager should recall the deliverables, even it involves a cost overrun. Approaching management may be the next step. Terminating the project is not called for, and it will be unethical to wait for the procuring organization to do their testing and find out the defects in deliverables.
[Professional Responsibility] [Prof. Responsibility]

43. B - Teaming agreements are an input to the Conduct Procurements phase. When such arrangements are in place, the buyer and seller roles will have already been decided by executive management.
Teaming agreements are also an input in the Plan procurements process.
[Refer PMBOK 4th Edition, page 331, 319] [Project Procurement Management]

44. A - Analogous duration estimating is used when there is limited available information about a project. This is especially true in the early phases of a project. In such instances, a previous similar project is used as a basis for estimating.
[Refer PMBOK 4th Edition, page 149] [Project Cost Management]

45. C - If there are significant differences in pricing by sellers, it usually indicates that the procurement statement of work was defective or ambiguous, or that the sellers misunderstood or failed to respond completely to the procurement statement of work. In such instances, an investigation needs to be launched to understand the reasons for the differences.
[Refer PMBOK 4th Edition, page 332] [Project Procurement Management]

46. A - Unplanned training takes place in a number of ways that include observation, conversation, and project management appraisals conducted during the controlling process of managing the project's team.
[Refer PMBOK 4th Edition, page 232] [Project Human Resource Management]

47. D - A process is considered as out of control if a data point exceeds a control limit or if seven consecutive data points are above or below the mean. Hence the process is out of control.
[Refer PMBOK 4th Edition, page 196] [Project Quality Management]

48. C - The Risk Urgency Assessment is a tool used in the Perform Qualitative Risk Analysis phase. It identifies risks requiring near-term responses that may be considered urgent to address.
[Refer PMBOK 4th Edition, page 293] [Project Risk Management]

49. D - Examples of Interactive communication are meetings, phone calls, video conferences.
Examples of Push communication are newsletters, memos, emails, faxes.
Examples of pull communication are intranet sites, e-learning and knowledge repositories.
[Refer PMBOK 4th Edition, page 256] [Project Communications Management]

50. A - The project manager, a team member or the project sponsor do not typically perform the role of lead negotiator on procurements. Due to the legal nature of the contractual relationship involved, a legal representative or a procurement administrator are involved.
[Refer PMBOK 4th Edition, page 333] [Project Procurement Management]

PMP Lite Mock Exam 17
Practice Questions

Test Name: PMP Lite Mock Exam 17
Total Questions: 50
Correct Answers Needed to Pass:
35 (70.00%)
Time Allowed: 60 Minutes

Test Description

This is a cumulative PMP Mock Exam which can be used as a benchmark for your PMP aptitude. This practice test includes questions from all PMBOK knowledge areas, including the five basic project management process groups.

Test Questions

1. Dina, the project manager of a hardware project, is performing a structured review of the procurement process. She would like to look into each document from the plan procurements process through the administer procurements process to identify failures. What tool should Dina use?

   A. Procurement audits in the close procurements process

   B. Performance reports in the conduct procurements process

   C. Negotiated settlements in the administer procurements process

   D. Procurement audits in the manage procurements process

2. You have presented a unique and verifiable product to your customers for their approval. Approval of this product may allow you to move on to your next phase. This unique and verifiable product is also known as:

   A. A plan

   B. A project

   C. A portfolio

   D. A deliverable

3. Experienced project managers always tell that accuracy and precision are not the same. Precise measurements may not be accurate and accurate measurements may not be precise. Which of the following statements about the precision and accuracy are CORRECT?

   A. Accuracy means the degree to which a set of inherent characteristics fulfill requirements and Precision means a category assigned to products or services having the same functional use but different technical characteristics

   B. Accuracy means the values of repeated measurements are clustered and Precision means the measured value is close to the actual value

C. Precision means the degree to which a set of inherent characteristics fulfill requirements and Accuracy means a category assigned to products or services having the same functional use but different technical characteristics

D. Precision means the values of repeated measurements are clustered and Accuracy means the measured value is close to the actual value

4. You are in the middle of a risk assessment meeting with key stakeholders, customers and project team leaders. While identifying and assessing risks, you have realized that two key stakeholders are overemphasizing the impact of a risk. What is the BEST step you must take to avoid unfairness or bias when assessing risks?

A. Implement assumptions analysis to explore the validity of assumptions

B. Develop a risk response strategy to eliminate threats

C. Perform qualitative risk analysis to identify risk attitudes

D. Perform sensitivity analysis to establish which risks have the most impact on the project

5. Erica is working for a kitchen tools manufacturing project, which is intended to make modern cooking ovens. This project is very important for the company as well as for Erica's career. Although, the project scope statement was defined very well and requirements were gathered from stakeholders in the planning phase, many design change requests have come in from customers during project execution. Which of the following tasks Erica must perform to avoid scope creep caused by uncontrollable changes?

A. Perform verify scope process and process all changes through the plan risk responses process

B. Perform integrated change control process and process all changes through the perform quality control process

C. Perform scope control and process all changes through the integrated change control process

D. Perform scope control and process all changes through the verify scope process

6. There is a heady demand for new houses in your city's expensive neighborhood. RECON, a construction company employed you as a project manager to assess the benefit of building new energy efficient houses in that neighborhood although it takes more expensive technology to build those. You have

started gathering data to perform the detail payback analysis to submit a report to the management. Since the full financial impact of energy efficient house building is difficult to estimate, you would like to prepare a rough cost-benefit analysis and include it with the report. Which of the following describes the effort you are undertaking in this scenario?

A. You are developing a business case to provide as an input to the develop project charter process

B. You are developing a cost management plan to provide as an input to the estimate costs process

C. You are developing a risk management plan to provide as an input to the perform quantitative risk analysis process

D. You are developing a cost-benefit analysis to provide as an input to the plan risk management process

7. Jared is in the execution phase of a residential housing construction project. He has been informed of major scope changes from stakeholders in the middle of the project. These changes involve regulatory requirements from local authorities that may impact not only the scope but also the cost and duration of the project. What should be the FIRST approach from Jared in considering these changes?

A. Meet with the change control board to solicit some ideas on the new project plan

B. Create a report detailing the impact of scope changes on project parameters such as cost, quality and schedule

C. Add new tasks to the project plan and assign resources to account for regulatory changes

D. Escalate the scope changes to the sponsor and steering committee for their decision

8. You are working in an Information Technology project as a project manager to develop a shopping website for your customers. Some key stakeholders in the project suggested scope changes to improve the look and feel of the website. Your team has analyzed the impact of these changes and presented to the change control board for approval. What should be your next step if the change control board accepts all proposed changes?

A. Implement the change request and update stakeholders

B. Review change control board decisions and inform stakeholders for their input

C. Conduct a team status meeting to update the progress on change requests

D. Revise cost estimates, schedule dates, resource requirements and planning documents

9. Jane is worried about her project because many of her tasks are slowly moving and two critical tasks may have the chance of slippage. She conducts a thorough resource analysis and finds out that there are five resources who will be free next week. She would like to use this as an opportunity to assign those resources to finish her tasks early and prevent the project completion date from slipping. This effort is an instance of which of the following risk response techniques?

A. Transferring

B. Sharing

C. Enhancing

D. Accepting

10. Debby has been working as a project manager for a company that designs precision instruments for research labs. Her company is in the process of bidding for a project being proposed by Food and Drug Administration. Although her company has experience in designing research instruments, it lacks specific expertise to perform this project. As a project manager what should Debby do in this situation?

A. She must escalate this issue to the management for their advice

B. She must bid for the project but provide facts to the buyer

C. Since the company lacks expertise, she must not bid

D. Since the company has prior experience in the instrument design, she must bid

11. You are meeting with your stakeholders to gather requirements for your project. You are well aware that collecting requirements include both product and project requirements. All of the following tools can be used to gather, define, and analyze project requirements from stakeholders EXCEPT:

A. Surveys

B. Facilitated workshops

C. Decomposition

D. Prototypes

12. In a textile manufacturing project, a team divided the whole project work into 35 work packages and assigned a few work packages to the design department for review. After reviewing, the manager of the design department has recently requested the team to further divide the work packages into more manageable work components for estimating and scheduling the resources. In this scenario, which of the following

techniques should the team use to complete the manager's request?

A. The rolling wave planning

B. The parametric estimating

C. The precedence diagramming method

D. The bottom-up estimating

13. You are working as a project manager for MALTEX, an IT organization having a projectized organization structure. You have recently started managing a project that involves stakeholders from within and outside your organization. The stakeholders external to your organization are very critical as their interests are negatively affected by the project. You are making serious efforts to gather their expectations and influence levels early in the project to make sure that their voice is heard and proper communication needs can be planned in the future phases of the project. The outcome of your effort can be documented in:

A. The stakeholder management strategy & stakeholder register

B. The project scope document & The project management plan

C. The stakeholder register & The project management plan

D. The stakeholder document & stakeholder communication plan

14. You have been managing a Federal highway construction project which is intended to improve the transportation between north and south regions of a country. Being in the execution phase, the change control board has approved many change requests generated from stakeholders including the highway transportation agency. At least half of those requests were made to bring the quality of the micro texture of the road aligned with the quality levels incorporated in the project management plan. What is the next course of action from you in managing such requests?

A. Initiate a defect repair to repair the road or completely pave a new road

B. Initiate a corrective action to bring the future quality of the road in line with the project management plan

C. Initiate a change request to bring the road quality in line with the project management plan

D. Initiate a preventive action to reduce the probability of negative consequences associated with the poor quality of the road

15. Joe vigil has been managing a project for Exton Oil Corporation. This project involves redesigning gas pumping stations across the state. The redesigning involves new gas pumps, security cameras, convenience

stores, and the use of environmentally friendly materials in the construction. While the redesigning work is underway, Joe's design engineer suggests a secondary alarm system for gas pumps to alert the attendant incase of a spillage. Although this suggestion is not in project requirements, Joe is impressed with the engineer's recommendation. What should be the next step for Joe in regards to the engineer's suggestion?

A. Initiate the formal change control process to find the impact of his recommendation

B. Approve his recommendation and allocate resources and funds

C. Create an issue log to document the engineer's suggestion for future use

D. Reject his recommendation as it requires additional funding

16. To communicate with stakeholders on the resolved issues and the issues that are hard to resolve, you use an issue log in your project. Since you assign an owner for every issue and resolve it by proactively working on it, your stakeholders actively support all your efforts in managing the project. This method of actively resolving issues and reducing risks to the project is known as:

A. Planning risk management

B. Issue management

C. Scope verification & Control

D. Managing stakeholders expectations

17. You have been assigned as the project manager for a software development project and in the process of communicating with stakeholders to address their issues and influence their expectations. Which of the following documents help you and your team to carry out this effort?

A. The Issue log, Project charter, and Configuration management system

B. The Issue log, Change log, and Project management plan

C. The Project risk register, Work performance information, and Accepted deliverables

D. None of the above

18. Changes in the projects are inevitable. So, project managers must develop or use a system to manage centrally and control those changes. There are four types of changes that need to be controlled in a project. Project changes, deliverable changes, process changes, and baseline changes. The impact of each of these changes must be evaluated and approved and rejected changes must be communicated to all stakeholders as and when required. Which of the following helps to control the above mentioned changes?

A. Configuration control and Control chart

B. Configuration control and Change control

C. Control chart and Cost control

D. Change control and Control chart

19. Two of your expert team members have been in a heated argument over the use of a new software product for your research project. Recently you noticed, that the argument instead of increasing creativity, causing conflict between the team members. To prevent the conflict from escalating, you want to resolve it by evaluating alternatives and open dialogue. All of the following statements about a conflict are false EXCEPT:

A. Conflict resolution should focus on past events

B. Conflict is a team issue

C. There are eight general techniques to resolve conflicts

D. Conflict resolution should focus on personalities

20. Project managers must look for non-value added activities in different phases of a project. It is estimated that about 20% of all project activities do not add any value to the project especially in manufacturing. These activities include excessive inspections, needless procedures and redundant documents. Elimination of these non-value added activities are part of the continuous process improvement, which is the means for improving the quality in all project processes. Keeping this in mind, what should a project manager do in his/her project during execution to process non-value added activities?

A. Use flow charts in the plan quality process to avoid non-value added activities

B. Use the process analysis in the perform quality assurance process to isolate non-value added activities

C. Use the Pareto chart in the perform quality control process to eliminate all non-value added activities

D. Use cause and effect diagrams in the perform quality control process to identify non-value added activities

21. Which of the following is neither input to nor output of the close procurements process?

A. Updates to lessons learned documentation

B. Contract change documentation

C. Negotiated settlements

D. Updates to procurement files

22. Some tools or techniques can be used across different project processes to plan, execute or control the characteristics of project elements. Which of the following is used as a tool in both quality control and plan quality processes?

   A. A run chart

   B. A control chart

   C. A Pareto chart

   D. A variance chart

23. In an underground highway construction project, stakeholders have suggested many changes to the project scope. As you already defined the cost baseline in your project, you would like to revisit the baseline to see how these changes impact the overall cost of the project. So, you have started doing impact analysis to determine the impact and inform concerned stakeholders of all approved changes and corresponding costs. You must use the following to carry out such process:

   A. Scope control process

   B. Configuration control process

   C. Control costs process

   D. All of the above

24. Which of the following statement represents McClelland's motivational theory?

   A. Individual needs can be classified as either achievement, affiliation, or power

   B. Employees chose responsibilities instead of salary hikes

   C. People try to work hard when their basic needs are satisfied

   D. Most people dislike work and try to avoid it

25. There has been budget cuts across all agencies in your organization. The program management office has started re-prioritizing all organization's projects due to lack of funds. Projects with unrealistic expectations, huge budgets, and incomplete requirements are the first ones to be terminated. Due to high budget, your project is on the list for early termination and that requires early closing of all your contracts in the project. Which of the following statements about early termination of contracts is TRUE?

   A. Early termination of contracts is a part of the close project or phase process.

   B. When contracts are terminated early, seller must pay all costs incurred

C. Early termination of contracts is a part of the close procurements process

D. When contracts are terminated early, buyer need not pay anything to the seller

26. Which of the following statements are NOT true considering the planned value, the earned value, the schedule variance and the cost variance of a project?

A. The cost variance is the difference between the earned value and the actual cost

B. The schedule variance is the difference between the earned value and the planned value

C. The earned value is the value of work to be completed in terms of the approved budget

D. The planned value is the budget authorized to the work to be performed

27. You are working as a project manager for a wind powered vehicle manufacturing project, which is in its planning phase. You carefully gathered all your requirements from your key stakeholders and prepared a system requirements specification and project requirements specification documents. While presenting your documents to the project team, a project team member who is very enthusiastic about the project started

talking about the duration estimates for each activity. Which of the following statements indicate your response to your team member?

A. WBS creation and Schedule development must be done after estimating durations

B. Schedule development and Costs estimation must be done before estimating durations

C. Scope definition, WBS creation, Quality planning, and Communication planning must be done before estimating durations

D. Scope definition, WBS creation, Activity definition, and Activity sequencing must be done before estimating durations

28. Rosanne is an experienced project manager working for a pharmaceutical project. This project involves two big vendors to supply chemical products with specific composition for preparing drugs. While reviewing documents to see how the seller is performing, she noticed that some of the contractual terms were not met by the sellers. Since it is first time violation, she would like to initiate a corrective action to bring the performance of the seller consistent with the statement of work. Which of the following are NOT outputs of Rosanne's effort?

A. Work performance information and Approved change requests

B. Procurement documentation and Seller performance evaluation documentation

C. Procurement documentation and Organizational process assets update

D. Change requests and Project management plan updates

29. The project charter defines the overall scope and objectives of a project. Considering different inputs to the project charter, which of the following is NOT a correct statement?

A. Government or industry standards cannot be used as an input to develop a project charter

B. The description of the product to be delivered is an input to the develop project charter process

C. Organizational process assets are input to the develop project charter process

D. When projects are executed for external customers, a contract is used as an input to the charter

30. Kristin is working as a project manager for a City public utilities improvement project. Since this project involves many stakeholders from inside and outside of the project, she is in the process of developing a strategy to identify all stakeholders. Which of the following is the BEST strategy to identify all stakeholders?

A. Identifying all stakeholders using a stakeholder analysis matrix

B. Identifying key stakeholders first and interviewing them to expand the list until all stakeholders are identified

C. Identifying all stakeholders using a stakeholder register

D. None of the above

31. Close project or phase is the process of completing and concluding all activities across all project groups to officially close the project. Which of the following activities are NOT performed in the closing project or phase process?

A. Actions required to transfer completed products to operations

B. Actions required to archive project information

C. Actions required to audit project success or failure

D. Actions required to accept the deliverables

32. Which of the following activities fall under the planning process group but not under the project time management?

A. Estimating the type of materials and equipment needed to perform project activities

B. Formalizing the acceptance of completed deliverables

C. Identification of various activities to produce the project deliverables

D. Developing a detailed description of the project and product being developed

33. James has been managing a hotel construction project in a busy street. He is in the process of estimating activity durations for building walls and calculates the most likely estimate as 15 days. If pre-fabricated material is used, it would take no more than 12 days to finish the work. However, the work may be delayed and could take up to 18 days if less experienced construction workers are used to build the walls. But, the engineer in-charge of the work estimates the duration as 8 days when pre-fabricated material is used. What is the expected duration of building walls using the three-point estimate, if the engineer's estimation is assumed correct?

A. 12 days

B. 11 days

C. 15 days

D. 14 days

34. Rodney is in the process of preparing the project performance report for the team meeting. He is expecting many questions from his stakeholders on the budget and schedule. He calculates the following values; Budget at Completion (BAC) = $22,000, Earned Value (EV) = $13000, Planned Value (PV) = $ 14000, Actual cost (AC) = $15000. What is the Estimate at Completion (EAC) for the project if the work is performed at the budgeted rate?

A. $24,000

B. $36,000

C. $22,500

D. $37,000

35. In your project, two dependent tasks have 3 days lag time. If the relationship between them is finish-to-start, the successor task may start:

A. 3 days after the predecessor task is scheduled to start

B. 3 days before the predecessor task is scheduled to start

C. 3 days before the predecessor task is scheduled to finish

D. 3 days after the predecessor task is scheduled to finish

36. Many organizations favor fixed-price contracts because the performance of the project is the responsibility of the seller. Which of the following is the characteristic of a firm fixed price contract?

A. The buyer must precisely specify the number of resources to be used for procurement

B. The buyer must precisely specify the service or product to be procured

C. The buyer must precisely specify the time for completing the contract

D. The buyer must precisely specify the price of the contract

37. Decision making is an important skill a project manager must possess to manage and lead the team. Which of the following is NOT a part of the six-phase decision-making model ?

A. Solution evaluation planning

B. Solution action planning

C. Problem solution generation

D. Problem solution escalation

38. You applied for a project coordinator position in your organization. You have recently met with your director to learn more about the job functions of that position. Your director indicates that it is the functional managers who control the resources and not you in your new position. Which of the following represents the organization structure that you will be working in if you are chosen as a project coordinator?

A. Projectized

B. Weak matrix

C. Balanced matrix

D. Functional

39. A process in a mobile phone manufacturing project has an upper control limit of 0.12. What is the standard deviation of the process if the upper control limit is set at 3 Sigma?

A. 0.5

B. 0.4

C. 0.12

D. 0.36

40. Chris works as a project manager for UNISTEEL, a steel melting shop. He was assigned by his Executive Project Manager to study and prepare a report on the defects that eroded the blast furnace lining which has caused a drastic decline in production. Since this report will be used by the management to control the process and material quality, Chris performed a careful study and uncovered two factors related to refractories that caused majority of the lining problems. Which of the following statements BEST illustrate the technique Chris must have used in this scenario?

A. A Pareto chart indicates that 80 percent of the problems are due to 20 percent of the causes

B. A cause and effect diagram indicates how various causes show the history and variation of defects

C. A Pareto chart identifies the possible relationship between changes observed in two independent variables

D. A cause and effect diagram indicates how various factors or causes can be linked to potential problems

41. Cindy has been working in a manufacturing project as a project manager. This project is designed to produce high quality semiconductors to use in computers. Since semiconductors are produced from silicon wafers, she contracted a company to provide silicon wafers to the project on an ongoing basis. Due to unknown reasons from the contractor, low quality wafers have been transferred to the project compromising the electrical performance of semiconductors. Overwhelmed by the complaints from the computer division, Cindy is obligated to correct the manufacturing defects to avoid future

liabilities. In this scenario, the costs incurred by Cindy is known as:

A. External failure costs or Cost of nonconformance

B. Appraisal costs or Cost of nonconformance

C. Prevention costs or Cost of conformance

D. Internal failure costs or Cost of conformance

42. You, as an independent consultant, are working with a project manager of a spacecraft parts manufacturing project to make sure that the team comply with organizational quality policies and procedures. Since parts made in this project must adhere to high precision and accuracy, you are documenting the gaps within the processes and procedures to improve the quality for customer acceptance. Which of the following best represents the project management activity you are doing?

A. Statistical sampling

B. Quality audits

C. Quality control

D. Inspection

43. You have been managing a research project that is intended to create Genetically Modified fruits using Genetic Engineering techniques.

Since many legal issues are involved in this process, you created contingency allowances by using different quantitative analysis methods to account for cost uncertainty. You have just wrapped-up a brainstorming session with your team in the execution phase to monitor new risks evolved in the project over past few weeks and to establish new risk response plans. What should you do if you want to allocate more contingency reserves to account for new risks?

A. Perform the reserve analysis to compare the amount of contingency reserves remaining to the amount of risk remaining

B. Perform Monte Carlo analysis to compare the amount of contingency reserves remaining to the amount of risk remaining

C. Perform the variance and trend analysis to compare planned results to the actual results

D. Perform the quantitative risk analysis to determine the outstanding risks

44. In a small office construction project, the following activities are scheduled in sequence. i) Digging and pouring footings - 5 days ii) Working on the slab and pouring - 3 days iii) Framing the floor - 5 days iv) Wall framing - 4 days v) Roof framing - 6 days vi) Insulation and drywall - 7 days vii) Interior doors and trim - 3 days viii) Hardware and fixtures - 2 days. What

is the minimum time to complete the project if all activities are on a critical path except number viii, and activity iii is delayed by 1 day?

A. 32 days

B. 33 days

C. 34 days

D. 35 days

45. Analyzing the situation, differentiating between wants and needs, and focusing on interests and issues rather than on positions are critical elements in:

A. Team building

B. Planning

C. Decision making

D. Negotiating

46. In a ship design project, a project manager is in the process of negotiating with a consulting company to ensure that project receives certified and specialized consultants for creating the hull design. The project manager wants to make certain that the consultants will be able to work until their assignments are completed. He is using all his negotiation skills and interpersonal skills to get competent staff on time. Based on the scenario described above, the project manager is engaged in:

A. Acquire project team process

B. Resource gathering process

C. Develop human resource plan process

D. Manage project team process

47. You have recently acquired a project to develop Organic products for a retail store. You are making informal conversations and luncheon meetings with all your senior functional managers to understand various factors that impact the allocation of resources to the project. Which of the following BEST describes the activity you are undertaking?

A. You are using organizational process assets to manage your project team

B. You are using the observation and conversation to manage your project team

C. You are using the networking technique to develop the human resource plan

D. You are making use of your interpersonal skills to develop your project team

48. The organization's safety and health policy, ethics policy, project policy, and quality policy can be used in a project to influence it's success. All these policies are a part of:

A. Organizational process assets

B. The project management plan

C. Enterprise environmental factors

D. Historical databases

49. Velvet is working for a chemical industry and her management proposed two different projects to manufacture Benzene for commercial use. After doing financial analysis, the financial advisor provided her the following statistics about the projects. Project-1-60% probability of success with a profit of $500,000 and 20% probability of failure with a loss of $200,000; Project-2-30% probability of success with a profit of $300,000 and 30% probability of failure with a loss of $400,000; Based on the information above, Velvet must choose:

A. Either project-1 or project-2

B. Neither project-1 nor project-2

C. Project-2

D. Project-1

50. You are managing a highly complex drug manufacturing project and your sponsor is highly motivated and influential. You are optimistic about the outcome of the project, however, you are not sure about the project approval requirements that measure the success of the project. So, you would like to document the name of the person who signs off the project and the criteria that constitutes the success of the project. Which of the following documents should you use to incorporate project approval requirements?

A. The scope document

B. The project charter

C. The approval requirement plan

D. The project management plan

PMP Lite Mock Exam 17
Answer Key and Explanations

1. A - A procurement audit is used as a tool in the close procurements process. Procurement audits are carried out to identify successes and failures that warrant recognition. When this tool is used, all procurement processes are thoroughly checked and corresponding documents are verified for problems. Therefore, procurement audits in the close procurements process is the correct answer. [PMBOK 4th edition, Page 343] [Project Procurement Management]

2. D - A unique and verifiable product produced in each phase or end of the project is known as a deliverable. Deliverables are produced from the Direct and Manage project execution process. [PMBOK 4th edition, Page 87] [Project Integration Management]

3. D - Accuracy and Precision are not the same. Precision means the values of repeated measurements are clustered and Accuracy means the measured value is close to the actual value. [PMBOK 4th edition, Page 190] [Project Quality Management]

4. C - After identifying risks, the project manager must prioritize risks for further analysis by assessing and analyzing the impact of each risk. It is often possible that during the risk assessment, risk attitudes may introduce bias into the assessment of identified risks. So project managers must identify and manage risk attitudes during the qualitative risk analysis. So, you must perform the qualitative risk analysis to avoid bias during assessment. [PMBOK 4th edition, Page 289] [Project Risk Management]

5. C - All scope changes must be controlled in a project using the control scope process. But, the scope control must also ensure that all changes requested by customers go through the perform integrated change control process. This way, scope creep can be avoided and project changes can be managed. Hence, Erica must perform scope control and process all changes through the integrated change control process. [PMBOK 4th edition, Page 125] [Project Scope Management]

6. A - An organization's business need may arise due to advances in the technology, a demand from the market or a legal requirement. The business need along with the cost-benefit analysis are documented in a business case. A business case determines whether the project worth the investment. Payback analysis is also part of a business case. The business case and other documents are used as an input to the develop project charter process. Hence, you are making efforts to build a business case to provide as an input to the develop project charter process. [PMBOK 4th edition, Page 75] [Project Integration Management]

7. B - Any scope changes in a project must go through the integrated

change control process to determine the impact on project parameters such as cost, quality and schedule. After finding the impact, the changes should be presented to the change control board for their review. Then, all approved changes must be planned and resources must be allocated. Therefore, the first step for Jared is to create a report detailing the impact of scope changes on project parameters such as cost, quality and schedule. [PMBOK 4th edition, Page 94] [Project Integration Management]

8.   D - Approved change requests require changes to cost estimates, resource requirements, schedule dates and activity sequences. You should incorporate these revisions first before asking your team to implement the changes. Stakeholders can be updated after carrying out the changes. So, the first step you should do is to revise the estimates and baselines. [PMBOK 4th edition, Page 94] [Project Integration Management]

9.   C - Availability of free resources can be considered as an opportunity or a positive risk. There are four risk response planning strategies available to deal with opportunities. Exploit, Share, Enhance and Accept. Enhancement is used to increase the positive impact of an opportunity. Allocating more resources to complete a task is considered as an opportunity enhancement. Therefore, Jane is using the enhancing risk response strategy. [PMBOK 4th edition, Page 305] [Project Risk Management]

10.   C - Bidding a project without enough experience is against the PMI code of conduct. Project managers must not bid on any work that their organization is not qualified to perform. A project manager must not do this knowingly. Hence Debby must not bid on this project. [PMI code of Ethics and Professional Conduct] [Prof. Responsibility]

11.   C - Both product and project requirements are gathered from stakeholders during collect requirements phase. This effort is undertaken during project planning. Interviews, facilitated workshops, surveys, prototypes and group creativity techniques are used as tools to define and analyze requirements. Decomposition is used only to breakdown the work and not to gather requirements. Therefore, Decomposition is the valid answer. [PMBOK 4th edition, Page 105] [Project Scope Management]

12.   A - Carefully read this question. The manager requested to divide the work packages into more manageable components for estimating the resources. The define activities process is used to divide the work packages into more manageable activities for estimating, scheduling, and executing the project work. These activities are the lowest components of a work breakdown structure. The tools used in this process are 1) Rolling wave planning 2) Decomposition 3) Templates and 4) Expert judgment. Hence, the team must use the rolling wave planning to fulfill manager's request. [PMBOK

4th edition, Page 133] [Project Time Management]

13. A - Carefully read this question. You have just started managing this project and you are in the process of documenting the influence and expectation levels of stakeholders. You are performing this process to plan for future communications. So, you are still in the identify stakeholders process of the initiation phase of the project. The outputs of this process are the stakeholder management strategy and stakeholder register. Hence, your findings must be documented in these two documents. Therefore, the stakeholder management strategy & stakeholder register are correct answer options. [PMBOK 4th edition, Pages 250, 251] [Project Integration Management]

14. B - Change requests are initiated and submitted to the change management board. Once change requests are approved, the project manager must give a documented direction to prevent, correct or repair based on the approved changes. In this scenario, the quality of the road appears to be deviated from the project management plan. So, you must initiate a corrective action to assure future quality measurements align with the project management plan. You can initiate a corrective action or defect repair later to correct the quality of the already paved road. But, you must initiate a corrective action first. [PMBOK 4th edition, Page 83] [Project Integration Management]

15. A - Change requests should always be recorded in written form and entered into the change management system to find the impact of the change on the scope, budget, schedule and quality. So, Joe must initiate the formal change control process. After approval from change control board, Joe can allocate resources and funds to the change. Hence, Joe must initiate the change first. [PMBOK 4th edition, Page 94] [Project Integration Management]

16. D - Clarifying all stakeholders issues and resolving them on time is done throughout the life cycle of the project. If issues are not resolved, they become the source for conflicts. So project managers must manage stakeholders expectations to overcome risks and enable stakeholders to be active supporters of the project effort. Therefore, you are managing stakeholders expectations in this scenario to reduce risks. [PMBOK 4th edition, Pages 261, 262] [Project Communications Management]

17. B - Communicating with stakeholders to address their issues is done during manage stakeholders expectations process of the communication management. The documents used as an input to this process are the issue log, change long, project management plan, stakeholder register, stakeholder management strategy and organizational process assets. Therefore the Issue log, change log and project management plan help you to carry out this effort. [PMBOK

4th edition, Page 263] [Project Communications Management]

18. B - Configuration control is focused on the specification of both the processes and deliverables where as change control is focused on project changes and the product baselines. So, a configuration control with a change control system must be implemented to handle all those changes. [PMBOK 4th edition, Page 94] [Project Integration Management]

19. B - Conflicts are unavoidable in the project environment. Project managers must make sure that conflicts are resolved as early as possible. To resolve conflicts they must use direct and collaborative approach. Conflict resolution must not focus on personalities and past events. There are six different conflict resolution techniques in use. A Conflict is not an individual issue, it is always a team issue. [PMBOK 4th edition, Pages 239] [Project Human Resource Management]

20. B - Continuous process improvement is an iterative task that is carried out throughout the project. In this scenario, the question specifically asks about the execution phase of the project. Perform quality assurance is the only quality process in execution. This process is undertaken in the execution phase to eliminate waste and non-value added activities. An important tool used for this purpose is the process analysis. Hence, project managers must use process analysis in the perform quality assurance process to isolate non-value added activities.

[PMBOK 4th edition, Page 204] [Project Quality Management]

21. C - Contract change documentation is an input to the close procurements process. Procurement files and Lessons learned documentation are updated during the close procurements process. But, negotiated settlements are used as tools to close procurements. Hence, it is the answer. [PMBOK 4th edition, Page 343] [Project Procurement Management]

22. B - Control charts are used to decide whether a process is steady or showing any abnormal condition. Upper and lower control limits are set for the process and characteristics that go beyond the limits are analyzed. Control charts are used in both plan quality and quality control processes as tools to judge the quality performance. [PMBOK 4th edition, Pages 196, 209] [Project Quality Management]

23. C - Control costs process involves many activities such as influencing the factors that change the cost baseline, managing the actual changes, and informing stakeholders of approved changes and corresponding costs. Since you are in the process of managing the changes and informing them to the stakeholders, you are in the control costs process. [PMBOK 4th edition, Page 179] [Project Cost Management]

24. A - David McClelland's motivational needs theory states that human motivation is shaped by three needs

1) achievement 2) power and 3) affiliation. A person's motivation and effectiveness in certain jobs are influenced by these three needs. Hence 'Individual needs can be classified as either achievement, affiliation, or power' is the correct answer. [http://www.netmba.com/mgmt/ob /motivation/mcclelland/] [Project Human Resource Management]

25. C - Early termination of contracts is a special case of procurement closure. This effort is done during close procurements process. When contracts are terminated early, based upon the contract terms and conditions, the buyer may have to compensate the seller. Therefore, early termination of contracts is a part of the close procurements process' is a true statement. [PMBOK 4th edition, Page 342] [Project Procurement Management]

26. C - Earned value is the value of the work completed. This value is often expressed in terms of the approved budget assigned to the work completed. The earned value is measured against the performance measurement baseline. Therefore, 'Earned value is the value of work to be completed in terms of the approved budget' is NOT a true statement. All other statements are correct. [PMBOK 4th edition, Page 182] [Project Cost Management]

27. D - Estimating activity durations is done during planning phase of a project. Since project manager has just developed requirements, the

scope must be defined and the WBS must be created immediately. Based on the WBS, activities must be defined and sequenced. After sequencing, resources and duration for each activity must be estimated. So, the team member must know that many activities need to be done before estimating durations. Therefore, 'Scope definition, WBS creation, Activity definition, and Activity sequencing must be done before estimating durations' is the correct response from you in this situation. [PMBOK 4th edition, Page 43] [Project Time Management]

28. A - Evaluating the performance of the seller is done during administer procurements process. If the contractual terms are not met by the seller, a corrective action can be initiated. If there are severe violations, contract can be terminated based on the language used in the contract. Procurement documentation, Seller performance evaluation documentation, Change requests, Project management plan updates and Organizational process assets updates are outputs of this process. Work performance information and approved change requests are inputs to this process. Since they are not outputs of this process, work performance information and approved change requests are the correct answers. [PMBOK 4th edition, Pages 338, 339] [Project Procurement Management]

29. A - Government or industry standards are part of enterprise environmental factors and enterprise

environmental factors are used as inputs to the develop project charter process. So 'Government or industry standards cannot be used as an input to develop a project charter' is NOT a true statement. [PMBOK 4th edition, Pages 74, 75] [Project Integration Management]

30.   B - Identification of stakeholders is an important part of the initiation phase of the project. Stakeholders can be external or internal to the organization. A project manager must identify all potential stakeholders very early in the life of the project. The stakeholder register and stakeholder analysis matrix are prepared after identifying the stakeholders. So, they cannot be used to identify stakeholders. In this scenario, identifying key stakeholders and interviewing them to expand the list until all stakeholders are included is considered as the best strategy. [PMBOK 4th edition, Page 248] [Project Integration Management]

31.   D - Actions required to transfer completed products to operations, actions required to archive project information, and actions required to audit project success or failure are carried out in the close project or phase process. But, actions required to accept the completed deliverables are executed in the verify scope process. The completed deliverable are then transferred to the close project or phase process. Therefore, actions required to accept the deliverables are not done in the close project or phase process. [PMBOK

4th edition, Page 100] [Project Integration Management]

32.   D - Identification of various activities to produce the project deliverables is done in define activities process of the project time management. Estimating type of materials and equipment needed to perform activities is done during estimate activity resources process. This is also a part of the project time management. Formalizing the acceptance of completed deliverables is done during the Monitoring & Controlling phase of the project, which is also a time management process. Developing a detailed description of the project and product being developed is done during the define scope process. This is also a planning activity, however, it falls under project scope management. Hence, 'Developing a detailed description of the project and product being developed' is the correct answer. [PMBOK 4th edition, Page 112] [Project Scope Management]

33.   D - If the engineer is correct, the optimistic estimate can be taken as 8 days. The pessimistic estimate is still 18 days and the most likely estimate is 15 days. Using the PERT or the three-point technique, the expected activity duration is calculated using the formula $Te = (To + 4Tm + Tp)/6$, where Te is the estimated duration, To is optimistic duration, Tm is the most likely duration and Tp is the pessimistic duration. Hence, $Te = (8 + 60 + 18)/6 = 14$ days (approximately.) Therefore, 14 days is the correct answer. [PMBOK 4th

edition, Page 150] [Project Time Management]

34. A - If the project work is performed at the budgeted rate, the Estimation at Completion can be determined using the formula (EAC) = AC + BAC - EV; Substituting all these values in the equation EAC = $15000 + $22,000 - $13,000 = $24,000. Therefore Estimate at completion = $24,000. [PMBOK 4th edition, Page 184] [Project Cost Management]

35. D - In a finish-to-start relationship, the successor task starts after the predecessor task finishes. The lag time gives a delay in the successor activity. So, the successor task may start 3 days after the predecessor task is scheduled to finish. [PMBOK 4th edition, Page 140] [Project Time Management]

36. B - In a firm fixed price contract, the buyer must precisely specify the product or service to be procured. Any changes in the contract require additional cost to the buyer. So, buyers must be careful while preparing the statement of work. [PMBOK 4th edition, Page 322] [Project Procurement Management]

37. D - In a six-phase decision making model, the project manager must define the problem first. After defining, he/she must generate problem solution, generate ideas to action, plan solution action and plan solution evaluation. Once the solution is implemented, he must evaluate the outcome and process. Therefore, except problem solution escalation all

other phases are part of this model. [PMBOK 4th Edition, Appendix-G] [Project Human Resource Management]

38. B - In a weak matrix organization structure, project manager works more like a coordinator to organize different activities and do not have direct control over the resources. Project team members report to functional managers and their progress is measured by the functional managers. Therefore, weak matrix is the correct answer. [PMBOK 4th edition, Page 28] [Project Framework]

39. B - In quality control operations, the upper control limit of a process is set at 3 Sigma, where Sigma is the standard deviation. In this case, 3 Sigma = 0.12, therefore, the Sigma or the standard deviation = 0.4 [PMBOK 4th edition, Page 209] [Project Quality Management]

40. A - In this scenario, Chris is using a quality control technique to carry out his study. A Pareto chart is based on the Pareto law which shows that 80 percent of the problems (lining problems) are caused by 20 percent of the causes (two factors). Since, Chris's study is similar to Pareto law, it best illustrates the study he carried out. [PMBOK 4th edition, Page 211] [Project Quality Management]

41. A - In this scenario, Cindy is performing warranty work to correct manufacturing defects. These defects are identified by external customers and the costs are known as external failure costs. These costs are also known as costs of nonconformance because the product did not meet the quality requirements. The cost of nonconformance is a part of the cost of quality. Therefore, Cindy is incurring external failure costs or cost of nonconformance. [PMBOK 4th edition, Page 195] [Project Cost Management]

42. B - Making sure that the project team comply with organizational quality policies and procedures is done in the perform quality assurance process. Quality audits are one of such techniques in which a structured review is performed by independent consultants or contractors to identify all shortcomings in carrying out quality policies and procedures. These efforts should be used later to improve the product quality and reduce the cost of quality. Therefore, you are performing quality audits in the perform quality assurance process. [PMBOK 4th edition, Page 204] [Project Quality Management]

43. A - Many risks evolve over the course of any project. Project managers must monitor and control those risks and plan risk responses. The reserve analysis is used as a tool in Monitor and control risks process. This technique is used to compare the amount of contingency reserves remaining to the amount of risk remaining throughout the execution of the project. Hence, you must perform the reserve analysis first to decide on the contingency allowances. [PMBOK 4th edition, Page 311] [Project Risk Management]

44. C - A critical path has a zero total float. That means, any delay in the critical path activity delays the project finish date. In other words, critical path gives the minimum time required to complete a project. So, adding the duration for all critical path activities give the minimum time required as 33 days. If activity iii is delayed by one day, the total duration or the minimum time required to complete the project will also be delayed by one day, thus making it 34 days. [PMBOK 4th edition, Page 155] [Project Time Management]

45. D - Negotiation is a strategy used to bring compromise between two parties with opposing interests. Analyzing the situation, differentiating between wants and needs, focusing on interests and issues rather than on positions, asking high and offering low, and listening are very important skills in negotiation. [PMBOK 4th edition, Appendix G] [Project Human Resource Management]

46. A - Negotiation skills are used by project managers throughout the project. In this scenario, the project manager is negotiating with vendors to get talented consultants in sufficient number within the scheduled time. This process ensures the availability of scarce resources during critical phases of the project. This effort is done during acquire project team process. Negotiation is used as a tool in the acquire project team process. Hence, the project manager is engaged in the acquire

project team process. [PMBOK 4th edition, Pages 227, 228] [Project Human Resource Management]

47. C - Networking is a technique used to develop the project human resource plan. This technique is used by many project managers to understand the factors that impact the allocation of resources. Luncheon meetings, conferences and events are various forms of networking. Hence, in this scenario, you are making use of the networking technique to develop the human resource plan. [PMBOK 4th edition, Page 222] [Project Human Resource Management]

48. A - Organizational process assets can be used to influence project's success. Organizational standards and policies such as safety and health policy, ethics policy, quality policy, and project management policy are a part of the organizational process assets. [PMBOK 4th edition, Page 32] [Project Framework]

49. D - Profit or loss from a project = (Expected profit * probability of profit) - (Expected loss * probability of loss). So, for project-1, the profit or loss = (500000 *0.6 - 200000 *0.2) = 300000 - 40000 = $ 260,000 profit. For project-2, the profit or loss = (300000 *0.3 - 400000 *0.3) = 90000- 120000 = $ -30,000 = $30,000 loss. Hence, Velvet must select project-1 which can yield profit. [Project initiation methods] [Project Framework]

50. B - Project approval requirements must be documented early in the project during the initiation phase. These requirements show the requisites for project success, the names of persons signing off the project and deliverable requirements. Since the project charter is created in the initiation phase of the project, the project manager must include these requirements in the charter. Hence, the project charter is the correct answer option. [PMBOK 4th edition, Page 79] [Project Integration Management]

PMP Lite Mock Exam 18
Practice Questions

Test Name: PMP Lite Mock Exam 18
Total Questions: 50
Correct Answers Needed to Pass:
35 (70.00%)
Time Allowed: 60 Minutes

Test Description

This is a cumulative PMP Mock Exam which can be used as a benchmark for your PMP aptitude. This practice test includes questions from all PMBOK knowledge areas, including the five basic project management process groups.

Test Questions

1. 1.) You are working in a matrix project environment where functional managers have control over the resources. You are well aware that not acquiring the project team timely for a project will result in changes to the schedule, cost, and quality. So, to acquire the project team from functional managers the best technique you should use is:

    A. Pre-assignment

    B. Virtual teams

    C. Negotiations

    D. None of the above

2. A project to construct a high-rise building is progressing very well. Stakeholders are proactive in identifying issues related to the quality of the structure, walls and floors. As a project manager, you are conducting meetings to clarify or resolve their issues. Although, you are committed to manage stakeholders concerns, you learned that some critical issues need to be deferred to the next phase of the project for resolution. What should you do in this situation?

    A. You must not defer any stakeholder issues but look for alternate methods

    B. You must escalate these issues to the sponsor for his advice

    C. You must work with stakeholders to defer those issues

    D. You must request the stakeholders to retract their issues

3. Marvin has been working for a retail company as a project manager. With his positive thinking and good managerial skills he turned many potentially disastrous projects into successes. Because of his expertise, the company high level executives offered him a group project manager position for a newly started environmental project. However, Marvin learned that in his newly assigned project he may have to offer bribes to get the Government

licenses. What should Marvin do in such a situation?

A. Reject the offer because project managers should not engage in an unethical conduct

B. Accept the offer because project managers must obey their higher-ups

C. Accept the position and offer bribes because project managers must complete projects on time and within budget

D. Investigate to find out if it is customary to offer bribes in that part of the country

4. You want to recognize your team's hardworking members. Being the project manager, you want to motivate your team members by rewarding one individual every month with a 'Project star of the month' award for his/her demonstrated and continuous effort. But, your sponsor opposes your idea of awarding your team members. Which of the following could be the reason for such resistance from your sponsor?

A. Awarding every month may take away the budgeted money allocated for the project

B. Awarding one individual may impair the team integrity

C. Project manager must get the approval from all stakeholders before rewarding

D. Money instead of award should be given to get maximum benefits from team members

5. Rina and Gimo are the senior developers in a website development project. They have been arguing over the best web design product to use in support of the new website they will be developing. As the project manager, to make a decision and reduce the conflict, you use a forcing approach. What is the important characteristic of this approach?

A. Forcing to close the project

B. Highlighting areas of agreement rather than areas of disagreement

C. Asserting one's viewpoint at the expense of others

D. Withdrawing from the actual conflict

6. You are in the final phase of a low cost car manufacturing project. This project, as designed, has delivered a low cost car that runs on the battery. However, to close this project, many administrative standards are required to be followed in order to avoid auditing from Government authorities. Since your organization possesses experts who have tremendous knowledge in closing procedures and standards, you would like to use them to close this project. This effort is an instance of:

A. Using enterprise environmental factors in closing the project

B. Using expert judgment in closing the project

C. Using organizational process assets in closing the project

D. All of the above

7. Nancy is engaged in the construction of three unique office buildings. Although construction sites are located in various places, she has been managing each team very efficiently to complete the work on time and within the budget. Which of the following statements describe the effort that Nancy is doing?

A. Construction of each building is an operational work because it is repetitive in nature

B. The building construction is considered neither as a project nor as an operational work

C. Construction of all three buildings is considered as one project

D. Construction of each building is a project because each building is unique in nature

8. There are several communication methods used to share and distribute information to stakeholders, team members and management. Which of the following communication methods are used during execution

phase to notify the public about environmental changes your project is going to cause after implementation?

A. Pull communication

B. Interactive communication

C. Informal communication

D. Push communication

9. Lesley is managing a software development project for the World Climate Control Organization. Since her team members are dispersed across the globe, she would like to set up online conferences in next two months to let everyone in her project know what is going on and what their role is within the project. She wants to use these conferences as team development activities to learn and exchange information in the project. To schedule such activities, which of the following should she use to know the availability of team members?

A. Project charter

B. Resource calendars

C. Responsibility assignment matrix

D. Project staff assignments

10. Two of your team members in your Software development project are not performing well. The initial assessment from your project leader indicates the lack of skills as the main reason for their low performance. In

order to complete their tasks and overall project on time, you want to improve their skills by online training. Since you are in the execution phase of the project, you must document the training requirements in the following document:

A. Enterprise environmental factors

B. The human resource management plan

C. Team performance assessments

D. Project staff assignments

11. Which of the following statements are NOT true considering the management of risks in a project?

A. The affect of various risks on project scope, cost and quality is numerically analyzed in the perform quantitative risk analysis process

B. A contingency plan is created to handle known risks in a project

C. The assumptions analysis is a technique used in identify risks process

D. The risk register is updated in all risk management processes except in plan risk management

12. You have been chosen by a program management office (PMO) to write a purchase order for your expertise in business writing. You have learned that the PMO has already selected a seller for a software product and would like to award the procurement contract to the selected seller as a purchase order which you must prepare. In this scenario, the PMO is administering:

A. The close procurements process

B. The administer procurements process

C. The plan procurements process

D. The conduct procurements process

13. Randy, a senior project manager, is using a lessons learned knowledge management system to document the findings in a precision instrument manufacturing project. He is using the information from his team which has identified causes of product quality variance using a control chart and the details regarding corrective actions chosen to reduce the variance and improve the product quality. Which of the following should Randy use to add this information to the lessons learned?

A. Organizational process assets in the quality control process

B. The process improvement plan in the plan quality process

C. Organizational process assets in the quality assurance process

D. The process improvement plan in the quality control process

14. Shawn is in the execution phase of his project. He is getting unexpected requests from his stakeholders about the project progress. All of the following can be used by Shawn to respond to their requests EXCEPT:

A. The project management plan

B. The stakeholder register

C. Organizational process assets

D. Performance reports

15. You are working in a Lab-EX, a laboratory experiment project to gather the impact of a virus on male human bodies. This project needs local Government approval for carrying out the tests on live persons. However, you were informed by the local authorities that it would take at least three weeks to get the authorization for such approval because of the documents involved in the review and approval process. Considering this as a risk to the project, you would like to send paper work ahead of time to reduce the approval time to one week. Which of the following describe the risk response techniques being used in this scenario?

A. Risk mitigation

B. Risk reduction

C. Risk accept

D. Risk avoid

16. A drug manufacturing project requires many pharmaceutical chemicals for synthesizing to produce an active ingredient or a drug. You are managing a contractor to supply all these chemicals in your drug manufacturing project. Recent quality testing of the drugs raised concerns over the quality of the materials supplied by the contractor. Which of the following must be done to make sure that all contractual obligations are followed by the contractor?

A. Escalate this issue to the sponsor and submit all drug testing reports

B. Reject all poor quality drugs and penalize the contractor

C. Convene a meeting with stakeholders and communicate the findings

D. Carryout audits and inspections to verify compliance in the seller's deliverables

17. A project manager is spending majority of his funding in the current phase of his project. Not only she is spending her money but also managing various resources in the project. What is the stakeholder influence on the project now compared to earlier phases?

A. Cannot be determined

B. More

C. Less

D. Same

18. You are working for FALCON highway construction agency as a project cost estimator. The agency started a highway construction project which is in it's planning phase. The rough order of magnitude (ROM) cost estimate for the project is expected to be between 3 and 5 million dollars in the planning phase with a ROM of -25% to +25%. What will be the ROM estimate in the execution phase if it changes to -10% to +10%?

A. Between 3.1 and 4.1 million dollars

B. Between 3.6 and 4.4 million dollars

C. Between 3.9 and 4.1 million dollars

D. Between 3.4 and 4.4 million dollars

19. You are the project manager of a business that sells software contracting services to Banks. Recently, Fourth National bank has requested you to submit a proposal for their mortgage project that has been published for the bid. They have also requested you to register the name of your business on the list of qualified sellers. Which of the following statement about qualified sellers list is true?

A. Qualified sellers list is the list generated from procurement negotiations and represents an output of the conduct procurements process

B. Qualified sellers list gives the listing of vendors who have been selected to perform the work with the organization and represents an input to the plan procurements process

C. Qualified sellers list gives the listing of vendors who have been pre-selected for their past experience with the organization and represents an input to the conduct procurements process

D. Qualified sellers list is the list generated out of bidder conferences and represents an output of the conduct procurements process

20. Which of the following is NOT an input to the Direct and Manage project execution process?

A. Issue and defect management procedures

B. Consultants

C. Stakeholder risk tolerances

D. Project files from prior projects

21. Project-A has an initial investment of $10 million, out of which $3.5 million has already been spent. This project gives a good control for the stakeholders on the revenues collected from oil and gas industry. Project-B, with the same goal as project-A requires only $7.5 million for completion if it starts now. Which project should you choose based on the information presented above?

   A. Project-B

   B. Both projects

   C. Project-A

   D. None of the above

22. Debbie, an IT project manager, is in the planning phase of a shopping website development project. A junior project manager, who has been working under her authority, started developing procedures to indicate how the integrity of cost and schedule performance baselines should be maintained in the project. Where should the junior project manager store these procedures?

   A. In the project human resource plan

   B. In the project scope statement

   C. In the project management plan

   D. In the project communication plan

23. Your organization has recognized a need to replace the legacy manufacturing system with a modern software application to reduce delivery delays and process downtime. Your IT director anticipates a project to fulfill this business need, however, he warns that the new project's budget cannot exceed $75,000 due to shortages in the department budget. He also indicates that no additional staff will be allocated to this project other than the existing IT staff. If you are assigned as a project manager to this project, you would document these initial project conditions as:

   A. Project assumptions in the project charter

   B. Project restrictions in the project management plan

   C. Project constraints in the project charter

   D. Project conditions in the project cost management plan and human resource management plan

24. All of the following are outputs belong to the Create WBS process, EXCEPT?

   A. The requirements traceability matrix

   B. The project scope statement

   C. The codes of account identifiers

D. The technical reference information

25. You are a senior project manager working for RETAMART, a retail shopping network that sells various consumer products. As part of the expansion plan approved by the board of directors, you have been assigned as a project manager for a new plant. Due to transportation problems, the project has undergone delays and the Schedule Performance Index (SPI) is found to be at 0.6 and the cost performance index (CPI) at 0.7. However, you expect some improvements over next few weeks that may change schedule performance index to 1.1 and cost performance index to 0.9. Which of the following statements will be true if your anticipated changes materialize?

A. The project will be overspent and behind schedule

B. The project will be on schedule and under budget

C. The project will be overspent but ahead of schedule

D. The project will be under budget but behind schedule

26. Jen works as a project manager for the National weather agency. She has been managing a project which was designed to find the impact of climate changes on Northern mountains. The initial study established two months

delay for the testing equipment to reach mountains due to road construction. However, a recent assessment has shown a significant drop in the delay time because of rapid progress in construction. Which of the following steps should Jen take next to account for the change in the delay time?

A. Distribute the information

B. Conduct a stakeholder meeting

C. Create a new project plan

D. Update the risk register

27. The method used in the plan quality process to identify the factors that may influence specific variables of a product under development is known as:

A. The forecasting technique

B. The control chart

C. The statistical sampling

D. The design of experiments

28. A team member in your project is constantly providing incomplete deliverables and not performing well. Instead of releasing him from the project, you would like to give him one more chance for improvement. You meet with him and say " You need to complete your deliverables because our Director would like to have the project on time". What form

of project management power are you exercising in this scenario?

A. Referent

B. Formal

C. Reward

D. Expert

29. Dana works for a Federal agency that manages mission critical projects. As a project manager, she is responsible for all communication needs in her data center project, which has started recently. This project involves many stakeholders, customers, external vendors and team members. Since conflicts are inevitable in such a huge project, she has decided to provide her project team the details of the issue escalation process including the names of the chain of command to escalate the issues that cannot be resolved at a lower level. Dana must use the following document to store this information:

A. The project charter

B. The communication management plan

C. The issue log

D. The project scope document

30. Project managers must obey the Code of the Ethics and Professional Conduct. They must maintain both aspirational as well as mandatory

standards at all times. Avoiding these standards will be subjected to disciplinary procedures. But, PMI code may not apply to:

A. Non PMI members who apply to commensurate a PMI certification process

B. Non PMI members who serve PMI in a volunteer capacity

C. Non PMI members who hold a PMI certification

D. Applies to all of the above

31. You are in the process of collecting and disseminating performance information to the stakeholders in the project. You want to predict the future performance of the project based on the current information. This performance information includes status reports, current status of risks, and summary of changes approved in the period. Which of the following methods help you in predicting the future performance of the project?

A. A time-series method

B. A pareto chart

C. A run chart

D. A work breakdown structure

32. When the budget is determined for a project, costs are estimated for all activities in the project and aggregated

to establish a cost baseline. Which of the following statements about the cost baseline is NOT true?

A. The project cost performance is measured against the cost baseline

B. The cost baseline is an output of the determine budget process

C. The cost baseline includes all authorized budgets including management reserves

D. The cost baseline is in the form of an 'S' curve

33. The RACI chart is an example for a responsibility assignment matrix (RAM). The letters R and C in RACI chart stand for

A. Responsible and consult

B. Resource and consultant

C. Responsible and categorize

D. Resource and consult

34. The number of communication channels depends on the number of team members in any project. If five team members are released from a team of 25, how many communication channels remain in the project?

A. 300

B. 625

C. 190

D. 400

35. All of the following statements about project management process groups are correct EXCEPT:

A. All of the project groups would repeat for each subproject in a large project

B. The project management process groups are not project phases

C. There are five project management process groups required for any project

D. Project process groups are often performed only once in each phase

36. You are in a meeting with your senior manager who has been helping you to organize and manage a team of IT people with numerous backgrounds. While you are discussing the creativity and breakthrough performance your team is demonstrating now, your senior manager indicates that your team has moved from the storming to the performing stage. Which of the following explains the characteristic of the performing stage?

A. In the performing stage, the team completes the work and disbands as a project team

B. In the performing stage, the team function as a well organized unit and resolve issues effectively

C. In the performing stage, the team begins to work together and trust each other

D. In the performing stage, the team starts to focus on the project work and technical decisions

37. No matter how good you are in communicating, information distribution to stakeholders as planned is a challenging task. Many tools are used in a project for effective information distribution that includes all of the following EXCEPT:

A. Visual aids

B. Encoding and Decoding

C. Press releases

D. Portals

38. Mary is a project manager for an infrastructure upgrade project in a Government agency. She has recently realized that a critical scheduled task exceeded the deadline and the stakeholders are on top it. The resource manager has permitted to use three more resources to work and complete the delayed task. Although, the attempt from the resource manager helps her, Mary is concerned about the task because:

A. Allocating more resources may result in rework

B. Allocating more resources may shorten the duration but results in increased risk or cost

C. Resources may need training to complete the task

D. Allocating more resources need stakeholders approval

39. All of the following are tools of the control schedule process EXCEPT:

A. Parametric estimating

B. What-if scenario analysis

C. Schedule compression

D. Variance analysis

40. You are working with your customers on completed deliverables in your Electronic parts manufacturing project. Since these parts are exported to other countries, they need more testing before your customers accept them. In this scenario, which of the following statements about the completed deliverables is CORRECT?

A. Completed deliverables not accepted by customers must be forwarded to the close project or phase process

B. Deliverables formally accepted by customers must be moved to organizational process assets

C. Deliverables formally accepted by customers are forwarded to the verify scope process

D. Completed deliverables not accepted by customers must require a change request for defect repair

41. You are managing a heavy equipment manufacturing project that involves many mechanical, electrical as well as IT staff. Your team prepared a schedule network diagram using duration estimates with dependencies and constraints. Your team also calculated the critical path for the project using late and early values. Today, your project office has indicated about the non-availability of some of the resources you planned for the project. Now, you explore the possibility of modifying the schedule to account for limited resources. What is your best possible step in such a situation?

A. Recalculate critical path using the critical chain method

B. Perform resource leveling to account for limited resources

C. Use crashing or fast tracking to level resources across the project

D. Apply leads and lags to develop a viable schedule

42. You are working as a project manager for a High yield crop development project. Data from the weather agency shows an unfavorable weather pattern for next few months. As a senior project manager, you want to assess the feasibility of the schedule under adverse conditions and provide some insights to your team. This way, your team can prepare some reserves and plan risk responses if unfavorable conditions exist during execution. Which of the following techniques should you use to assess the feasibility of the schedule?

A. Pareto charts

B. Variance analysis

C. Crashing

D. Monte Carlo analysis

43. All of the following activities are performed in the close project or phase process EXCEPT

A. Activities that fulfill the exit criteria of the project

B. Documenting the reasons for deliverables which were rejected

C. Activities which are needed to transfer the completed products to operations

D. Documenting the reasons for projects terminated early

44. Your project team has recently identified a risk in the software development project and decided not to change the project management plan to deal with the risk. The risk response strategy your team used in this scenario is an example of:

    A. Mitigate

    B. Transfer

    C. Avoid

    D. Acceptance

45. Which of the following is neither an input to nor an output of the develop project charter process?

    A. A project charter

    B. Professional and technical associations

    C. A business need

    D. A project statement of work

46. It is a well known fact that employees working in Government entities feel more financially secure compared to the staff working in private firms. According to Maslow's hierarchy of needs, based on the said statement, which of the following needs are NOT satisfied for employees in private firms?

    A. Job needs

    B. Physiological needs

    C. Safety needs

    D. Esteem needs

47. You have just completed the first phase of a multi-phase project. You have performed the earned value measurements and found out that The CPI is 0.79, the SPI is 0.98 and has been increasing during the course of the project. Your next phase plane should focus first on which element of the project?

    A. Quality

    B. Resources

    C. Schedule

    D. Cost

48. A project manager has just started planning his project. If he knows very limited information about his project, he must use the following technique to estimate the duration for each activity:

    A. Four-point estimating

    B. Three-point estimating

    C. Analogous estimating

    D. Parametric estimating

49. You are in the verify scope process of your Electronic goods manufacturing project. While reviewing some

products, you have noticed that the tolerance for one product is 0.01% less than what was listed in the requirements documentation. This deviation may not be a problem for the customers and it may not negatively impact the operations. What is your best immediate action in such a situation?

A. Notify the customers about the deviation

B. Change the project management plan to allow for small deviation

C. Reject all products and restart the project

D. Discuss with your team about the quality testing

50. You have recently taken over a troubled automobile project which has gone out of control. The project team missed many deadlines and stakeholders were not happy with the project progress. As an experienced project manager, your first priority is to bring the schedule into alignment with the project plan. You would like to use what-if scenario analysis to see how various factors affected the project schedule so that you can develop a plan to reduce the impact of adverse conditions on the project schedule in future. What would be your next course of action once you determine the factors that created schedule overrun?

A. Prepare a resource breakdown structure to identify resources used

B. Update activity lists to incorporate new activities into the schedule

C. Generate change requests to update the schedule baseline

D. Develop project schedule network diagrams to determine the total slack

PMP Lite Mock Exam 18
Answer Key and Explanations

1. C - Project managers can use pre-assignment, virtual teams or negotiations as tools or techniques for acquiring the project team. However, negotiation is the best tool to acquire the project team from functional managers to ensure that the project receives appropriate staff in the required time frame. Therefore, negotiations is the correct answer. [PMBOK 4th edition, Page 227] [Project Human Resource Management]

2. C - Project managers must actively communicate and work with stakeholders to meet their needs and address their issues as they occur. However, there might be occasions when some issues need to be resolved outside the project and some need to be deferred to the next phases of the project. In such cases, project manager must work with stakeholders to defer those issues. He must not escalate these issues to the sponsor without talking to the sponsors first. Asking the stakeholders to withdraw their issues is not recommended. [PMBOK 4th edition, Page 261] [Project Communications Management]

3. A - Project managers must adhere to code of ethics and professional conduct. They must maintain fairness and honesty. Since the new job requires some illegal and unethical activities, Marvin must reject the offer. [PMI's code of Ethics and Professional Conduct] [Prof. Responsibility]

4. B - Project managers must make sure that rewards should not hurt team cohesiveness. Sometimes this type of award lacks transparency and may create problems within the team and the team's integrity may be lost due to team member of the month award. Hence, project managers must work on the rewarding behavior that everyone can achieve. Therefore 'Awarding one individual may impair the team integrity' is the prime reason to oppose project manager's idea. [PMBOK 4th edition, Page 234] [Project Human Resource Management]

5. C - Project managers must resolve conflicts as early as possible to improve productivity and generate positive working relationships. Forcing is a conflict resolution technique in which one's view point is pushed at the expense of others. This type of approach offers win-lose solution. Hence 'Asserting one's viewpoint at the expense of others' is the correct answer. [PMBOK 4th edition, Page 240] [Project Human Resource Management]

6. B - Projects are closed during the close project process. Only tool which is used in this process is the expert judgment. Expert judgment can be obtained from consultants or industry experts. These experts make sure that all project standards are followed when they are closed. In this scenario, you want to use experts from your own organization in

closing the project. [PMBOK 4th edition, Page 101] [Project Integration Management]

7. D - Projects are temporary and unique in nature where as operational work is repetitive in nature. Since Nancy is working to construct three unique buildings and each has a definitive beginning and a definitive end, each effort is considered as a project. Portfolio refers to collection of projects or programs to meet business objectives which may not be dependent. So, in this scenario, 'Construction of each building is a project because each building is unique in nature' is more appropriate and a valid answer. [PMBOK 4th edition, Pages 5, 8] [Project Framework]

8. A - Push communication is used to send information to specific recipients who need to know. Push communication is done using letters, faxes and memos etc.. Pull communication is used for large volume of information. The methods for this kind of communication include internet sites and blogs etc. Since you want to notify public about the environmental changes, you must use pull communication methods. [PMBOK 4th edition, Page 256] [Project Communications Management]

9. B - Resource calendars are used as tools in the develop team process to know the availability of team members for team development activities. The responsibility assignment matrix gives the

responsibilities assigned to various team members. Project staff assignments give details of individual assignments and project organization charts display team members and their reporting relationships. The project charter does not give any of that information. Hence, Lesley must use resource calendars to know that information. [PMBOK 4th edition, Page 231] [Project Human Resource Management]

10. B - A human resource management plan is a part of the project management plan. All training needs, reward information, disciplinary actions are documented in the human resource plan. During execution, additional training requirements can be added to this plan as a result of team performance assessment. Hence, you must use the human resource management plan to document the training requirements. [PMBOK 4th edition, Page 231] [Project Human Resource Management]

11. B - Risks that are identified and analyzed are known as known risks. So, it is possible to plan for known risks. However, risks that are unknown cannot be managed like known risks. These unknown risks need a contingency plan to manage whenever they occur. Hence, 'A contingency plan is created to handle known risks in a project' is NOT a true statement. [PMBOK 4th edition, Page 275] [Project Risk Management]

12. D - Sellers are selected and procurement contracts are awarded to

selected sellers in the conduct procurements process. Contracts can be awarded in the form of a purchase order. Since PMO selected you to write the purchase order, it is in the process of conducting procurements. [PMBOK 4th edition, Page 333] [Project Procurement Management]

13.   A - Since Randy is using product quality variance information and corresponding corrective action information, he and his team are in the process of quality control. In quality control, all quality activities and their results are recorded to assess the quality performance. Corrective actions are taken to bring the quality on track. Lessons learned databases are part of organizational process assets and these assets are updated in the quality control process. Hence, Randy must update organizational process assets in the quality control process. [PMBOK 4th edition, Page 214] [Project Quality Management]

14.   B - Since Shawn is in the execution phase and stakeholders are requesting project information, he must be in the distribute information process. The project management plan, organizational process assets and performance reports are inputs to this process. So, Shawn must use any of the above documents to respond to their requests. The stakeholder register is an output of identify stakeholders process and it does not give any information about the project progress. Hence, 'The stakeholder register' is the correct answer. [PMBOK 4th edition, Page

258] [Project Communications Management]

15.   A - Since the delay in the approval process delays the project, you want to reduce the delay to reduce the impact on the project. Because this is a negative risk, the valid risk response strategies are avoid, transfer, mitigate or accept. Risk mitigation techniques are used to reduce the probability and impact of negative risks than trying to repair the damage after risk has occurred. In this case, you are reducing the approval time by sending paperwork early to avoid delays in the project. Hence, the risk mitigation technique is the correct answer. [PMBOK 4th edition, Page 304] [Project Risk Management]

16.   D - Since the drug testing raised doubts over the chemicals supplied by the contractor, you must ensure that contractor is following the quality requirements by inspecting and auditing sellers deliverables. You can also include seller's personnel during auditing. All other actions including meeting with the sponsor and stakeholders can be performed later, if the seller is not following the contractual requirements. Therefore, 'Carryout audits and inspections to verify compliance in the seller's deliverables' is the first action required from you. [PMBOK 4th edition, Page 339] [Project Procurement Management]

17.   C - Since the project manager is spending his money and managing resources, he is currently in the execution phase of the project.

Spending levels are maximum in the execution phase. Stakeholder influences on the project decrease over the life of the project. Hence, stakeholder influence is less now compared to previous phases. [PMBOK 4th edition, Pages 16, 17] [Project Framework]

18. B - Since the Rough Order of Magnitude (ROM) in the planning phase is -25% to +25%, the estimated value + 1/4th of the estimated value = 5 million dollars. Therefore, the estimated value(5/4) = 5 million dollars and the estimated value = 4 million dollars. In the executing stage, the ROM estimated value = estimated value +or -10% of estimated value = 4 + or - .4 = 4.4 to 3.6 million dollars. Hence the ROM estimate in the executing stage will be between 3.6 to 4.4 million dollars. [PMBOK 4th edition, Page 168] [Project Cost Management]

19. C - Sometimes, based on the past experience, organizations would like to choose pre-selected sellers for their work. Qualified sellers list is one such list where sellers are pre-screened and procurements are directed to them. This process is done during conduct procurements process and qualified sellers list is an input to this process. [PMBOK 4th edition, Page 330] [Project Procurement Management]

20. B - Stakeholder risk tolerances are a part of enterprise environmental factors. Issue and defect management procedures and project files from prior projects are a part of Organizational process assets. Since,

organizational process assets and enterprise environmental factors are input to the Direct and manage project execution process, all options mentioned above are inputs to this process except consultants. Consultants are used as tools to manage the project execution. Hence, consultants are NOT an input to the process. [PMBOK 4th edition, Pages 85, 86] [Project Integration Management]

21. C - Sunk costs are costs that are already incurred in the project. These costs should not be taken into account during project evaluation. For Project-A, $3.5 million are sunk costs. So, the costs needed to complete this project are only $6.5 million. But, Project-B requires $7.5 million to complete. Since project-A requires less funds compared to project-B, you should choose project-A instead of project-B. [http://www.digitalpurview.com/project-selection-method/] [Project Integration Management]

22. C - The baselines change only when a change request is generated. A project management plan documents the instructions to handle changes to performance baselines. These baselines include scope, cost and schedule baselines. Therefore, the junior project manager must store these procedures in the project management plan. [PMBOK 4th edition, Page 99] [Project Integration Management]

23. C - The budget restrictions and staffing restrictions must be known early in the project. These restrictions are also known as constraints which form the boundary of the project. Constraints must be documented as early in the project as possible. Since Project charter is the first document prepared in the project, all constraints must be recorded in the project charter to get an agreement from stakeholders. Hence, you must document these conditions as project constraints in the project charter. [PMBOK 4th edition, Page 77] [Project Integration Management]

24. A - The code of account identifier and the technical reference information are included in the WBS dictionary, which is an output of the create WBS process. The project scope statement is also generated as an output of the create WBS process. The requirements traceability matrix is an output of the Collect Requirements Process. Hence, this is not an output of the Create WBS process. [PMBOK 4th edition, Pages 121, 122] [Project Scope Management]

25. C - The cost performance index above 1 indicates that the project is under budget and the schedule performance index above 1 indicates that the project is ahead of schedule. If all of your anticipated changes happen to be true, the project will be overspent but on schedule because the schedule performance index will be greater than 1. [PMBOK 4th edition, Page 183] [Project Cost Management]

26. D - The delays are considered as risks to the project. In this scenario, the reassessment indicated a drop in the risk (delay time) compared to the initial risk identification. The risk reassessment is done in the monitor and control risks process and the outcome of the risk reassessments updates the risk register. Therefore, Jen must take steps to update the risk register. Other steps can be taken after updating the risk register. [PMBOK 4th edition, Page 311] [Project Risk Management]

27. D - The design of experiments is a quality planning tool to identify the factors that may influence specific variables of a product under development. This tool is used to determine the number of quality tests in a project. [PMBOK 4th edition, Page 197] [Project Quality Management]

28. A - The Five powers of a project manager are 1)Formal:- Based on project manager's position 2) Reward:- Giving rewards for obeying instructions from the project manager 3) Penalty:- Based on the ability to penalize team members for their mistakes 4) Expert:- Using project manager's expertise 5) Referent:- Based on the ability to refer to the authority of someone in a higher position (like a Director in this case). So, you are using the referent power in this scenario.
In this case, the project manager was exercising the power of penalty. [Project manager powers (http://www.deepfriedbrainpmp.com /2011/02/powers-of-project-

manager.html)]   [Project Human Resource Management]

29.   B - The issue escalation process must be documented during the planning phase of a project. The issues that cannot be resolved at a lower level can be escalated using a chain of command within a stipulated time frame. This information is part of the communication management plan. Hence, Dana must document this information in the communication management plan. [PMBOK 4th edition, Page 257] [Project Communications Management]

30.   D - The PMI code of conduct applies to all PMI members, non-members who earned a PMI certification, non-members who apply to become a PMI certified and who serve PMI in a volunteer capacity. It may not apply to non-PMI, non-PMI certified project managers. Hence, 'Applies to all the above' is the best answer. [PMI code of Ethics and Professional Conduct] [Prof. Responsibility]

31.   A - The process of collecting and disseminating performance information to the stakeholders is done during report performance process. This process uses communication methods, forecasting methods, the variance analysis and reporting systems as tools for predicting the future of the project. Since a time-series method is one of such forecasting techniques, it is the correct answer. [PMBOK 4th edition, Page 270] [Project Communications Management]

32.   C - The project cost baseline includes all authorized budgets excluding management reserves. Management reserves are not included to measure the cost performance of a project. Therefore, 'The cost baseline includes all authorized budgets including management reserves' is not a true statement. [PMBOK 4th edition, Pages 174, 178] [Project Cost Management]

33.   A - The responsibility assignment matrix (RAM) is used to show the relationship between resources and work packages. A RACI chart is an example for RAM and the letters in RACI chart stands for responsible, accountable, consult, and inform. Therefore, 'Responsible and Consult' is the correct answer. [PMBOK 4th edition, Page 221] [Project Human Resource Management]

34.   C - The total number of communication channels in a project can be determined using a formula $n(n-1)/2$ where n represents the number of team members. In this scenario, since 20 team members exist after relieving 5, total number of communication channels left = $20(19)/2 = 190$. Hence 190 is the correct answer. [PMBOK 4th edition, Page 253] [Project Communications Management]

35.   D - There are five project management process groups that are required by any project and each group would repeat for each subproject. Project management process groups are not project phases. They are often iterated prior to completing the project. Hence, 'Project process groups are often performed only once in each phase' is not a true statement. [PMBOK 4th edition, Page 41] [Project Framework]

36.   B - There are five stages of team development: Forming, Storming, Norming, Performing and Adjourning. In the Forming stage, the team works independently; In the Storming stage, the team begins to understand the project work; In the Norming stage, the team begins to learn one another; In the performing stage, they work as a well organized unit and show the maximum performance; In the Adjourning stage, the team completes the work. Therefore 'In the performing stage, the team function as a well organized unit and resolve issues effectively' is a true statement. [PMBOK 4th edition, Page 233] [Project Human Resource Management]

37.   B - To distribute information effectively to stakeholders, project managers use variety of tools such as sender-receiver models, visual aids, information distribution tools, portals, press releases, email, faxes and other electronic tools. Encoding and decoding are parts of communication model. They are not tools for information distribution. [PMBOK 4th edition, Page 260] [Project Communications Management]

38.   B - To meet schedule constraints, schedule compression techniques are used to reduce the schedule duration. The crashing and fast tracking are two

such techniques. Crashing involves allocation of more resources to reduce the duration. Crashing always does not produce a desirable result and may result in increased risk. Providing training is not a problem from project manager's point of view. Stakeholder's approval is not required when resources are not allocated. So, Mary's concern is only about increased risk or cost due to allocation of more resources to the task. [PMBOK 4th edition, Page 156] [Project Time Management]

39.   A - Variance analysis, Schedule compression and What-if scenario analysis are used as tools to the control schedule process. Parametric estimating is not a tool to this process. [PMBOK 4th edition, Page 160] [Project Time Management]

40.   D - Verify scope is the process of formalizing the acceptance of finished deliverables. In this process, stakeholders or customers give formal acceptance to the completed deliverables and deliverables not accepted by them must initiate a change request for defect repair. The accepted deliverables must be forward to the close project or close phase process. Therefore, 'Completed deliverables not accepted by customers must require a change request for defect repair' is the correct answer. [PMBOK 4th edition, Page 125] [Project Scope Management]

41.   A - A critical chain method is used to prepare a schedule network diagram with limited resources. A network diagram is prepared initially and the critical path is then calculated. Availability of resources is entered and resource-limited schedule is prepared. Duration buffers are used in critical chain method. Hence, recalculating the critical path using the critical chain method is the next best step. [PMBOK 4th edition, Page 155] [Project Time Management]

42. D - What-if scenario analysis is used to prepare a schedule under different scenarios. The outcome of the what-if scenario analysis assesses the feasibility of the project schedule if adverse conditions exist. Monte Carlo is one of such techniques in which questions like "what if something happens" are asked and the feasibility of the schedule is assessed. Hence, you must use Monte Carlo analysis in this scenario. [PMBOK 4th edition, Page 156] [Project Time Management]

43. B - When a project is in its closing phase, all activities needed to complete the project across project management processes are finalized. Detail reasons should be documented when projects are closed early. All activities involved in exit criteria of the project must be performed. Since the reasons for not accepting the deliverables is documented in verify scope process, there is no need to document the reasons again in the closing phase. Hence 'Documenting the reasons for not accepting the deliverables' is the correct answer. [PMBOK 4th edition, Pages 99, 100] [Project Integration Management]

44. D - When risks cannot be eliminated from the project, it is advisable to accept them. In this scenario, your team is unable to identify suitable response strategy. Hence, risk acceptance is the correct strategy to plan for. [PMBOK 4th edition, Page 304] [Project Risk Management]

45. B - A project statement of work and a business need are inputs to the develop project charter process. A project charter is an output of the develop project charter process. Professional and technical associations are used as tools to gather expert opinions while developing a charter. Hence, 'Professional and technical associations' is the correct answer. [PMBOK 4th edition, Page 77] [Project Integration Management]

46. C - According to Maslow's motivational theory, there are five types of human needs 1. Physiological needs:- Without these needs such as air and food, human survival is not possible. 2. Safety needs:- Personal security and financial security are safety needs. 3. Social needs:- Family and Friendship, and sense of belonging to a group, etc..4) Esteem needs:- Self-esteem and self-respect are esteem needs 5) Self-Actualization:- Desire to become more and more what one is, to become everything that one is capable of becoming. Based on the statement it can be concluded that for employees working in private firms, the safety needs are not satisfied. [PMBOK 4th Edition, Appendix-G]

[Project   Human   Resource Management]

47.   D - A Schedule Performance Index (SPI) of less than one indicates that less work has completed than planned and a Cost Performance Index (CPI) of less than one indicates a cost overrun for the work completed. In this scenario, cost overrun is more compared to the schedule delay. Therefore, you must focus on the cost of the project to reduce it for next phase. [PMBOK 4th edition, Page 182] [Project Cost Management]

48.   C - When there is a limited amount of information available about a project, analogous estimating is used to estimate the activity durations. This estimating technique uses parameters such as budget, complexity and size from previous projects to estimate the duration. Since the project manager has just started planning and he knows very limited information, he must use analogous estimating. [PMBOK 4th edition, Page 149] [Project Time Management]

49.   A - When you find a defective product, you must notify customers immediately even if the deviation may not affect customers. As a project manager, you must maintain honesty and should not hide facts. After notifying customers, the project manager must discuss with the team and change project management plan based on the customer's input. Hence, the first step you must take in this process is to notify the customers about the deviation. [PMI code of

Ethics and Professional Conduct] [Prof. Responsibility]

50.   C - You are in the process of determining the status of the project schedule and influencing the factors that caused schedule changes. Based on the scenario, you are currently in the control schedule process. What-if analysis is used in control schedule process to see how various factors influence the schedule. One output of this process is to generate change requests to correct the schedule. Hence you should generate a change request to update the schedule baseline. [PMBOK 4th edition, Page 160] [Project Time Management]

ADDITIONAL RESOURCES

Exam Taking Tips

Studying for a multiple choice exam entails preparing in a unique way as opposed to other types of tests. The PMP exam asks one to recognize correct answers among a set of four options. The extra options that are not the correct answer are called the "distracters"; and their purpose, unsurprisingly, is to distract the test taker from the actual correct answer among the bunch.

Students usually consider multiple choice exams as much easier than other types of exams; this is not necessarily true with the PMP exam. Among these reasons are:

- Most multiple choice exams ask for simple, factual information; unlike the PMP exam which often requires the student to apply knowledge and make a best judgment.

- The majority of multiple choice exams involve a large quantity of different questions – so even if you get a few incorrect, it's still okay. The PMP exam covers a broad set of material, often times in greater depth than other certification exams.

Regardless of whether or not multiple choice testing is more forgiving; in reality, one must study immensely because of the sheer volume of information that is covered.

Although four hours may seem like more than enough time for a multiple choice

exam, when faced with 200 questions, time management is one of the most crucial factors in succeeding and doing well. You should always try and answer all of the questions you are confident about first, and then go back about to those items you are not sure about afterwards. Always read *carefully* through the entire test as well, and do your best to not leave any question blank upon submission– even if you do not readily know the answer.

Many people do very well with reading through each question and not looking at the options before trying to answer. This way, they can steer clear (usually) of being fooled by one of the "distracter" options or get into a tug-of-war between two choices that both have a good chance of being the actual answer.

Never assume that "all of the above" or "none of the above" answers are the actual choice. Many times they are, but in recent years they have been used much more frequently as distracter options on standardized tests. Typically this is done in an effort to get people to stop believing the myth that they are always the correct answer.

You should be careful of negative answers as well. These answers contain words such as "none", "not", "neither", and the like. Despite often times being very confusing, if you read these types of questions and answers carefully, then you should be able to piece together which is the correct answer. Just take your time!

Never try to overanalyze a question, or try and think about how the test givers are trying to lead astray potential test takers. Keep it simple and stay with what you know.

If you ever narrow down a question to two possible answers, then try and slow down your thinking and think about how the two different options/answers differ. Look at the question again and try to apply how this difference between the two potential answers relates to the question. If you are convinced there is literally no difference between the two potential answers (you'll more than likely be wrong in assuming this), then take another look at the answers that you've already eliminated. Perhaps one of them is actually the correct one and you'd made a previously unforeseen mistake.

On occasion, over-generalizations are used within response options to mislead test takers. To help guard against this, always be wary of responses/answers that use absolute words like "always", or "never". These are less likely to actually be the answer than phrases like "probably" or "usually" are. Funny or witty responses are also, most of the time, incorrect – so steer clear of those as much as possible.

Although you should always take each question individually, "none of the above" answers are usually less likely to be the correct selection than "all of the above" is. Keep this in mind with the understanding that it is not an absolute rule, and should be analyzed on a case-by-case (or "question-by-question") basis.

Looking for grammatical errors can also be a huge clue. If the stem ends with an indefinite article such as "an" then you'll probably do well to look for an answer that begins with a vowel instead of a consonant. Also, the longest response is also oftentimes the correct one, since whoever wrote the question item may have tended to load the answer with qualifying adjectives or phrases in an effort to make it correct. Again though, always deal with these on a question-by-question basis, because you could very easily be getting a question where this does not apply.

Verbal associations are oftentimes critical because a response may repeat a key word that was in the question. Always be on the alert for this. Playing the old Sesame Street game "Which of these things is not like the other" is also a very solid strategy, if a bit preschool. Sometimes many of a question's distracters will be very similar to try to trick you into thinking that one choice is related to the other. The answer very well could be completely unrelated however, so stay alert.

Just because you have finished a practice test, be aware that you are not done working. After you have graded your test with all of the necessary corrections, review it and try to recognize what happened in the answers that you got wrong. Did you simply not know the qualifying correct information? Perhaps you were led astray by a solid distracter answer? Going back through your corrected test will give you a leg up on your next one by revealing your tendencies as to what you may be vulnerable with, in terms of multiple choice tests.

It may be a lot of extra work, but in the long run, going through your corrected multiple choice tests will work wonders for you in preparation for the real exam. See if you perhaps misread the question or even missed it because you were unprepared. Think of it like instant replays in professional sports. You are going back and looking at what you did on the big stage in the past so you can help fix and remedy any errors that could pose problems for you on the real exam.

10209119R0

Made in the USA
Lexington, KY
04 July 2011